BUSINESS COMMUNICATION

ABOUT THE AUTHORS

Roy W. Poe is president of the McGraw-Hill Continuing Education Company. He was awarded the bachelor of science and master of science degrees by Oklahoma State University and has completed postgraduate courses at the University of California in Berkeley and other universities. He was awarded an honorary doctor of commercial science degree by Fort Lauderdale University in 1966. He has taught in high schools, business colleges, community colleges, and universities and has served as associate dean of Golden Gate College, as supervisor of training for the Veterans Administration in San Francisco, and as director of the former Gregg College in Chicago. Before assuming his present position, he was editorial director of the Gregg Division and later vice president and editorial director of the McGraw-Hill Book Company. In addition to lecturing at numerous universities and at business and education seminars throughout the country, he has written articles for various professional publications and is coauthor of *Gregg Notehand.*

Rosemary T. Fruehling is associate professor and coordinator of the Secretarial Science Department at the County College of Morris in Dover, New Jersey. She was awarded the associate in science degree by Virginia Junior College, Virginia, Minnesota, and the bachelor of science and master of arts degrees by the University of Minnesota in Minneapolis. She has taught business and office education courses in several high schools, including the St. Louis Park (Minnesota) High School, where she organized and conducted a cooperative training program for office education students. In addition, she has taught graduate classes in universities, lectured at numerous business and education seminars throughout the country, and served as training consultant for a number of business firms. In 1952 she was listed in *Who's Who of American College Leaders* and in 1971 was presented the "Outstanding Educator in America" award. She has written articles for professional journals and is coauthor of *Business Correspondence/30* and *How to Write Effective Business Letters.*

BUSINESS COMMUNICATION
a problem-solving approach

ROY W. POE

ROSEMARY T. FRUEHLING

GREGG DIVISION

McGraw-Hill Book Company

New York   St. Louis   Dallas   San Francisco   Düsseldorf
Johannesburg   Kuala Lumpur   London   Mexico
Montreal   New Delhi   Panama   Rio de Janeiro
Singapore   Sydney   Toronto

BUSINESS COMMUNICATION: A Problem-Solving Approach

1 2 3 4 5 6 7 8 9   HDBP   2 1 0 9 8 7 6 5 4 3

DESIGNER: JOHN L. HORTON

Library of Congress Cataloging in Publication Data

Poe, Roy W, date.
  Business communication.

    1. Commercial correspondence. I. Fruehling,
Rosemary T., joint author. II. Title.
HF5721.P6   651.7'5   72-5658
ISBN 0-07-050360-5

PREFACE

This is a different kind of book about business writing. It came about from the authors' conviction that one becomes an effective writer only when he's personally involved with what he's writing about.

The "No Formula" Approach to Business Writing

Writing a letter or a report is a very personal thing. Communications are written by and to people, and the content of a particular message depends on how the writer feels about his subject, how well he knows his reader, and what the attitudes and policies of the organization he represents are. A good communication is never the result of following a formula: "Do this in the first paragraph, do that in the next paragraph, and close the letter like this."

Suppose a dozen people who heard a speaker at a convention decide to write him about his talk. Although all twelve letters may have some common characteristics—courtesy, tact, friendliness, and so on—no two will be exactly alike. They will vary in approach, length, and emphasis. Some letters will be highly personal because the writers are friends (or want to be friends) of the speaker; some will be critical; some will be laudatory. Although each letter will be different, all may be "good" letters, depending on what each writer wants his message to convey. This is why there are few hard-and-fast rules about business writing. Writing a letter or a report involves a good deal more than following a "recipe." If a communication is to have individuality (and a good one always does), it must be created—and created out of experience. Without experiencing the situation, the writer is likely to wind up with a to-whom-it-may-concern letter or report.

On-the-Job Writing Versus Classroom Writing

The business writer on the job has a distinct edge over the student of business writing in the classroom. The employee is immersed in each situation that calls for a letter or a report. He is "living" his subject. He knows what prompted the communication to which he is responding or the background of a situation calling for the initiation of a letter or report. He usually knows something about the person he's writing to. He understands thoroughly what mission the message is to accomplish and something about the language that best fits the occasion. And, most important of all, because his company holds him responsible for constructing communications that will do the job, he writes with "success consciousness."

One of the difficulties of teaching business writing is that it's hard to create situations in which the student knows enough about the communication situation to produce an effective message. Generally, he is asked to read the "rules" for good writing, study examples of letters and reports that someone has created out of situations of which he isn't a part, and then try his hand at solving communication problems in abstract situations.

In this book we've tried to change the pattern. We've created communication situations in which the student can become personally involved—situations that are typical of those the business writer faces every day. These situations, which we call "cases" although they can probably be more accurately described as vignettes, follow the general background for business writing and introduce the principles of letter and report writing. In each of these cases, the student "feels" the climate of the communication situation and experiences the firing-line reaction that the practicing writer feels. Usually we offer one or more "wrong" solutions to the case problem; then we analyze each solution, telling the student what is wrong with it. Finally, we offer a recommended solution (sometimes two) and identify the features that make it a successful communication. These analyses become the instructional medium as opposed to "textbook lectures" that are often abstract. This pattern gives the student maximum *involvement,* which we think is the best way in which he can learn the writing craft. In the classroom tryouts of the manuscript, we learned that this problem-solving approach to effective writing really does work.

Special Features of This Book

The book has several distinctive features:

1. The student starts to analyze and write letters and reports almost immediately. We don't believe in "lecturing" for a third of the book before getting the student into the action.

2. We ask the student to imagine himself in various business positions—assistant office services manager, supervisor of records management, assistant manager of a resort hotel, assistant to the president of a publishing house, assistant personnel manager, and so on. The communications he deals with in each of these positions are directly related to the functions an employee holding the job would perform.

3. We avoid putting letters into strict categories—adjustment letters, credit and collection letters, sales letters, and so on. Such letter "types" are virtually unknown outside textbooks. In a business office, most letters simply can't be "typed." We believe there's no such thing as an "adjustment" letter, for example. Adjustment letters, credit letters, collection letters, and sales letters are all letters to customers. In fact, one letter often sells, "adjusts," collects, and builds good business relations—all in the same message.

4. We provide a good quantity of practical exercises—projects in which the student is on the firing line. Suggested solutions to the projects will be found in the *Instructor's Manual and Key,* which also contains a number of suggestions for teaching the course.

5. We introduce memorandums at the very beginning. Memorandums are internal letters, and many business writers prepare more of them than they do letters to be mailed outside the company. We think it's time this type of communication receives the emphasis it deserves.

Roy W. Poe
Rosemary T. Fruehling

CONTENTS

BUSINESS COMMUNICATION

part

1

BACKGROUND FOR BUSINESS WRITING

UNIT 1 SAY IT SIMPLY

Many people think there is a language unique to the world of business, a language characterized by words and phrases that make the writer appear to be profound, highly educated, "businesslike." The reason people think so, of course, is that so many communications written by business executives are verbose, stilted, impersonal, and murky in meaning. The writers often seem to intentionally aim at bewildering their readers.

"BUSINESS LANGUAGE" AND CLARITY

The best writers, in or out of the business world, are those who don't put on airs or beat around the bush; the worst are those who try to show their cleverness with words, the breadth of their vocabulary, and their "executiveness."

Case Example

The Strongheart Company, of Memphis, is planning to build three new warehouses in Indiana—one each in Indianapolis, Fort Wayne, and Gary—and management is talking with Brady Construction Company about building them. Representatives of Brady have been invited to visit Strongheart the week of April 11 to discuss warehouse space needs with those responsible for receiving, storing, and shipping goods. R. J. Simmons, executive vice president of Strongheart, must write to the appropriate executives in his company, asking them to make sure they and their key people are on hand the week of April 11 and, in the meantime, to update information on space needs they previously reported. Here is Mr. Simmons' memo.

TO: Messrs. Wilson, Conover,   FROM: R. J. Simmons
         Himmelfarb, and Gagne

SUBJECT: Visit With Brady Construction   DATE: March 12, 19—

To alleviate the shortage of warehouse space, Mr. LeFevre and the writer have initiated preliminary negotiations with Brady Construction Company for the construction of three new warehousing complexes in Indianapolis, Fort Wayne, and Gary; and it is mandatory that we must know the requirements for space needs no later than March 16. Representatives of Brady plan to visit our premises during the entire week of April 11 to contact each one who has responsibilities for Receiving, Storing, and Shipping Departments, and you must check your calendars now immediately, informing the writer of plans you may have arranged to be absent from your desk during that period.

2

Brady appears to be eminently qualified to undertake the design and construction of these facilities; our previous meetings with their representatives were encouraging.

R.J.S.

cc: S. LeFevre

Did you enjoy reading the memorandum? What's more important, was it clear and easy to read? Probably not, right? This memorandum, typical of many written in business every day, is an example of that so-called "business language" we spoke about. Notice the words and phrases that complicate the message:

alleviate the shortage	*warehousing complexes*	*contact*
initiated	*mandatory*	*eminently qualified*
preliminary negotiations	*premises*	

Also note the long, involved sentences (the memo has only three sentences, each containing several thoughts) and the roundabout way of expressing ideas:

plan to visit our premises. Just say *will be here.*
during the entire week. The week of April 11 is clearer.
now immediately. Either *now* or *immediately,* not both.
informing the writer. Better: *telling me.*

The meaning is also obscure. For example, what did the writer mean by "informing the writer of plans you may have arranged to be absent from your desk during that period"? Didn't he really mean, "Check your calendars now and let me know whether you plan to be here"?

Finally, the memo is badly organized. For example, there is no good reason to discuss Brady's qualifications at the end of the memo. This remark should be placed near the discussion of who Brady is and the purpose of the representatives' visit. The last thought to be left with the readers is their responsibility for updating their reports and clearing their calendars for the April 11–15 meetings.

What might Mr. Simmons have said in his memorandum?

TO: Messrs. Wilson, Conover, Himmelfarb, and Gagne   FROM: R. J. Simmons

SUBJECT: Visit With Brady Construction   DATE: March 12, 19—

Mr. LeFevre and I have had two meetings with representatives of Brady Construction Company about our plans to build new warehouses in Indianapolis, Fort Wayne, and Gary. We like their proposal and think we may have found the right people to do the job for us.

Some of the Brady men will be here the week of April 11 to learn more about our specific requirements. They are particularly interested in the procedures for receiving, storing, and shipping goods. To get ready for their visit, we'll need an updated estimate of our space needs in those three locations. Will you please reexamine your earlier reports and, where appropriate, revise your figures. I'll need your new estimates by March 16.

It is very important that you and your principal foremen and supervisors be available April 11 to 15 for individual conferences with the Brady men. If for any reason you plan to be away from your desk during that week, please let me know at once.

R.J.S.

cc: S. LeFevre

Isn't the second memorandum much smoother and easier to read and understand? Notice its directness and simplicity, prime qualities of effective business communications.

If you think the first example is exaggerated, you are mistaken. Much of the writing in business, government, and other organizations is similarly complicated by such gobbledygook. (Webster defines *gobbledygook* as "wordy and generally unintelligible jargon.")

Look at this example from a government official's memorandum.

Because of our industry knowledge and working relationships, our agency can and must be in the position of providing valid criteria directed to the consideration that unless the standards, programs, laws, and regulations that our government generates as they apply to business and industry, in its multiple role of perhaps being a polluter and at the same time being a supplier of equipment and systems to correct pollution, are clearly prepared and interpreted and in fact within a time frame that industry can actually implement, they serve no useful purpose.

After reading this statement two or three times, you get the impression that the writer believes his agency should clarify its regulations on pollution. But you aren't quite sure, and neither were those who received the document. Besides hiding his thoughts behind a cloud of stiff and pompous words, the writer has tried to say everything in one sentence. It's hard *not* to confuse the reader when your sentences run this long (90 words)!

Let's take another example.

Case Example

You're a customer service correspondent in the home office of the Champion Sporting Goods Company. Recently you've had several complaints from customers (schools, retail stores, government agencies, etc.) that refunds due them for overpayments or for returned merchandise are very slow in reaching them. They say your competitors are much faster. Your boss decides that each district office of Champion should prepare its own refund checks so that customers will get them quicker. He writes the following memo to the district managers telling them about the new procedure.

TO: All District Managers   FROM: Joseph Barnes

SUBJECT: Refunds   DATE: March 19, 19—

Effective June 1st and thereafter issue all checks for any amount written out to customers for overpayment of their accounts or for returned merchandise from your office directly to the customer without having to go through the home office.

We feel that this plan and procedure will not only help to improve customer relations substantially but will also close the gap on one of the important areas where our company compares unfavorably with other companies in its contacts with customers.

However, you may or may not find in your previous or committed routine that this is feasible. This new practice may be too time-consuming. Comment on same at the bottom of this memo and return it to me. Please do this by return mail, as we hope to effectuate this new procedure immediately. Thank you for your cooperation.

You can quickly see that the message is somewhat garbled and will require some time for the district managers to decipher. Note the following:

Effective June 1st and thereafter. The words *and thereafter* are not needed; *June 1st* should be *June 1.*

issue all checks for any amount. The word *checks* is sufficient.

written out to. The words *written out* are unnecessary.

without having to go through the home office. This phrase is not needed. If the checks are to go directly to customers, they obviously cannot go through the home office.

but will also close the gap on one of the important areas where our company compares unfavorably with other companies in its contacts with customers. This is a long, involved way of expressing a simple thought: *but also will give us an edge on our competitors.*

in your previous or committed routine. This phrase says nothing and should be omitted.

by return mail. Obviously the writer wants immediate action, and he is more likely to get it if he says *today* or by *Wednesday, the 26th.*

as we hope to effectuate this new procedure immediately. Why not, *We want to start this plan at once?*

How do you like this revision of the memo—without the gobbledygook?

TO: All District Managers   FROM: Joseph Barnes

SUBJECT: Refunds   DATE: March 19, 19—

Beginning June 1, please send all refund checks to customers directly from your office. This procedure should speed up the process and get rid of the complaints we've had from some of our customers.

The idea should work; let's give it a try. Let me know if you run into any problems.

DEADWOOD

The gobbledygook example above contains not only pompous and meaningless words but simple words that are merely *deadwood*—words occupying space without adding to clarity. It's been said that the typical business communication could be reduced by one-third simply by removing deadwood.

Case Example

Look at the following sentence from a meeting announcement.

In the event that you can attend the meeting, plan in advance to offer some concrete suggestions on how to reduce the cost and expense of overtime in the Office Services Department.

Let's eliminate some of the deadwood.

In the event that. Just say *If.*

plan in advance. Plan is sufficient; *in advance* is not necessary because planning is something that is done in advance.

concrete suggestions. Why *concrete?* Why not simply *suggestions?*

cost and expense. In this case, the words *cost* and *expense* mean the same thing; use one or the other but not both.

We arrive at a simple, direct message that anybody can understand immediately.

If you can attend the meeting, plan to offer suggestions on how to reduce overtime expense in the Office Services Department.

Here are other examples of deadwood in business writing.

Deadwood	Replacement
a philanthropic gift	*a gift*
according to our records	Can usually be eliminated.
actually, we have no basis for	Omit *actually.*
attached hereto	Omit *hereto.*
basic essentials	*essentials.* If something is essential, it must be basic.
during the time that	*while* or *when*
first and foremost	*first* or *most important*
I am of the opinion that	*I think*
I wish to inform you	Omit.
in compliance with your request	This phrase usually is not needed.
in this connection, I propose that	*I propose that*
it is my personal opinion	*Personal* is unnecessary.

meet together	*meet.* People cannot meet separately.
rules and regulations	These terms often mean the same thing.
subsequent to	*after*
true facts	*facts.* All facts are true.
we are at the present time	*we are* or *we are now*
we are not in the position to	*we* can't
we regret to inform you	*unfortunately* or *we're sorry that*
your check in the amount of $75	A check is always for some amount. *Your check for $75* is better.

"HORSE-AND-BUGGY" WRITING

When some people write letters, they seem to be still wearing high-button shoes and long gold watch chains. These horse-and-buggy writers outdo each other in Victorian courtesies.

Case Example

My dear Sir:

Yours of the first received and contents duly noted. In reply would state that as per agreement the undersigned agrees to perform indicated services in accordance with prior instructions.

Thanking you for past favors, I remain,

Yours truly,

Would you ever write such a message? Of course not, but many people still cling to the ''grand style'' of the horse-and-buggy era. Wouldn't you write the message this way?

Dear Paul:

I was glad to have your letter and to know that we've come to an agreement. You can count on our living up to our part of the bargain.

Thank you for giving us this chance to work with you.

Sincerely,

Following are a few of the horse-and-buggy expressions that are still with us. Use their up-to-date replacements.

Horse-and-Buggy	Up-to-Date
advise	tell
at hand	I have
beg to advise, state, suggest, etc.	Omit.
favor us with a reply	please write
has come to hand	has arrived

Horse-and-Buggy	Up-to-Date
hereby advise	Omit.
herewith rendered	here is
I deem	I think
I seek your kind indulgence	I hope you understand
in due course	by next Monday
kindly	please
order has gone forward	order was sent
under date of	July 12
under separate cover	separately
up to this writing	until now
with your kind permission	may I
your kind (or esteemed) favor	your letter

JARGON

Another enemy of clarity is jargon—the specialized language of a profession or trade.

Case Example

Many companies do not elect to close the factory overhead applied and factory overhead control accounts monthly. In that eventuality, since the natural procedure would be to record variances at the time of closing these accounts, such companies develop the variance analysis monthly in memorandum form, report to the parties concerned, and defer the general journal entries until the year-end closing. Since the variance analyses previously demonstrated constitute a form of worksheet, it is not necessary to have a formal closing of the books in order to develop the information for reporting purposes.

The above paragraph from an accounting report may be quite clear to an accountant, but to the man who doesn't know the accountant's language, it is meaningless. Every profession has its own jargon, and as long as its members are communicating with one another, jargon isn't a problem. But when we write letters and reports to people outside our field of work, we must remember that our jargon may seem like gobbledygook to them. To a publisher, *halftone* is a very ordinary word, but the layman has to be told that it is a photograph. *Actuary* is a strange term to most people, but every good insurance man knows that an actuary is a person who computes insurance premiums. *Machine language* is a term that is meaningful only to those who work with computers. A credit man does not write to the man in the street about the *aging of accounts receivable,* nor does a stockbroker use such terms as *odd-lot differentials, noncumulative preferred stock,* and *over-the-counter stock* when writing or talking to a new investor.

If you want to keep your writing simple, then, make sure you choose words that your reader understands.

VOGUE WORDS

Not long ago it became fashionable, especially in government circles, to tack the suffix *-wise* onto certain words—*businesswise, profitwise, policywise,* and so on. Although such words can help to shorten a message, they also complicate it. Compare:

> Profitwise, it was not a good decision.
> The decision brought our profit rate down.

Another fad, equally disturbing and still in vogue, is the use of such ''ize'' words as *optimize, maximize, definitize, finalize,* and *circularize.* Not only do most such words fail to save space, but they also tend to interfere with clarity. Compare the following trio of offenders with their replacements.

> VOGUE WORDS
>
> To optimize the utilization of the equipment available, the budget department has resorted to overtime.
> It is requested that a decision be finalized in the immediate future.
> Please definitize the procedures.
>
> WITHOUT VOGUE WORDS
>
> The budget department is working overtime in order to make the most efficient use of its equipment.
> May we have a final decision by May 16?
> Please state the procedures explicitly.

Some words are like fashions—they come and go. And too many writers tend to pick up the vogue words and use them to prove they are in fashion. As this book is written, some of the vogue words are *viable, synergism, expertise, cognitive, interface, relevant, accountability, parameter, charismatic, polarize, escalate, overkill,* and *coexistence.* Of course, such words are perfectly good if the user is certain that his reader or listener understands them, but the trouble is that vogue words look and sound impressively profound. And once a vogue word takes hold, it is beaten to death—often as much through misuse as overuse. An example of the misuse of a vogue word is *parameter.* Many people use it as a synonym for *perimeter,* which it is not, of course.

WRITING FOR EASY READING

''I must write with pains so that my reader may read with ease,'' said Robert Louis Stevenson. The distinguished author meant that he wrote to someone and not for himself. If this advice is sound for the fiction writer, it is even more appropriate for the business writer. Those who receive a great deal of correspondence want to grasp each writer's ideas as quickly as possible, take the necessary action, and move on to the next job. They don't have the time or the desire to plow through verbose or stilted communications. Thus you should prefer the simple expression to the complex, the direct route to the circuitous one.

It may surprise you to learn that people with the largest vocabularies are often the most readable writers; they have learned that it is the simple word that stirs the emotions and puts feeling into communications. The skilled writer knows that *conflagration* means *fire,* but he will choose the latter. By the same token, he will avoid using *subsequent to* for *after, edifice* for *building, cognizant* for *aware, determine* or *ascertain* for *find out, maximal* for *complete, nominal* for *small, conjecture* for *guess,* or *ameliorate* for *improve.*

When you were very young, you may have used the pompous expression, "Kindly extinguish the nocturnal illumination," and howled with laughter when your friends couldn't translate it as "Please turn off the light." Or, "Mater requested that I expedite the purification of the walking surface" for "Mother said to mop the floor and be quick about it." These examples are *supposed* to be funny; unfortunately, we can find similar ones in today's letters and reports that weren't meant to be but are.

Beware, then, of accepting the idea that there is a "business language" reserved for the exclusive use of those engaged in commerce. There is no such thing—only a personal writing style adapted to business situations.

■ ■

PROJECTS

A Rewrite the following in simple, easy-to-understand language.

1 In a subsequent memo, we will evaluate the relative desirability of various and sundry investments in effectuating the overall objectives of the company.

2 It is apparent and obvious, therefore, that sound knowledge of letter composition and cultivation of the accurate thinking by which it must be accompanied should constitute an exceedingly worthwhile accomplishment.

3 Verification that functional requirements of products are satisfied at minimal cost is established by design value reviews prior to final engineering release.

4 A number of business decisions are capable of easier resolution as a consequence of advance cost estimates.

5 Many top-management groups seek to inject more incentive into pay practices by gearing increases to differences in performance.

6 Business failure itself is an everyday occurrence in our country.

7 The two most important considerations in determining the internal communications system or systems that will be most appropriate for a given organization are speed and cost.

8 Mere availability of potential statistical method has not led automatically to practical applications.

9 What is the receptivity of the organization to change?

10 Clear-cut job descriptions, preferably in writing, for all supervisory personnel are indispensable to manager development.

B See if you can reduce the number of words in each of the following, at the same time making each statement clearer and more to the point.

1 We are making this analysis for the purpose of providing a basis for improving the sales picture.

2 In the majority of instances, we ship goods to our customers under a c.o.d. arrangement.

3 In view of the foregoing facts and figures, it seems appropriate to suggest an entirely new customer-service policy.

4 I have your letter of September 14 before me and am happy to tell you that we will be able to supply the uniforms you want in the colors and sizes you requested in your letter.

5 Would it be possible, do you think, for you to engage the Crown Room for our use as the meeting place of our task force on May 19?

6 It is the consensus of opinion of our Personnel Relations Committee that work stoppages would decrease impressively and substantially if the equipment were kept in constant and complete repair.

7 Are you sending the invitations out in the mail in plenty of time so that those who are being invited will have sufficient advance notice in which to respond?

8 The accountants in our department individually and collectively agree with the decision arrived at to cease and desist the practice of amortizing product-development costs over a five-year period.

9 The regional managers held a meeting for the purpose of discussing the distribution of sales territories in the various geographical areas.

10 Mr. Collard gave a talk on the growing increase in the popularity of bonus compensation systems for personnel in management positions.

C Suggest one or two words that can be substituted for each of the following expressions. You may want to indicate that the expression can be omitted altogether.

1 in regard to *or* in reference to

2 along the lines of

3 due to the fact *or* for the reason that

4 in favor of

5 in order to

6 in the majority of instances

7 in the neighborhood of

8 in view of the above

9 on behalf of

10 Hoping to hear from you, I remain

11   with the exception of

12   attached (or enclosed) please find

13   enclosed herewith

14   continued patronage

15   I have your letter

16   subsequent to

17   taking the liberty of

18   would like to state (and all the would-like-to's and wish-to's)

D   Tell why each of the following expressions is redundant.

1   new innovations

2   absolutely necessary

3   ask the question

4   consensus of opinion

5   enclosed you will find

6   necessary requirements

7   other alternative

8   reasonable and fair

9   temporarily suspended

10   totally unnecessary

E   Study the following; then rewrite each, removing unnecessary words. In some cases, you may wish to substitute a different term.

1   exactly identical

2   basic fundamentals

3   connect up

4   free gratis

5   repeat back

6   past experience

7   four in number

8   at a distance of 40 miles

9   at a price of $175

10   the color of the Gizmo is dark green

11   round in shape

12   throughout the entire year

13   during the year of 19—

14   came at a time when

15   if it is possible, please

16   the reason is due to

17   in view of

18   according to our records

19   at all times

20   during the time that

21   held a meeting

22   in this day and age

23   made the announcement

24   at an early date

25   due to the fact that

26   a substantial number of people are of the opinion

27   fully cognizant of

28   encounter difficulty in

F   See if you can think of a simpler word for each of the following. (For some, you may need more than one word.)

1   acquiesce

2   aggregate

3   apparent

4   approximately

5   ascertain

6   assist

7   commensurate with

8   communicate with

9   conclusion

10   construct

11   demonstrate

12   difficult

13	discrepancy	21	modification	29	render
14	disseminate	22	permit	30	submitted
15	equitable	23	preclude	31	subsequent to
16	equivalent	24	predisposed	32	sufficient
17	expiration	25	previous to	33	terminated
18	initiate	26	procure	34	transmitted
19	inquire	27	provided	35	utilization
20	interrogate	28	purchase	36	verification

G   Rewrite the following letter, using today's language.

Dear Madam:

Yours of February 1st at hand and contents noted. In reply would wish to state that your order for 20 Executive Desk Planners will be shipped to you in due course. It is anticipated that you will have receipt by February 11 or at an earlier date; if not, I beg your indulgence.

In this connection, would state that you will be billed at the price of $3.20 each, less trade discount of 30 percent. Hoping this is satisfactory and thanking you in advance for your esteemed patronage, I remain,

Yours truly,

H   Rewrite the following memo, which requires some reorganization of ideas.

TO: All Personnel   FROM: Lester Mapes
SUBJECT: Interoffice Mail   DATE: March 3, 19—

Interoffice envelopes are provided to all departments by the mail room. If you have a shortage of these envelopes, they can be obtained from Mr. Hudson.

Because of the excessive cost of using envelopes designed for purposes other than interoffice mail (letter envelopes, etc.), it is requested that interoffice envelopes be used whenever practical.

■ ■

UNIT 2   SAY IT CLEARLY

In Unit 1 we said that the best business writers write so that people on the run can read their messages with ease and with understanding. We pointed out that gobbledygook, deadwood, outdated phrases, and jargon are arch-enemies of the good writer. In this unit we're going to talk about other factors that affect readability.

GRAMMAR AND READABILITY

Even though grammar and punctuation are unattractive to many of us who have struggled with them unsuccessfully for years, they are not unimportant. Poor grammar and punctuation can destroy the clarity of a communication. Perhaps even more important, they can destroy the reader's confidence in the writer and his firm.

That's reason enough to be correct in grammar usage. Another reason is that when you make errors in grammar, you distract the reader. Have you ever heard a speaker who, by a nervous tic, slovenly stance, or sloppy dress, diverted your attention so that you had trouble listening to what he said? Bad grammar and punctuation can cause the same distraction.

Case Example

Dear Mr. Grubbs,

I am delighted to tell you that every member of our advertising staff plan to attend the July workshop in Columbus, some of them will go for two days and others for three. You will be interested to learn that Mr. Aiken will accompany George Bok and I to the meeting.

Concerning the program. We look forward to hearing Dr. Pressey on research. He spoke at the Marshalltown conference a year ago and our people commented "they would like to hear him again." This is their chance.

Yours very truly,

We won't bother to point out the mistakes in grammar and punctuation; they will be obvious to you. No matter what one's title is in an organization or what rung of the company ladder he is on, as long as he uses company letterhead, the firm—as well as the writer—is subject to criticism and a "bad press" when letters such as the one above slip through.

Many prospective executives shrug off the importance of having strong language skills on the theory that they will have secretaries who know all the dos and don'ts of grammar. As experienced executives know, however, not all secretaries are expert grammarians. Nor does every young executive have his own secretary; instead, he may have to write his communications in rough draft and turn them over to typists who do not touch up work but return it precisely as given to them.

If you feel insecure about your grammar usage and mechanics of style, there's still time to remedy the situation. Several good programmed books (self-study) could help enormously. On the job, you can make it your business to study the style of work of good writers in your company.

SENTENCE STRUCTURE AND READABILITY

Sentence structure, including the length and variety of your sentences, is a crucial factor in the readability of your communications. And since long sentences require deep concentration by the reader, the good writer looks for opportunities to break them up. When a sentence grows to about 20 words—roughly two typewritten lines—start thinking how you might trim it.

Case Example

> Because more than one freight classification may apply to the same type of goods, the traffic manager can effect further savings by a careful auditing or checking of freight bills the company is called upon to pay, since these charges are complicated and involved and errors are often made in computation as well as in classification.

Notice how much clearer the author's ideas are when broken down:

> Because more than one freight classification may apply to the same type of goods, the traffic manager can effect further savings by a careful auditing of the company's incoming freight bills. Since the charges in such bills are complicated, errors in computation and in classification are often made.

Short sentences can be most effective. It is said, for example, that the most powerful sentence in the English language is ''Jesus wept''—just two words. And grammatically incomplete, short statements (called *elliptical expressions*) can occasionally be used with good results.

> We certainly can, Mr. Salinger.
>
> We promise—October 3 at the latest.
>
> Mail it today. Please.
>
> I agree.
>
> When?

Overusing short sentences or elliptical expressions, however, makes a message choppy and disconnected. Compare the following.

CHOPPY

Dear Mr. Talbot:

The error in your June statement was our error. We admit it is ours. We are enclosing a corrected statement. Your records and ours now agree. Thank you. We appreciate your help.

Sincerely,

SMOOTHER

Dear Mr. Talbot:

The error in your June statement is ours, and we are enclosing a corrected statement showing that your records and ours now agree.

Thank you for your help.

Sincerely,

For easier reading, confine each sentence to a single thought or to very closely related ideas. Since your reader can digest only a reasonable amount of information in one gulp, strive for bite-size sentences. The following college catalog course description is an illustration of a writer taking too big a bite in one sentence.

> This course is an important elective offering, as demonstrated by an experimental research project conducted as a master's thesis, planned to provide social-work students with necessary firsthand experience of being in a group that is constantly examining itself and its members, since the experiencing, studying, and learning of these processes is related to the increasing use of group methods in all the social services and, further, because this experience can greatly enhance a student's self-awareness and authentic presentation of self, both of which are highly desirable components of the professional practice of social work.

Give the reader a breather from time to time. Constructing reasonable sentences not only forces you to organize your information more intelligently but also helps the reader to enjoy and understand the message.

PARAGRAPHING AND READABILITY

Long, fat paragraphs discourage the reader. Haven't you found yourself putting a book away simply because it opened with a long descriptive paragraph? Paragraphs extending to four or more inches of single-spaced type aren't necessary. Somewhere in a lengthy paragraph there is usually an opportunity to begin a new paragraph. Since short paragraphs are visual rests for your reader, consider him by including them in your writing.

Case Example

> Many persons believe that the inventions created by man are causing too much shifting of jobs and are causing unemployment. As each new invention becomes popular, more workers lose their jobs. They also believe that when there is a depression, new inventions should be registered with the government and not introduced and put to use until prosperity comes. Others, however, feel that progress should not be hindered. They believe that, in the long run, machines create more jobs than they destroy. For example, the discovery of electricity and the invention of the electric light threw many persons out of work, but on the other hand, thousands of newly trained workers were needed in the factories that manufactured electrical goods. The invention of the automobile threw carriage makers out of work, but it eventually caused many more men to be employed as automobile workers than had been employed previously as carriage makers. Today skilled workers are learning how to perform other kinds of tasks within their factories. The industries created by the invention of the automobile, radio, motion picture, airplane, computer, and television have created, in turn, hundreds of thousands of jobs.

How might the above paragraph be revised and divided so that it is more readable and understandable?

> Many persons believe that man's inventions are causing a shifting of jobs and unemployment. As each invention becomes popular, more workers lose

their jobs. People also believe that when there is a depression, inventions should be registered with the government but not introduced until prosperity returns.

Others, however, feel that progress should not be hindered. They believe that, in the long run, machines create more jobs than they destroy. For example, the discovery of electricity and the invention of the electric light threw many persons out of work, but on the other hand, thousands of newly trained workers were needed in the factories that manufactured electrical goods. The invention of the automobile threw carriage makers out of work, but eventually it caused many more men to be employed as automobile workers than had been previously employed as carriage makers.

Today skilled workers are learning how to perform other kinds of tasks. The industries created by the invention of the automobile, radio, motion picture, airplane, computer, and television have created, in turn, hundreds of thousands of jobs.

Just as you present only one main idea in a sentence, so you should develop only one main thought in each paragraph, making everything in the paragraph contribute directly to that central idea.

When one business writer was asked how he writes such effective letters and reports, he said, "I grab the reader firmly by the hand, and I hang on to him until I'm finished." That's good advice. One way to "grab the reader by the hand and hang on" is to bridge the gap between sentences by using connectors, or transitional expressions, such as the following:

TO SHOW CAUSE AND EFFECT

| accordingly | as a result | hence | therefore |

Mr. Balfour requested that we send copies of the report to all new managers. Therefore, we made an extra fifty copies.

TO SHOW EXCEPTIONS TO WHAT HAS BEEN SAID

| but | even though | on the contrary | otherwise |
| conversely | however | on the other hand | |

We can, as you suggested, be ready to move by October 6. However, a move at that time would delay customer billings.

I agree that Meredith has a better college record than Lacey. On the other hand, he has virtually no experience in COBOL.

TO INDICATE TIME, PLACE, OR ORDER IN RELATION TO WHAT HAS GONE BEFORE

above all	finally	in summary	still
after all	first	meanwhile	then
again	further	next	too

Entering the Latin American market is not as simple as it sounds. First, there is the problem of translations. Then there is the matter of finding suitable manufacturing capabilities. Above all, we must face up to the fact that we have no distribution outlets there.

TO INTRODUCE EXAMPLES

| for example | for instance | namely | that is |

Many functions could be merged immediately; for example, receiving and marking could be placed under one supervisor.

BREVITY AND READABILITY

Rarely is there any excuse for a letter to exceed one page. Most letters can be cut about a third without suffering in meaning. The misconception therefore arises that short letters are the best letters. Not necessarily. In fact, brief letters can be less readable than those that are too long.

Brevity is carried too far when information needed to make the message clear is left out. Also, leaving out friendly words and phrases that do not contribute to meaning but contribute to goodwill or favorable acceptance is an expensive word-saving tactic. Removing deadwood that contributes neither to better understanding nor to good human relations is, however, a form of brevity well worth practicing. Brevity should never be at the expense of completeness. You may find that a somewhat longer letter is much clearer and more readable. That's what we really want, isn't it?

Case Example

If a furniture manufacturer has to tell a dealer that his order for a coffee table can't be filled because the company has discontinued a particular line, he could accomplish the objective of brevity with this letter.

> Dear Mr. Angevine:
>
> We can't fill your order and are therefore canceling it. Sorry.
>
> > Sincerely yours,

But this writer has left too many questions unanswered, the most important of which is "Why?" And he has also passed up the opportunity to make or keep a friend—a friend who might be a customer for other products he has to sell. Let's try again.

> Dear Mr. Angevine:
>
> About six months ago we decided to discontinue our Conger red maple table line because most of our customers quit ordering it.
>
> You can probably get what you want, however, from the White Mountain Furniture Manufacturing Company, Plymouth, New Hampshire. At least they were able to fill a similar order I referred to them in November.
>
> Good luck—and thanks for thinking of us!
>
> > Sincerely yours,

The second letter is longer, you will notice, but a lot more effective.

How long should a letter be? There is no better answer than "long enough to do the job it sets out to do." Some of the most successful sales letters written by *Esquire, Look, Time* and Haband (a mail-order clothing firm) are four or five pages long. On the other hand, some very brief letters accomplish their mission in grand style. H. L. Mencken, the great literary figure, received many letters from people taking him to task about his newspaper and magazine articles on religion, women, politics, and other subjects. His answer to all these critics was very brief:

> Dear Madam (or Sir):
>
> You may be right.
>
> H. L. Mencken

ACTION VERBS AND READABILITY

Some writers make their messages dull and tedious to read by overusing passive verbs. By using such verbs as *is being credited, has been sent, was filled, were checked, are being processed,* and *have been assigned,* the writer misses the opportunity to add punch to his writing.

Notice how the writer gave life to the following sentences by using active verbs.

> *Jean transcribed the letters. Jean* is the subject, the "doer" of the action; *transcribed* is the "action" verb; and *letters* is the direct object, the "result" of the action.
>
> *Miss O'Brien gave Mr. Stevens the memo. Miss O'Brien* is the subject, the "doer" of the action; *gave* is the "action" verb; *Mr. Stevens* is the indirect object, the person to whom Miss O'Brien gave the memo; and *memo* is the direct object, the thing that Miss O'Brien gave to Mr. Stevens.

A less skillful writer would make the above active sentences passive by:

1. Making the direct object or, if there is one, the indirect object the subject of the sentence.
2. Using a "being" verb (*be, am, is, are, was, were, been*) before the main verb.
3. Using a past participle (a verb form that can be used with *has, have,* or *had*) as the main verb.
4. Using *by* with the subject.

> *The letters were transcribed by Jean.* Note that the writer made *letters,* which was the direct object in the active sentence, the subject; used the "being" verb *were* with the past participle *transcribed;* and used *by* with *Jean,* the subject—the "doer" of the action—in the active sentence.
>
> *Mr. Stevens was given the memo by Miss O'Brien. Mr. Stevens,* which was the indirect object in the active sentence, is the subject. Also note the use of *was* with the past participle *given* and the use of *by* with *Miss O'Brien.*

Unless there is a definite advantage to emphasizing the result or the receiver of an action instead of the doer, you should avoid using passive sentences. But in stating a formal policy or regulation, for example, you may find a passive sentence preferable to an active one.

> *Smoking in the stockroom is prohibited.* This passive sentence is more tactful and less antagonizing than an active sentence, such as "The management prohibits smoking in the stockroom."

LOGIC AND READABILITY

When faulty logic slips into your writing, the readability of your messages suffers.

> Argyis and Company employs 200 men and 100 women; therefore, Argyis and Company discriminates against women.

Or you may be guilty of non sequiturs. The term *non sequitur,* meaning "it does not follow," applies to situations where the writer omits steps in his reasoning and makes it difficult or impossible for the reader to see the connection between statements.

> Our company is moving out of this building to Lafayette Street, and I am planning to buy a Buick.

The writer may have meant something like this:

> Our company is moving out of this building to Lafayette Street. Since there's no bus or subway service from my house to Lafayette Street, I'm going to need a car to get to work. I'm thinking of buying a Buick.

Still other defects in readability are due to conclusions based on false assumptions, half-truths, and fuzzy reasoning.

Case Example

An author submitted a manuscript to a publisher, requesting a personal interview to discuss it as soon as it was received. The editor wanted to write the author that he had received the manuscript, but he also wanted to avoid a personal interview. (He receives dozens of manuscripts every day and can't possibly see in person everyone who wants a work published.) He wrote the author as follows:

> It is our policy never to grant an interview with an author prior to acceptance of his manuscript.

What's wrong with the statement? In the first place, it simply isn't true. Publishers jump at the chance to talk with authors who have been consistently on the best-seller lists or who dominate the headlines in politics, entertainment, science, and the arts. Obviously the editor meant that he didn't think an interview with this author would be productive. Straight thinking would have required the editor to admit to himself that he wouldn't refuse *everybody* an appointment who wanted to see him—only those who didn't appear to have anything to offer him.

What might the editor have said? Something like this would have been more logical.

> Please give me several days to examine your manuscript thoroughly and to share it with others here. After we've given your work a careful evaluation, I will write you to tell you whether a meeting would be desirable.

Case Example

Charles Renault, a retail furniture dealer, wrote to a wholesaler asking for an extension of 30 days in paying his invoice for goods purchased a couple of weeks ago. He also requested the usual discount of 4 percent, even though he knew he wasn't entitled to it. The wholesaler, although willing to grant the 30-day extension, did not feel that he could allow the discount because the purpose of a discount is to encourage prompt payment. If an exception were granted, the wholesaler's other customers would also have to be given the same privilege and the whole idea of discounts for quick payment would be lost. The account supervisor who wrote to Mr. Renault said:

> Although we will be pleased to grant you an extension of 30 days in paying your account, I must tell you that the discount is not permitted. Discounts are given only to our prompt-paying customers, and it is they whom we must favor.

The writer is not logical when he implies that Mr. Renault is not a prompt-paying customer simply because he asked for an extension and a discount to which he was not entitled. Mr. Renault was presumptuous, perhaps, in asking for this special favor—he knows the rules, too—but that is no reason to brand him a slow-paying customer. The two issues are the purpose of a discount and the fair and equal treatment of all customers—not who is a prompt-paying customer and who is not.

The account supervisor might better have written this:

> Dear Mr. Renault:
>
> Of course we're glad to give you an extra 30 days on your account.
>
> We've had to make a hard-and-fast rule about discounts, giving them only when payment is received within the allowed 10-day period. If we made exceptions, a lot of our customers whom we've denied discounts would be unhappy; and, at the same time, those who are entitled to discounts would feel we were penalizing them. Possibly you've experienced this situation in your own business and know why we cannot change our discount policy.
>
> Sincerely yours,

Case Example

A mail room supervisor, angry because many employees brought mail to her department after the announced closing hour of 4:30 and expected it to be sealed, stamped, and mailed the same day, issued this memorandum.

> TO: All Employees   FROM: Jane Dobson
> SUBJECT: Mail Deadline   DATE: May 5, 19—
>
> This is to inform all parties that mail cannot be accepted after 4:30 each day. This policy has been in effect for over two years, but it is still being violated by many people. Only special-delivery letters will be received.

What's wrong with this thinking? In the first sentence the supervisor said that mail cannot be accepted after 4:30, but in the last sentence she said that special-delivery letters would be received. What the supervisor probably meant was that ordinary mail received after 4:30 would not be sealed, stamped, and sent out that day (presumably, it would lie in the mail room until the next morning); however, special-delivery letters would be sent out after 4:30.

And what was meant by "but it is still being violated"? Probably that nobody paid any attention to the policy when it was announced two years ago. The mail room supervisor might have been more successful if she had issued the much more logical message that follows. People tend to cooperate more readily when they understand why they are asked to do things.

TO: All Employees   FROM: Jane Dobson
SUBJECT: Mail Deadline   DATE: May 5, 19—

Will you please help us?

A couple of years ago, we set a policy that when ordinary outgoing mail is received in the mail room after 4:30, it is held for processing and mailing until the next day. The reason is that our employees leave at 5 and we are not authorized to keep them beyond that hour. Therefore, we set 4:30 as the cutoff point for ordinary mail, to allow ourselves a full 30 minutes to get everything processed.

Of course you may bring your outgoing mail to us up to 5, and we'll put it in safekeeping. But we won't try to get it to the post office until the next morning.

Special-delivery letters are exceptions to this policy. We will get those out the same day we receive them, even if they arrive in the mail room after 4:30.

APPEARANCE AND READABILITY

Some communications fall in the hard-to-read category simply because of the way they look. Poor typing (bad erasures, strikeovers, smudges), unbalanced margins, inconsistent spacing—all decrease readability.

Case Example

Here is an example of a letter that was carelessly written and even more carelessly typed. The person to whom the letter is addressed had sent a check for $8 to a magazine publisher for a subscription to a particular periodical. But he forgot to state what magazine he wanted and the publisher issues several at the $8 rate. Of course, the subscriber should have been more specific, but this is no excuse for the reply he received.

Dear Sir:

I'm sure if someone sent you a payment of $8 you'd want to know what it was for. So do we.

We received this among on 1/26/68 but allthough we have written to your twice, you have not as yettold us how to apply it. Apparently it is intended for a subscription to Garden Week, but we have no openaccount fore that magazine in your name.

In the m antime, I fear we may be sending you bills...or that you are not getting a servicd to which you are intitled. So would you please let me know if your payment is to cover a bill..to enter a new subscription...to renew a subscription..or for any other purpose. MOST IMPORTANT; please tell us the exact mailing address.

Your prompt answer, jotted on this letter and returned in the enclosed envelop will be most welcome, Then we'll be able to straighten out the matter in a hurry.

                    Most cordially,

                    Sue Farnsworth

                    Sue Farnsworth
                    Circulation Credt

After studying the illustration carefully, you will probably agree that the writer is capable of writing a good letter. The tone is fine (note that this was the third time Miss Farnsworth had written to the addressee; yet she showed no irritation or anger), and the writer obviously means well. Unfortunately, she could hardly have been more careless in attending to the important details of grammar, punctuation, and typing. Such imperfections insult the reader by implying that he won't recognize poor quality. (As a point of interest, because this letter was so carelessly written, the addressee sent it to an executive in Miss Farnsworth's company, a publishing house, with a bitter denunciation of the firm's correspondence standards. You can imagine the repercussions!)

DISPLAY AND READABILITY

The readability of many communications (especially memos and reports) can be enhanced by itemizing information that lends itself to 1–2–3 listings.

Case Example

Dear Miss Hardaway:

Our experiment with centralized files pointed up three basic problems which caused us to abandon the idea in our company. The physical difficulty of employees' getting to and from the files was a serious drawback. The distance was sometimes great, and the result was a considerable amount of traffic and delay. Messenger service didn't solve this particular problem either.

Another problem was that different departments have different needs. Where one department called for information in terms of geographical location, another asked for the same information by subject. This created much confusion and resulted in duplication of files. Interestingly, one of the most serious problems (and this surprised us) was that some departments didn't want other departments to have access to their records. While it was unlikely that one department would have need for another department's confidential files, the suspicion prevailed nevertheless that people were getting information they were not entitled to.

If you get to Cleveland sometime soon and have a little time, I'd like to show you the setup we have now. It works like a charm and has solved most of the problems referred to above.

Sincerely yours,

What do you think of this revision of the preceding letter?

Dear Miss Hardaway:

Our experiment with centralized files pointed up three basic problems which caused us to abandon the idea in our company.

1. Physical Problem. The physical difficulty of employees' getting to and from the files was a serious drawback. The distance was sometimes great, and the result was a considerable amount of traffic and delay. Messenger service didn't solve this particular problem, either.

2. Varying Needs of Departments. We learned very quickly that different departments have different needs. One department called for information in terms of geographical location; another asked for the same information by subject. Such variation created much confusion and resulted in duplication of files.

3. Departmental Access to Records. Interestingly, one of the most serious problems (and this surprised us) was that some departments didn't want other departments to have access to their records. Although it was unlikely that one department would need another's confidential files, the suspicion prevailed nevertheless that people were getting information they weren't entitled to.

If you get to Cleveland sometime soon and have a little time, I'd like to show you the setup we have now. It works like a charm and has solved most of the problems referred to above.

Sincerely yours,

Some writers prefer to number every paragraph in a memorandum in order to make follow-up references easier. For example, it is handier to refer to "item 4 in your July 21 memo" than "your statement concerning back-ordering procedures in the Connecticut and Massachusetts offices in your July 21 memo." Enumerations tend to clutter when they are overused, however; they should be used only when they will help the reader stay on course.

In long or involved memos and letters, sideheadings help to guide the reader, as shown in the following example.

Case Example

TO: Daniel L. Haskell   FROM: Susan T. Frey

SUBJECT: Sales Personnel Study in   DATE: January 27, 19—
         Branch Offices

As you know, I recently spent a week in each of the three Western regional offices, talking with the managers and their field supervisors about their personnel turnover problems. Here is a brief report.

LOS ANGELES

Los Angeles is short two salesmen (and has been since October), and the Bakersfield and Riverside territories have been left virtually uncovered since that time. One other salesman, Arnold Hooper (San Diego), is on the verge of resigning.

The Problem

The reasons given for the resignation of Alger (Bakersfield) and Hughes (Riverside) were just about identical: dissatisfaction with basic salary, inequitable incentive arrangement, and low mileage allowance. I understand that both received a substantial increase in salary from Jefferson Life, our major West Coast competitor.

While Hooper does not emphasize money as the basis for his unrest, it is certainly a major factor. Hooper's problem seems to be his inability to accept supervision, at least from the present field manager.

Recruiting

The Los Angeles office has found no effective sources of recruitment of new salesmen, relying almost entirely on newspaper ads in the Sunday *Times* and word-of-mouth recommendations of other salesmen. There do not appear to be any likely candidates on the horizon.

PHOENIX

Phoenix is fully staffed at the moment, although a couple of people are unsettled about their jobs (Millard in Phoenix and Carpenter in Flagstaff). The district manager told me that neither is performing up to his capacity and that their loss would not be a serious blow.

Recruiting

Phoenix seems to have no difficulty obtaining highly qualified candidates for sales positions. As a matter of fact, several applicants there look quite promising. This office has established exceptionally good relations with several colleges and universities in the area and obtains many candidates from these institutions.

SAN FRANCISCO

The San Francisco office is short one salesman; however, they have had several promising interviews and believe they will fill the vacancy before the end of the month. The situation here, however, is not so rosy as might be imagined.

The Problem

While San Francisco seems to have little trouble in filling their vacancies, the turnover rate is extremely high. Of the fifteen salesmen in this office, seven have been with the company less than a year, four less than two years, and only one more than five years. According to the exit interviews, most of those who leave the company do so because of dissatisfaction with salary and incentives. However, a number seem to have some difficulty getting along with their field managers.

RECOMMENDATIONS

I believe that we are in serious trouble in the matter of hiring and retaining an effective sales staff. Even among those people who choose to remain with the company, morale is low. To overcome the situation, I recommend the following:

1. Salary Study. That a study of salaries of our salesmen as compared with those in the industry as a whole and with several similar firms within each geographical district be undertaken.

2. Supervisory Training. That a how-to-supervise training program be established for district managers, field managers, and sales supervisors.

3. Personnel Recruitment. That a conference be held in each district under the supervision of our personnel department, instructing managers and field managers on the techniques of recruiting, testing, interviewing, and hiring salesmen.

4. Management Contacts. That more frequent contacts with management be provided all salesmen, through more frequent district and national conferences.

5. Field Memo. That a "field memo" or some such news-inspiration piece be distributed every month to field salesmen.

After you have read this report, I would like to talk with you further about some of the problems I found and enlarge on the recommendations I have made.

S.T.F.

The style of headings shown in the memo report above is most common but may vary considerably, depending upon personal preferences. Some writers prefer to put major headings in the left margin, as shown in the following excerpt from the same report.

TO: Daniel L. Haskell   FROM: Susan T. Frey

SUBJECT: Sales Personnel Study in   DATE: January 27, 19—
         Branch Offices

As you know, I recently spent a week in each of the three Western regional offices, talking with the managers and their field supervisors about their personnel turnover problems. Here is a brief report.

LOS ANGELES   Los Angeles is short two salesmen (and has been since October), and the Bakersfield and Riverside territories have been left virtually uncovered since that time. One other salesman, Arnold Hooper (San Diego), is on the verge of resigning.

The Problem   The reasons given for the resignation of Alger (Bakersfield) and Hughes (Riverside) were just about identical: dissatisfaction with basic salary, inequitable incentive . . . .

Displaying statistical data—no matter how simple—in tables increases the readability of letters and reports. Tables help the reader to understand at a glance information that he might find quite difficult to grasp in narrative form.

Case Example

As to advertising expenditures by media, in 19-2 we spent $15,000 on newspapers and magazines; $8,500 on radio and television; $18,000 on direct mail; $7,700 on transit advertising; $17,000 on premiums; and $6,400 on billboards. In 19-1 we spent $18,000 on newspapers and magazines; $10,000 on radio and television; $21,000 on direct mail; $3,500 on transit advertising; $12,000 on premiums; and $9,800 on billboards. For all media, in 19-2 we spent a total of $72,600 as compared to $74,300 in 19-1.

Compare this narrative style with the following table.

ADVERTISING EXPENDITURES, 19-2 AND 19-1

	19-2	19-1
Newspapers and Magazines	$15,000	$18,000
Radio and Television	8,500	10,000
Direct Mail	18,000	21,000
Transit Advertising	7,700	3,500
Premiums	17,000	12,000
Billboards	6,400	9,800
Totals	$72,600	$74,300

Would you agree that the information is easier to read in table form and that comparisons of yearly amounts are also easier?

■■■■■■■■■■■■■■■■■■■■■■■■■■■■■■■■■■■■■■

PROJECTS

A   Can you find the errors in the following?

1   Electronics, in addition to computer programming and refrigeration, are being offered by our training department.

2   Has there been any other complaints from our customers in the northwest region?

3   An art book or a one-volume encyclopedia seem to be appropriate gifts for subscribers.

4   Of the six different proposals we've received, the Kensington one seems to be the more attractive.

5   All of the accountants have been working overtime, some of them in the evenings and others on weekends.

6   Marty spoke to Tom and I about the shipping problem.

7   We are holding up invoicing ourselves.

8   Our chief economist is one of those who thinks he can predict with accuracy the capital expenditures in the construction industry.

9   This pay increase for production personnel is retroactive from July 15.

10   Stillman should of kept his word on the incentive rate.

11   The first installment will reach you Saturday, May 1 the second Saturday, May 14.

12   I did not attend the labor-management meeting therefore I am not certain of the outcome.

13   Please return to us for our records, the recently-revised training materials Mr. Harwell left with you.

14   Our aims at all times are these to give our customers the best service, to keep prices as low as possible, and making for ourselves a modest profit.

15   Sanborn asked the question what does cost reduction have to do with sales and there were several answers.

B   Rewrite the following, making any changes you feel will improve clarity.

1   Since an approved idea will win you a cash award, the amount depending on the value of your suggestion to the company, write your suggestions and drop your ideas in one of the suggestion boxes, and particularly welcome are suggestions that lead to improved quality or quantity of work, to reduced costs, or to improved relations with customers.

2   At a meeting of the board of directors, Mr. Ames, the corporation treasurer, brought an important problem to the attention of the board, pointing out that so far the company has been moving ahead haphazardly, with no blueprint or plan for its future operations and without control over its business costs, and contending that the corporation would be even more successful if it paid more attention to estimating, planning, and analyzing its costs and profits.

3   Actual costs are essential factors in income determination, but they leave much to be desired for other management purposes, as they reflect the inefficiencies of the period's operations are subject to seasonal fluctuations, and show the influence of unusual and nonrecurring events and thus they are decidedly poor guides for planning, control of costs, product costing, and establishment of selling prices.

4   About half of the fifty states have merit systems which require competitive examinations, New York being the first state to introduce the merit system and for over 75 years applicants for New York State employment have been required to pass tests other than those of political loyalty, so that today 70 percent of all jobs in the executive branch of the New York State government are filled through competitive examinations.

5   Salaries vary in different parts of the country and at different times, depending upon business conditions, the cost of living, and the supply of available trained office workers, being frequently determined by the ability and experience required by the position, but they have improved each year and, with more liberal allowances for sick leaves and vacations, are becoming quite respectable.

6   At a very minimum, the marketing organization should embrace such activities as sales, advertising, sales promotion, and market research, which is being "broken out" as a separate function in more and more companies and in many firms including the General Electric Company, product planning is also considered a marketing function as well as product service, especially where it is a factor in maintaining customer goodwill.

C   Rewrite the following, aiming at better variety of sentence length and paragraphing as needed.

1   The company contributes to still other benefit plans on your behalf. Because these plans bear no direct relationship to your employment with Polson's, Inc., they are given only brief mention here. These are state unemployment insurance, social security, and medicare.

2   He called in his chief accountant. He discussed the situation and his concern over his precarious profit position. The chief accountant pointed out that on several occasions he had recommended that the president establish a profit plan. He made it clear that this profit plan should be implemented by a detailed budget. The president countered with the opinion that the company was too small to warrant such elaborate procedures. He added ironically that the cost of such a program would probably wipe out the small profit which remained.

3   The next cause of delinquency in our customer accounts is laziness. Laziness is one of the most difficult causes of delinquency we have to cope with. Laziness is hard to grasp adequately. This is so because people who pay slowly through laziness are difficult to identify. Eventually we have to resort to harsher collection procedures. This is necessary simply because we have to show people that there is something worse in store for them if they don't pay their bills. This refers only to extreme cases.

4   Enclosed for your review and comment is a brief proposal from Lewis Markham. He has set up Personality Plus Institute. The purpose of this institute is to develop innovative programs on personal growth. In short, what must an individual do to sell himself? Mr. Markham is a full-time employee of Horizons Unlimited. He is also a part-time teacher at Ketchum College. I think you will be interested in this proposal.

5   There is a simple way to control the cost of telephoning. It is to schedule as many of your calls as possible in the evening. Many of your customers will be available to you in the evening. Evening rates for long-distance calls are lower than day rates. A great deal of money can be saved by telephoning your customers in the evening.

D   Some of the following sentences contain more than one idea. Rewrite them.

1   I look forward to our meeting in March, and in the meantime, I hope you will give some thought to the selection of a new agency.

2   It should not be necessary to assign guards for Saturdays and Sundays, and I suggest that we eliminate this expense.

3   We want you to come to see us in our new location, and I hope you will be completely satisfied with the Crawford-Gill line of maple tables.

4   I have clerked in stores, solicited door-to-door, and sold products on established routes, and I hope you will grant me an interview.

5   Fill in and return the card today, and remember that you get an additional 10 percent discount on all orders placed by August 1.

6   Won't you make use of Rayford's offer of a 10-day free examination by mailing the coupon today?

7   We want to congratulate you upon your successful completion of the Minnehaha Housing Project, and we hope the enclosed description of our expansion plans will encourage you to come to Des Moines to talk to us about our new shopping mall.

8   Employees have been particularly successful in making suggestions that bear some relation to their own work rather than to the work of others, but not eligible to receive awards are members of the methods staff and also those department heads and executives who are in a position to authorize the adoption of their own suggestions.

9   Here's a copy of Jefferson Federal's write-up and appraisal of the El Tiempo project, and you will notice that they have converted pesos to dollars.

10   Financial security for you and your family need no longer be a dream, and we hope you will stop in this month to learn firsthand how our Master Annuity can solve your money worries.

11   At any rate, I'm going to telephone you within a couple of weeks to see if you won't let me tell you more about Tuff Track Tires.

E   Read the following and see if you can supply connectors to bridge the gaps.

1   The language used in business communications obviously calls for precision. The word *nice*—what does it really say?

2   When you buy from a reliable merchant, you are encouraging good business practices. When you buy from an unethical dealer, you are approving his way of doing business.

3   If Winston Churchill, instead of speaking about ''blood, toil, sweat, and tears,'' had used such dreary words as, ''We shall all face difficult times,'' he probably would have made little impression. He would have had little success with big, fancy words.

4   A Federal Reserve bank does not provide service to the general public. It is a bank for banks; it provides the same services for its members that commercial banks provide for their customers.

5   About 90 percent of the goods and services produced in this country are produced by privately owned business enterprises. To a large extent, it is the owners and managers of business who are responsible for economic growth.

6   It has always been the first task of management to make profits for the company. And in their desire to increase the firm's income, managers are often thoughtless in handling employees, treating them as though they were just so many machines. Consideration is often given only to minimizing costs, no matter what effect such action may have on the income of the workers.

Workers usually see only one side of the picture. They believe all too often that the major purpose of the business is to provide them with jobs and are uninterested in and unsympathetic with management's desire to keep costs down and to make a profit.

7   No one knows for sure how much of our economic growth is the result of our having a free enterprise system. No one would deny that freedom to make our own economic decisions has contributed greatly to our economic progress.

8   Automation is eliminating two kinds of jobs in our company, the kind that does not require a great deal of skill, sometimes called semiskilled, and the monotonous kind where the worker performs the same task over and over.

F   Analyze the following for weak logic and other faults that hinder clarity; then rewrite as needed, supplying data to ensure clarity.

1   Your instructions were to ship 200 catalogs to Boston, 350 to Charleston, and 420 to Miami. I want to see what is happening to our shipments.

2   For example, of our 1,500 delinquent accounts about 10 percent have moved, leaving no forwarding address. We have an excellent record in collecting from our charge customers, but this situation is becoming increasingly serious and we can improve it.

3   In training a new man, your approach must be objective—it must be thorough and, above all, unselfish. It is only by giving of yourself, your time, and the benefit of your experience to the new representative that you can expect satisfactory results.

4   The new employee should be told about the importance of cooperation. Every worker is important, and this fact should be emphasized over and over again.

5

Dear Mr. Bradley:

I appreciate your comments about the delays you have experienced in recent weeks in receiving shipments from us.

We have always prided ourselves on the promptness with which we fill orders, but strikes and slowdowns in our industry have been all too common in the past five months. I hope you will bear with us during this present crisis.

Sincerely yours,

6   Potter's Mountain Inn has long been known as the complete convention center for business and professional groups such as yours. Whatever your preference in the way of sports, PMI has it. There's golf, tennis, swimming, water skiing, horseback riding, volleyball—you name it. And the big news is that it won't be long before we'll have winter sports, too.

7

To All Salesmen:

All credit cards bearing the company name must be surrendered to the accounting office immediately. In the future, if you wish to have credit cards, you must apply for them individually, paying the membership dues yourself (the dues are *not* legitimate company expenses).

You may retain the Air Travel and Hertz cards issued by the company.

8

DAILY CAFETERIA HOURS

Breakfast— 7:30–8:30

Lunch   —12:00–2:30

    Closed Mondays

9

PROPER PLANNING

One of the most significant phases for the new man is proper planning of time and activity. Show him how long-range and short-range plans are set up and used. Avoid criticism of the new man at this stage. Instead demonstrate the proper way to do things and compliment him on his progress whenever a sincere compliment is justified. Doing this, remember to compliment him for something he did well. Like, "That was an excellent presentation you made, John." Don't say, "You're a terrific salesman, John."

10   The purpose of this memo is to outline our objectives in the training of new field representatives because I want you to have the benefit of my observations in the recruiting, hiring, and training of new men.

G   The following letter was written to School and College Charms, Inc., by the president of a college students organization.

Gentlemen:

About a month ago I wrote for a free catalog, but I have not received it. I am particularly interested in the college pennant charm for William and Mary.

Is this charm available? If so, how much will it cost, including postage?

I would still appreciate having your catalog.

Very truly yours,

Here is the response as it was actually written (at the bottom of the student's letter).

```
Under sperate cover we are sending you a catalogue.  Please be advised that
we can give you a pennant with WM on it for William and Mary.  If you want it
in gold it will cost you $6.00 and 1.50 in sterling.  The pennant will be in
color and the WM will be in either gold or sterling according to  what you
order it in.
```

Criticize the response and then prepare the one you would have written.

H   Revise and set up the following memo so that it is easier to read and digest.

TO: J. N. Carey

FROM: (Your name)

SUBJECT: Customer Complaints on Elimination of Delivery Service

You asked for a report on the complaints of customers because of our elimination of delivery service. As you know, this new policy went into effect March 1 and we have had three months in which to assess its impact on our customers. As soon as the decision was made, I asked all employees who have contacts with customers—either by telephone or in person—to fill out a customer complaint slip (see attached) when the matter of delivery service was introduced.

At this time we have received 27 complaints. Six were from customers who have long-established charge accounts and are rated A-1. Seven were from newly established charge accounts (less than six months). 12 were from customers who could not be identified from our records and are presumed to be occasional cash shoppers. Two were from charge customers who have owed us money for 90 days or more and are rated as risky. Our total number of charge customers at this time is 7,003, and we estimate our cash customers each month to be about 35,000. If only 27 out of 42,003 have complained, we must assume that our new policy has had virtually no negative influence on customers and that we have weathered the initiation of this new policy well. Of course, we don't know how many customers opposed this policy and said nothing. However, it is significant that new charge accounts have not diminished during the past three months and store traffic is up slightly.

I recommend that we continue to keep records of customer complaints for three more months, say until September 15. At the end of that period if nothing more significant develops than we have already experienced, we can probably consider the matter closed.

■ ■

UNIT 3

SAY IT PERSONALLY

Although a letter speaks for the company on whose letterhead it appears, its personality is that of the writer. Some companies publish manuals that include model letters as well as secretarial hints; others issue bulletins that offer writing suggestions. Few, however, lay down a rigid company policy as to the style and organization of letters. Most business firms permit their writers almost complete freedom in expressing themselves to their readers. Although new writers often find their correspondence monitored by their immediate supervisors, the apprenticeship period is usually short.

PERSONALIZED LETTERS

If you have the idea that your letters must fit a mold and ''sound like the company is talking,'' get rid of it. Many business letters are personal letters, for correspondents soon become friends. A sales supervisor serving forty or fifty customers in a certain territory makes it his business to get to know them even though he may never meet them personally. It doesn't take him long to learn their special preferences, operating style, quirks, and general character. And his customers know him too. Once they do meet face to face, they are likely to learn about each other's family, hobbies, and favorite football team; and from then on, the letters they exchange are likely to be quite personal. Obviously, you should exercise taste and discretion when transacting company business by mail, but management encourages free expression.

If you want to make your letters warm and personal, treat your readers as individuals—living, breathing human beings who laugh, weep, love, get sick, make mistakes, get excited, get depressed, work, play, and crave attention.

Case Example

The customer-service correspondent for the Timely Publishing Company received a mild note of complaint, along with a check, from Professor Ogilvie, who had ordered a Timely book, *Introduction to Psychology,* and got a bill for $6.75. On the inside of the book jacket, however, Professor Ogilvie found the price was $6.50. When he sent his check, he asked for an explanation. The fact is that prices of books often increase after they are published, and it is not always possible to indicate the change on the flap of the book jacket.

> Dear Sir:
>
> This will acknowledge receipt of your inquiry under date of August 20 about the list price of McKeown's INTRODUCTION TO PSYCHOLOGY, which is indicated on the jacket of the book as $6.50 but which was invoiced to you at $6.75.

With regard to this matter, allow us to advise you that it is common practice in the publishing industry to change prices from time to time after a book is first printed because of increases in manufacturing costs and marketing costs. In the event a price is changed, however, every endeavor is made to remove the original price from the jacket before the book is shipped, but in this day and age books are often shipped prepackaged from the printing plant and thereby we are prevented from taking the original price off the jacket of the book. Thus, there will often be a discrepancy between the price printed on the jacket and the price indicated on the invoice.

Trusting this explanation will be satisfactory, I am

Very truly yours,

The trouble with this letter is that it is a ''to whom it may concern'' letter; it lacks the personal or human touch. The writer might as well have been issuing a bulletin to a thousand people. And it's too bad, because he has given a pretty good explanation of the difference between the bill Professor Ogilvie received and the price on the book jacket.

Such hackneyed, deadwood, and roundabout expressions (emphasized in the first unit) also destroy the human touch in business communications like this one. Did you notice these offenses in the letter to Professor Ogilvie?

This will acknowledge receipt of. A poor way to begin a letter to a customer-friend. Better: *I'm glad for the opportunity to explain* or *Thank you for asking about.*

your inquiry. Your letter or *your question.*

under date of. It is not necessary to refer to the date, but if it is done, here is a better way: *Thank you for your letter of August 20.*

indicated. Shown.

invoiced to you. This is jargon. Say *for which we charged you $6.75.*

With regard to this matter. Says nothing; leave out.

allow us. Meaningless.

advise you. Stilted. In this letter, these words can be omitted.

In the event. When.

every endeavor is made. We try.

in this day and age. Wordy and trite; say *today.*

discrepancy. Difference.

Trusting. Avoid participial constructions at the ends of letters. Say *I hope this explanation will be satisfactory.*

The tone of the letter is impersonal. The writer seems to have bent over backward to avoid talking to his reader as a person. Now let's look at how he might have humanized the letter.

Dear Professor Ogilvie:

It is easy to see why you were confused by the price of McKeown's INTRODUCTION TO PSYCHOLOGY, which is shown as $6.50 on the jacket and $6.75 on the invoice.

After a book is published, Professor Ogilvie, the publisher may have to change the price two or three times because of increased manufacturing and distribution costs. This is standard practice in the industry. When a price is changed, we snip the old price off the jackets of the books in our warehouse. We think we catch most of them. The big problem is that more and more of our books are prepackaged and shipped directly from the printing plant to the customer, and the printer doesn't provide this "snipping" service for us.

Thank you for giving us an opportunity to explain this price difference. I hope you will find Dr. McKeown's book ideally suited to your evening classes at Russell Sage. It is fast becoming the most respected introductory text in the field.

                                                  Sincerely yours,

What makes the second letter better? It is:

More readable. It not only flows better but also uses simple, everyday words everybody understands.

Individualized. Professor Ogilvie will feel this letter is meant especially for him. The first letter reads as if it were run off on a duplicating machine and sent "to whom it may concern"; the second sounds as if Professor Ogilvie really matters as an individual. Contrast "Dear Sir" with "Dear Professor Ogilvie," for example.

Conversational. In the opening, the writer admits that the professor isn't the only one confused by the difference in prices shown on the jacket of a book and on the publisher's invoice. He is saying, "That's a legitimate question—many people wonder about it, so you have company." And the opening sentence is more nearly what the writer would say to Professor Ogilvie if they sat down together.

Using Professor Ogilvie's name in the body of the letter also helps to convey a conversational, sincere tone. Overusing it, however, would make the letter sound insincere and phony.

We mentioned that the frequent use of personal pronouns gives warmth to a business letter and gives it a conversational tone. It also does something else: it helps the writer get away from stilted expressions and passive voice.

IMPERSONAL: Subject report was received and read carefully.

PERSONAL: I was glad to have your report, and I read it with great interest.

IMPERSONAL: In order to minimize costs, clerical productivity must be maintained at the highest possible level commensurate with equitable employment practices.

PERSONAL: If you want to keep costs down, you must get as much work out of your clerks as you can. But, of course, you've got to be fair about it.

IMPERSONAL: It is recommended that employees who are in disagreement with company policy concerning automobile leasing communicate with the Staff Marketing Vice President or the undersigned for clarification of the company's position.

PERSONAL: If you don't agree with our policy on car leasing, write or call John Burndy or me. We're eager to show you why we think the new plan is a good one.

Case Example

You are assistant to the national sales manager of the Yankee Manufacturing Company. Today you received a letter from Mrs. Lawrence Keith in which she asked for full details on one of your products, the Yankee Electronic Air Cleaner, which she is considering purchasing. Yankee publishes a booklet, *Your Guide to Cleaner Air,* which describes the Electronic Air Cleaner fully, but it is temporarily out of stock. You will send it to Mrs. Keith as soon as you receive a new supply. What do you think of this response?

> Dear Mrs. Keith:
>
> We have received your letter concerning the Yankee Electronic Air Cleaner and you will find full and complete answers to your questions about this cleaner in the descriptive booklet <u>Your Guide to Cleaner Air</u> which I will forward to you in a few days upon receipt of a new printing. In the meantime, allow me to tell you in answer to your questions that the Yankee Electronic Air Cleaner traps up to 95 percent of the smoke, grease, pollen, lint, soot, bacteria, and spores in the air, it measures only $20\frac{1}{4}$ by $31\frac{1}{4}$ by $8\frac{1}{2}$ and it will fit into the return-air duct of any central forced-air heating or air-conditioning system and is factory prewired and assembled.
>
> Hoping to be of further service to you, I remain,
>
> > Yours truly,

Would you agree that the main faults of the letter to Mrs. Keith are the following?

1. The tone is impersonal, lacking in freshness or warmth.
2. Many stale, trite, or otherwise unnecessary words and phrases are used.

> *full and complete.* These words mean the same thing; either would have been enough.
>
> *descriptive.* A good word, though somewhat lifeless. Substitute *colorful, interesting,* or another lively word.
>
> *forward to you.* A simpler, easier word than *forward* is *send.*
>
> *upon receipt.* Just say *when* (*when I receive*).
>
> *In the meantime.* A meaningless, unnecessary phrase.
>
> *allow me to tell you.* Deadwood.

3. The following awkward expressions cloud the meaning of the letter.

> *We have received your letter.* Obviously the letter was received; otherwise, there would be no reason for a reply.
>
> *in a few days upon receipt of a new printing.* A more readable way of expressing this idea is *just as soon as we receive a new printing in early July.*

Hoping to be of further service to you, I remain. This entire sentence is lifeless and out of date. To convey this idea, the writer might better say: *If I can be helpful to you in any other way, please feel free to call on me, Mrs. Keith.*

4. The first two sentences are too long, mainly because each contains more than one idea. Let's take the first one. The writer has actually included not two, but three, ideas in that sentence: (1) your letter received; (2) your questions answered in a special booklet; (3) will send booklet when it is available. If we leave the sentence alone but break it up into separate thought units, it would look like this:

> We have received your letter concerning the Yankee Electronic Air Cleaner. You will find full and complete answers to your questions about this cleaner in the descriptive booklet Your Guide to Cleaner Air, which I shall forward to you in a few days upon receipt of a new printing.

Of course, it is still a weak paragraph because the thoughts do not flow logically and smoothly, but it is now somewhat easier to read.

The entire job could be done, of course, in one single-idea sentence:

> You will receive within a few days our colorful booklet, Your Guide to Cleaner Air, which describes fully the Yankee Electronic Air Cleaner you asked about.

The second sentence also needs breaking up because it contains four separate thoughts: (1) what the cleaner does; (2) what the size is; (3) where the cleaner can be installed; (4) how the cleaner comes to the buyer.

The revision of sentence two, then, would look something like this:

> The Yankee Electronic Air Cleaner traps up to 95 percent of the smoke, grease, pollen, lint, soot, bacteria, and spores in the air. It measures only $20\frac{1}{4}$ by $31\frac{1}{4}$ by $8\frac{1}{2}$ and can be installed in the return-air duct of any central forced-air heating or air-conditioning system. The unit comes prewired and assembled.

5. The punctuation is poor. And, of course, the closing participial construction ending in a comma should be replaced by a complete sentence.

Here is the personalized letter to Mrs. Keith.

> Dear Mrs. Keith:
>
> You will receive within a few days our colorful booklet, Your Guide to Cleaner Air, which describes fully the Yankee Electronic Air Clearner you asked about.
>
> The Yankee Electronic Air Cleaner traps up to 95 percent of the smoke, grease, pollen, lint, soot, bacteria, and spores in the air. It measures only $20\frac{1}{4}$ by $31\frac{1}{4}$ by $8\frac{1}{2}$ and can be installed in the return-air duct of any central forced-air heating or air-conditioning system. The unit comes prewired and assembled.

Our dealer in Smithtown is Arrow Electronics, 347 East Grand. Why not visit him soon and let him show you the many superior features of the Yankee Electronic Air Cleaner? Ask for Mr. Magee; he'll be delighted to help you.

Sincerely yours,

Case Example

Suppose you are writing to one of your customers to thank him for his patience during a recent strike that prevented your filling his two-month-old order. What do you think of this?

Dear Mr. Ramada:

It is unfortunate that there was a delay in filling your order, which was caused by a strike in our plant. Many of our customers were inconvenienced, and they are to be commended for their patience during this critical period.

Sincerely yours,

Rather impersonal, wouldn't you say? The writer gives the impression that he is addressing a mass audience and in a rather guarded tone.

Here is a message with the appropriate human touch.

Dear Mr. Ramada:

You certainly were patient, Mr. Ramada, in waiting for us to fill your order delayed by the recent truckers' strike. The fact that you were inconvenienced, however, has been very disturbing to all of us. We'll try to make up for it on your very next order.

Sincerely yours,

In the example above, the writer acknowledges Mr. Ramada's patience, tells him that the reason for the delay was the truckers' strike, shows concern for inconveniencing him, and assures him of special attention on the next order. The message is friendly and human, but, most important, it respects the reader's intelligence.

Compare the following statements in terms of the effect the message is likely to have on the reader.

Impersonal	Personal
Carlton's display rooms are open to the general public Wednesday afternoons from 3 until 5:30.	If you can visit our display rooms on any Wednesday afternoon between 3 and 5:30, we'll be pleased to give you a personal tour.
Unfortunately, requests for copies of our contract forms cannot be granted.	If I could release copies of our contract, Mr. Burton, I would send them to you.

Impersonal	Personal
Our customers are advised to place their orders early because these Hogan irons are in short supply and great demand.	If you will get your order for Hogan irons to me right away, Mr. Krampft, you won't have any problem. Our supply is low, however, and we are receiving many orders for them.
Your letter stating that you received 12 Big Tom Lawn Mowers instead of 12 Big Tom Lawn Sweepers has been referred to me. This error is regrettable.	How in the world we managed to mix up your order so badly is a mystery to me. I assure you that I will certainly find out—but first, we are shipping you 12 Big Tom Lawn Sweepers today.
The beneficiary form X-388 is being returned because it has not been signed.	Please sign the enclosed beneficiary form, Miss Clark, and return it to me.

Case Example

Masterpiece Reprints, an art store, received the following letter.

Gentlemen:

I recently ordered a print of Marini's "Man on a Horse," and when it arrived, I was shocked to discover it was crushed and somewhat tattered. The tube in which the print was mailed appeared to be in good condition.

This is an expensive print ($18.95), and I do not understand how a company with your reputation could send out such shoddy merchandise. I am very distressed. What do I do?

Sincerely yours,

What do you think of the following response?

Dear Madam:

Reference is made to your complaint about the print of Marini's "Man on a Horse," which you state arrived in damaged condition.

This is to notify you that a replacement print is being sent at no cost to you.

Very truly yours,

Although the response contains the welcome news that the defective print is being replaced, it is cold and impersonal. When the customer's complaint is justified and the seller is making the adjustment, the writer should make every effort to build goodwill. He has nothing to lose and much to gain. Let's try it again.

Dear Mrs. Ortega:

You'll be pleased to know that this morning I mailed to you a new print of Marini's "Man on a Horse." It should reach you within a day or two.

It is hard to see how we at Masterpiece Reprints could have let a defective print get by us, Mrs. Ortega—we pride ourselves on our rigid standards of inspection—and I can only explain it by the unusually heavy orders we have had this month. At any rate, I'm grateful to you for giving me the opportunity to set matters right.

Will you return the defective print (we can get credit for it from our supplier)? We'll be glad to pay the postage.

Sincerely yours,

Note that the writer places in the first paragraph the good news that he is sending a new print to the unhappy customer. Mentioning this fact at the outset removes any doubt Mrs. Ortega may have about receiving a new print and prepares her for the explanation.

The letter is positive, friendly, personal. The writer is directing his remarks squarely at Mrs. Ortega, and his tactful way of explaining an unfortunate occurrence is likely to get the kind of response he wants—a satisfied customer who will continue to do business with Masterpiece Reprints.

PERSONALIZED MEMORANDUMS

Like business letters, most memorandums are more readable and persuasive when they are personalized.

Case Example

Martin Holcomb, director of marketing of the Cranston Rubber Company, prepared a memo report for the president concerning sales performance.

TO: J. W. Holmes   FROM: Martin Holcomb

SUBJECT: Sales Performance   DATE: January 12, 19—

Per-man sales performance was substantially improved during the past year. Volume is significantly higher (40 percent) with fewer representatives, leading to the conclusion that the caliber of sales personnel is superior to that in any previous period in Cranston history. Many attribute this to improved training and supervision.

M.H.

Pretty impersonal, isn't it? Now let's see how much more readable the report becomes when it is personalized. Note the direct wording and the use of *we* and *you*.

TO: J. W. Holmes   FROM: Martin Holcomb

SUBJECT: Sales Performance   DATE: January 12, 19—

Cranston is now enjoying the best sales force ever. Although we have 20 fewer representatives this year than last, our volume is up nearly 40 percent; so you can see that individual performance is much better. We believe the reasons are simply better training and supervision.

M.H.

■ ■

PROJECTS

A Rewrite the following paragraphs and messages, making them simple, personal, direct, and more appetizing to the reader.

1 During the next few months we will be conducting a survey to determine the type and extent of reporting that will be required to provide for effective marketing strategy and control in the future.

2 In connection with the foregoing, it is evident that further expansion of our services will tax our manpower resources to the limit. Consequently, we solicit the indulgence of those responsible for product planning.

3 Diversity of faculty background provides the students with the opportunity for breadth of view. The Committee, therefore, feels compelled to reiterate the admonition so frequently heard in academic circles against excessive inbreeding by the hiring of too many graduates of any one institution.

4 Reference is made to Contract H-4640, which was improperly executed. Signature should be affixed before resubmission.

5 Should further copies of the brochure be required, address requests to our Publications Office, specifying requirements.

6

Gentlemen:

Enclosed please find ten copies of our new and revised price sheet.

It will be noted that many items have been added to this sheet and that some items have been lowered in price and some increased.

Please discard all previous price sheets.

Thanking you for your cooperation, we remain,

                                        Very truly yours,

7

To All Dealers and Branches:

This is to advise that Omnibag Container Corporation is in process of moving to its new modern facilities near Raleigh, North Carolina. We confidently expect that this move will enable us to serve our dealers better.

Our new address will be P.O. Box 640, Raleigh, North Carolina 27602. Our physical location (to be used for freight shipments only) will be Highway U.S. 1-A South, Wake Forest, North Carolina.

Our telephone number is Area Code 919 556-5070. Our TWX number is 919 556-3062.

The Sales Department is moving February 15. All sales orders, phone calls, TWX, etc., after that date <u>must</u> be directed to the Raleigh address.

It will be helpful if you will advise your people of the above schedule so that correspondence may be handled without forwarding.

8 I have worked up a definition of capital budgeting to serve as a basing point for our further discussions on budgeting. I believe we must firm up such a definition as a starting point before we can proceed to the mechanics of more detailed requirements of a budgeting procedure.

9 This will acknowledge your letter of April 12 and inform you that a catalog was sent out today.

10 Diversification decisions must also be evaluated in terms of potential problems and disadvantages. Product diversification presents an added burden to both sales personnel and physical distribution facilities.

B Study the following memorandum; then rewrite it in a personal, human style. Organize and present the message so that it is easy to read and understand.

TO: L. N. Brazelle   FROM: Curtis Morgan
SUBJECT: Product Planning Conference   DATE: April 11, 19—

The undersigned has studied subject draft of the 19— Product Planning Conference and reacts favorably to it. The emphasis given to the increasing responsibility of the salesman in creating new markets is particularly noteworthy.

For your consideration three ideas are proposed. First, it is felt by the writer that there is a plethora of executive participation and a paucity of participation on the part of the field staff. It is recommended that a minimum of two full-length presentations from the field staff be included, and in this connection Morrie Cruikshank's market penetration study in the Northwest could be considered a possibility if it meets with your favor. Since the men are not felt to have seen Morrie's report, it is highly possible that they would be favorably impressed with what one man can accomplish when the job is approached with a definite and concrete plan.

Second, the number of speeches that are scheduled one after the other may become monotonous, and the writer is inclined to recommend interspersion of other types of programs as advantageous. The film that you and the undersigned saw (Creative Selling) in St. Louis at the convention last Christmas could possibly be scheduled on Wednesday forenoon just before the coffee break. Another suggestion that is relevant to variety is a panel. This panel could possibly be composed of the six regional managers. Their theme could be "Ask the Experts." Such a panel would give the salesmen an opportunity to query their superiors. For example, on policy, on procedural matters and routines, and on selling techniques. The panel mentioned could be inserted in the program before the luncheon on Thursday. Moose Marlin is a possible candidate to act as chairman of the panel aforementioned.

Third, it is noted that there is no program scheduled for the closing luncheon on Friday, and it is strongly recommended that we have J. B. make an oral presentation. Thirty minutes is recommended, and an appropriate topic is "Where We're Headed" or some other similar topic. It is believed that such a speech would provide a highly satisfactory capstone to the conference and send the men away with renewed confidence in the future.

It is requested that, should further comments be desired, you notify the undersigned, who will be willing to assist further as required. The initial effort is highly satisfactory in all respects.

C.M.

■ ■

UNIT 4   SAY IT POSITIVELY

Some people see only the dark side of things. They are consistently gloomy and negative. You can easily recognize them because when invited to an eight o'clock cookout they impulsively say, "No, I'm sorry I can't come at eight. But I could manage to get there around 8:20." Wouldn't it have been just as easy for them to have graciously accepted the invitation first and then asked if it would be all right to arrive a few minutes late?

PERSUASIVENESS

One of the oldest examples of bad salesmanship is the approach, "You don't want to buy a set of my encyclopedias, do you?" In putting the question negatively, the salesman has made it easy for the prospect to say no and has thereby lost the opportunity for the sale. The positive salesman is likely to say, "Would you like to see your children develop a real thirst for knowledge?" or "Would you like to be the proud owner of these 30 handsome volumes?"

Becoming adept in the art of persuasion, so important in all human relationships, requires positiveness—stressing the favorable and playing down the unfavorable. This is not to say that one should never be negative; sometimes a lusty no is the only appropriate response. Nor does being positive mean passing up the truth in order to win acceptance. If you receive an order for merchandise that you do not carry and you can offer no reasonable substitute, you would be wasting your time and that of your reader by beating around the bush. On the other hand, if you carry the article but are temporarily out of it, you can stress the positive.

Case Example

The Exact Time Watch Company has received an order from Dibble's Drug Store for six Dolly Madison clocks. Unfortunately, this particular model has been sold out, and a new shipment is not due for about ten days. Here is a letter to Dibble's Drug Store that emphasizes the negative.

> Gentlemen:
>
> I am sorry that we are out of stock on Dolly Madison clocks—we simply have not been able to keep up with the orders. I know it will disappoint you that we do not expect a new shipment from the factory for another ten days. Can you wait that long?
>
> Very truly yours,

Now let's try a more positive response.

> Dear Mr. Dibble:
>
> Thank you for your order for six Dolly Madison clocks. This model has been so popular this Christmas season that the factory is a little behind in filling orders.
>
> However, we expect a new shipment about November 14. In order to save you time, I am having your six clocks sent directly to you from the plant in Williamsburg so that you should have yours by the time we get ours.
>
> Sincerely yours,

Case Example

You are assistant to the sales manager of Peerless Hardware Corporation. One of your slow-paying customers, Riverdale Hardware Store, has been placed on a cash-only basis by the credit manager because of the difficulty your company has had collecting from this customer. Riverdale is not to receive shipments unless each order is accompanied by a check.

Today you receive a $76.60 order from Howard Malden, owner of Riverdale Hardware. In his letter Mr. Malden refers to "the enclosed check," but it is not enclosed. How would you answer his letter? Like this?

> Dear Sir:
>
> The check in the amount of $76.60, which you indicated you were sending with your order for two Peerless metal miter boxes, was not among the contents of the envelope.
>
> According to policy concerning your account, shipment of any order cannot be made unless it is accompanied by payment.
>
> Please advise.
>
> Sincerely yours,

If you suspect that Mr. Malden, by not enclosing his check, is trying to pull something, you might be tempted to write a letter like the one shown.

Mr. Malden's business is as good as anybody else's, however, if he pays cash for his merchandise. Your mission is to turn him down for credit but retain him as a cash customer.

Dear Mr. Malden:

It was a pleasure to receive your order for two Peerless metal miter boxes.

Your check for $76.60, which I'm sure you intended to enclose with your order, did not arrive. No doubt you have already discovered this oversight and have placed your check in the mail. In the meantime, I shall see that the two miter boxes are ready to ship just as soon as payment is received.

Thank you for your continued support of the Peerless line.

Sincerely yours,

The second letter delivers much the same message as the first, but the writer has searched for ways to soften the "no" he had to convey. He started on a positive note—a thank-you for the order, which is always appropriate. And notice how he handled the matter of the missing check; he made no accusations, only tactful inferences. He ended the letter on a friendly note.

Case Example

The Denison Company, a mail-order house, received the following letter.

Gentlemen:

I am building several cabins on Glazier Lake near Bradbury, Maine, and I am interested in buying wood-burning stoves, both heating and cooking, for them.

Do you have a special catalog describing your line of stoves, including prices? If so, please send it to the address above.

Yours truly,

What do you think of the following response?

Dear Mr. Walton:

I am sorry we do not print special catalogs for our stoves. Complete information is available, however, in our general catalog. This general catalog is being sent to you.

Sincerely yours,

Let's try another approach.

Dear Mr. Walton:

A full description of our line of wood stoves, both heating and cooking, will be found in our general catalog, which I am sending to you at once.

We have sixteen different models of wood heating stoves (pages 1190–1194) and twelve of wood cooking stoves (pages (1194–1197). I'm sure you will find exactly what you want from this wide selection. Complete price information accompanies each description, but you will want to know that you will get a 10 percent discount on quantities of six or more of each type of stove.

If, after examining the catalog, you need more information or assistance of any kind, please drop me a line. Or you may telephone me collect at (201) 239-2901.

Sincerely yours,

Remember, positiveness in business communications means emphasizing what you *can* do—not what you *can't* do.

Case Example

You are a sales assistant in the Erudite Book Company. The following letter, dated December 21, comes to your desk.

Gentlemen:

The junior high schools of Raleigh are setting up an occupations course at the ninth-grade level. We would appreciate your sending us examination copies of materials you feel appropriate for such a course.

We are interested in assembling materials and beginning work on the course right away; therefore, we would appreciate receiving the material as soon as possible.

Cordially yours,

Erudite publishes a good textbook on occupations, *Understanding Today's Occupations.* The current edition is quite old, but fortunately a new edition is at the printer's and will be ready in February—about two months from now. Following is a letter one publisher wrote in answer to a similar inquiry.

Dear Mrs. Pritchard:

Our guidance book for ninth-grade students is Understanding Today's Occupations, but the new edition is not due for publication until early February of next year.

This new edition will be a complete revision of Understanding Today's Occupations, First Edition, and will place greater emphasis on developing job concepts in addition to providing the students with information on various careers. To give you a preview of what the text will contain, I am enclosing a copy of the table of contents of the new edition.

Sincerely yours,

The response to Mrs. Pritchard is an example of accentuating the negative. The new edition of the book will be available in about two months; yet the writer makes that time seem a long way off. He should have spent his time convincing Mrs. Pritchard that the book will soon be available and that she ought to see the new edition before making a final decision.

Here is a positive response—the kind Mrs. Pritchard *should* have received.

Dear Mrs. Pritchard:

I am delighted to know that you are setting up an occupations course in the Raleigh schools. Fortunately, the new edition of our very successful ninth-grade book, Understanding Today's Occupations, is now at the printer and will be ready in very early February of next year. I hope this will be in time for your consideration because I think you will want to see this book before making your final selection.

Enclosed is a brochure that describes this new program. I am also sending you separately a copy of the current edition. I hesitate to send it to you—the new edition is so far superior—but I do want to get something into your hands so that you may get an idea of what topics are covered, the type of exercises, teacher aids, and so on. Incidentally, accompanying the new edition will be a laboratory manual, filmstrips, and overhead transparencies.

Let me know, please, in what other ways I can help you. I'll see that you get copies of the new materials just as soon as they arrive. In fact, I will have them sent directly from the printer.

Sincerely yours,

Observe the positive terms in the second letter:

I am delighted to know
Fortunately . . . will be ready
I hope this will be in time
I think you will want to see
Enclosed is a brochure . . . I am also sending you
I do want to get something into your hands
Let me know, please, in what other ways I can help you.
I'll see that you get copies
I will have them sent directly from the printer

Case Example

You are product manager of the Convivial Novelty Supply Company, with the responsibility of servicing customers in the northeast district. One of your customers, Miss Samantha Jallon, has written to complain about the inferior quality of the Halloween costumes you recently shipped. Although she says that all the costumes were sold, a few customers complained later about them, resulting, Miss Jallon says, in "loss of face and probably loss of business in the future." She maintains that you should give her a credit for $46.80, a 50 percent reduction, to compensate for her embarrassment.

After a thorough investigation, you decide that Miss Jallon is not justified in her complaint. The costumes are cheaply made, but they were priced especially low, too, which helped to account for their being the best-selling costumes you have handled. Many retailers purchased the same costumes and reported selling them with great success and satisfaction.

What do you think of this reply?

Dear Miss Jallon:

I am sorry indeed to have your complaint about the inferior Halloween costumes you claim you were sent. Your complaint has been investigated thoroughly, and we find no justification for your contentions.

May I expect your check for $46.80.

Yours very sincerely,

Although the writer had made up his mind to send a "no" answer, he could have written a much better letter. The positive writer would have avoided pointing the accusing finger with such terms as *your complaint* and *your contentions,* and he would not have referred to his product as *inferior.*

Here is what he might have written to Miss Jallon.

Dear Miss Jallon:

Thank you for your letter concerning the Halloween costumes you recently ordered. I am delighted that you were able to sell them all. Many of our customers reported similar success, with complete satisfaction from the parents and youngsters who bought them.

As you know, we purchased these costumes (identical in quality to those you purchased last year but lower in cost) at a very special price, and we were able to pass the discount on to our good customers like you. I have a feeling that if you explain to your customers that a $2.98 top price for a complete costume is quite a bargain—even for a one-time garment—they will understand and appreciate your position.

I will credit your account for $46.80, leaving a balance of $46.80. Please send us your check today in the enclosed addressed envelope.

Sincerely yours,

The second example is a no letter with a positive tone. Note that there is no mention of complaint or of shoddy merchandise and there are no accusations. The writer simply reasons with Miss Jallon in a friendly, direct, positive manner, expecting that she will quickly see his point of view.

HONESTY AND TACT

We often hear someone say that he believes in calling the shots as he sees them, meaning that he intends to be honest at all costs. Telling the truth is important, but let's recognize that being truthful or honest doesn't necessarily mean hitting a fellow between the eyes with a sledgehammer. For example, Mrs. Murphy, your robust neighbor, may be carrying a few more pounds than is becoming to her, but you wouldn't think of telling her that she is fat, obese, or overweight. If she asks (and *only* if she does!), you might hedge with such terms as "matronly" or "stout." We don't call our Congressman a politician or a bureaucrat if we wish to impress him. Nor do we refer to our elders as old people. A house purchased by a friend for very little money is not a cheap house—it's a modest home, an inexpensive house, a moderately priced house, a "real bargain." A stingy person is merely cost-conscious, budget-minded, or conservative with money. Here are other examples:

Sledgehammer	Gentler
dumb *or* stupid	less gifted
dyed hair	tinted hair
false teeth	dentures
fired (*from a job*)	released, separated
pushy	aggressive
secondhand car	used car
skinny	wiry, lean
stutter	speech impediment
ugly	plain

The communicator who has a tendency to boast about calling shots as he sees them must resist the temptation if he wants to win friends and influence people (which is what business is all about). Our point is that you can maintain your honesty and be tactful about it.

Being totally frank can sometimes cause irreparable damage to a company or a personal image, and it would be in the interest of good human relations and good business to take the gentle approach.

Not only should you avoid words that offend, but also you should stay away from words to which you know people react negatively. Some words are just naturally negative even when standing alone—*complaint, unsatisfactory, cheap, treason, absurd,* and *vicious,* for example. Other words are perfectly good in one context and abominable in another. For example, it is fine to tell a man who has asked for an appointment that you're *sorry* you can't make it on the date suggested. But when you write to a customer and refer to "the sorry way in which you have paid your account," then it becomes a different kettle of fish. The word *unfortunately* is a fine word if it is being used in reference to the writer, such as, "Unfortunately, I'll be out of town on the day you're coming to Lawrence." But when it is used to refer to the reader, it takes on a different tone: "You unfortunately left out some important details when you wrote." *Apology* can, likewise, be a negative word when it refers to the reader ("You owe us an apology"), but it has a positive ring when it refers to the writer: "Please accept my apology for the way in which your order was handled." The same is true of the word *failure.* It can be a pretty bad word when it identifies a shortcoming in a human being. But that depends on who that human being is. "Your failure to pay the invoice within the discount period" will antagonize the reader. Nobody wants to be told that he has failed. But when the writer admits failure, it becomes a perfectly good word: "Our failure to keep our side of the bargain is hard to explain."

You can avoid negative words and let your reader draw his own conclusions. For example:

Blunt	Tactful
You *failed* to enclose your check.	Your check did not arrive.
You *claim* that we made a *mistake* in our shipping charge.	I agree that there is a difference between your figure and ours, but . . .
You have *overlooked* the fact that there is a state sales tax on the merchandise.	You will see that we added the state sales tax to the bill, which . . .
Because you *delayed* so long in your response, Model GSF is out of stock.	If I had known your needs before November 20, I could have shipped Model GSF immediately.

Because we must try to achieve positive relationships with our business associates and customers, it makes good sense, wherever possible, to select words that nudge rather than sledgehammer our readers.

CUSTOMER SATISFACTION

Case Example

The Modern Press prints many books in binder form, such as cookbooks, "how to" books, laboratory manuals, and the like. After a book has been in print a few years, the publisher may decide to issue a new edition and let the old edition go out of print. The new edition may be of a different size and format, bearing little resemblance to its predecessor.

Such a situation is the subject of the exchange of letters that follow. A lady in Salt Lake City purchased the first edition of a loose-leaf cookbook. After she had used it for six or seven years, the cover began to fall apart, and she wrote the publisher the following letter.

Gentlemen:

I purchased the first edition of the <u>Martha Johnson Picture Cookbook</u> at a local bookstore about seven years ago, and I have enjoyed using it very much. Now the cover is falling apart (I suppose you would call it the binder), and I would like to have a new one for it.

Could I purchase a new five-ring binder from you? Please let me know how I go about it and what the price would be.

Sincerely,

Here is the response she received.

Dear Mrs. Hamm:

Thank you for your letter of November 2, concerning your <u>Martha Johnson Picture Cookbook.</u>

It is company policy to replace all defective books. However, the first edition is out of print and is no longer available. It has been replaced with a newer edition in a six-ring binder.

Therefore, I cannot send you a cover for your book.

I am sorry that I cannot help you. I know how difficult it must be to use a book in this condition.

Sincerely yours,

The general tone of the letter to Mrs. Hamm is good. The first paragraph expresses appreciation for the letter, and the last paragraph offers an apology that seems to indicate that the writer is sympathetic with the customer's problem.

Unfortunately, the writer misses the point in the second and third paragraphs. In the first place, the term *company policy* is irritating to most people; it induces visions of a big rule book the organization has prepared to hide behind when a no answer must be given. In the second place, the fact that the first edition is out of print and no longer available has little to do with the availability of a cover. After all, the contents may be out of print but extra covers might be available—not likely, but possible. Thus the customer's request was never really answered. All the publisher's correspondent had to do was say something like this:

> I wish we had a cover available to fit your edition of the <u>Martha Johnson Picture Cookbook</u>. Just to make sure, I checked with the bindery as well as with our warehouse, but there isn't a single one left.

In responding to communications from customers and others, some correspondents fail to deal with the question or request squarely and thus give no satisfaction to the person making the inquiry. Of course, it is not always possible to grant a request—thousands of requests that must be turned down are received by business firms every day. But actually saying no and avoiding the request entirely (as was done in the response to Mrs. Hamm) are two different things.

The fact that the letter to Mrs. Hamm was unsatisfactory is evidenced by the following letter she fired back to the publishing house—this time addressed to the president—along with the letter that she had received.

> Dear Sir:
>
> Isn't this the height of something? The more I think of it, the angrier I become.
>
> In my letter, I asked whether I could buy a five-ring cover to replace my very worn one. I was not fishing for a free replacement. I was told you do replace "defective" ones but that you can do nothing for me because my book is now out of print. I knew it was out of print; I merely wanted something to hold the pages of my well-used cookbook together.
>
> I hate to bother a man in your position, but perhaps you would be able to furnish a satisfactory answer. Is it possible to buy such a cover, and if so, what would be its cost? And how would I go about ordering it?
>
> Very truly yours,

How would you have answered the letter from Mrs. Hamm if you had been the president of the publishing house? He decided that enough damage had been done by the incomplete explanation she had received previously and that a mere apology would not do the job. Here is the letter he wrote:

> Dear Mrs. Hamm:
>
> I am sending you a new <u>Martha Johnson Picture Cookbook</u> with my compliments. I realize, Mrs. Hamm, that this is not a completely satisfactory answer to your problem, since you obviously want the cookbook you now have but with a good binder. Because I can't find a binder that fits your book, this is the least I can do to prove that I am sorry I cannot be of more help to you.
>
> Perhaps this new edition, which is larger and more complete, will in time become just as valuable as the cookbook you are now using. I hope so.
>
> Sincerely yours,

THE "CAN DO" SPIRIT

"The difficult we do immediately. The impossible takes a little longer." This famous slogan of what was then the United States Army Air Force during World War II has been picked up by many groups to show their "can do" spirit.

The "can dos" and "can't dos" have always been recognizable in most human endeavors. The "can't dos" search for ways to get around problems. The "can dos" search for ways to solve problems. Unfortunately, those who look for the escape hatch make up a good percentage of the business writing population. No doubt these are the same people who "duck out" on their responsibilities, no matter what they are doing. There is no reason to assume that those who give no more than they have to in performing their regular chores can be automatically transformed into "can do" types when they face a writing situation. Yet it is worth emphasizing that written words are taken much more seriously than spoken words, and the negative answer stands out much more glaringly when displayed in writing.

The "can do" business writer does a little more than he has to in answering the requests of his correspondents. If customers complain about poor service or faulty merchandise, he searches for explanations that will not only reassure his customers but, if possible, vindicate his company as well. If he must say no to unreasonable requests, he offers reasons and possible alternatives. If questions that do not pertain to the business in which he is employed are put to him, he does all he can to help the inquirer locate the information he needs. And while he is constantly aware of the importance of displaying a "can do" spirit in dealing with those outside his company, he knows that it is just as important for him to be interested, enthusiastic, and willing to help when a fellow employee asks for assistance in solving a problem.

Case Examples

The Turntable Record Shop received the following letter.

> Gentlemen:
>
> During the past several months I have heard Aaron Copeland's "Music From 'Our Town'" over a local FM station, and I am eager to have the recording. Unfortunately, none of the record shops in Broom County has it, nor can they find it in any catalog.
>
> Do you have a recording of this piece? If not, can you tell me how I can obtain one?
>
> Yours sincerely,

Unfortunately, the record referred to is not in stock in the Turntable Record Shop and no one in the store knows where it might be obtained.

Here is an example of a ''can't do'' letter—typical of thousands that prospective customers receive from business houses every day.

> Dear Mrs. Kraft:
>
> I am sorry we do not have in stock the recording you asked about.
>
> Yours truly,

The following letter takes a little more time to write, but it goes a lot further in building goodwill.

> Dear Mrs. Kraft:
>
> I wish I could help you locate a recording of Aaron Copeland's "Music From 'Our Town.'" Unfortunately, we do not have this recording in stock.
>
> I did find out that the recording was on the MGM label and went out of print about two years ago (it was part of an album, "Music From the Movies"). As far as I know, there are no plans to reissue this particular album.
>
> Have you tried the secondhand stores? Several carry a surprisingly large stock of old records, and many of our customers have picked up what they were looking for. In fact, Sullivan's, 416 Sheridan Road, Danville, has a good collection.
>
> Sincerely yours,

We can't say that every store or business can provide a personal service to everyone who makes an inquiry—often there are so many inquiries that a personal, helpful response is not feasible. But if there is time to write a personal response, the second example is a better model to follow than the first.

Following is another example of the ''can do'' spirit. The letter, written by an executive in a paper manufacturing firm, is in response to an inquiry about the availability of a booklet on the history of papermaking.

Dear Mr. Goodfellow:

Thank you for your interest in our booklet, A Brief History of Papermaking in America. We printed this piece several years ago and provided it free to thousands of schools and interested citizens. Unfortunately, our supply has long since been exhausted, and we have no plans to reissue the booklet.

A couple of years ago, arrangements were made with Zion Press to use our material in a book they were publishing, The Romance of Paper. It is a paperback, and I believe it sells for about $3. You might try your local bookstore for a copy or write directly to the publisher—16 Oakwood Avenue, Fort Madison, Iowa 52627.

Sincerely yours,

■ ■

PROJECTS

A   Rewrite the following, putting the messages in positive terms.

1   If you don't remit by August 14, you will not receive the 5 percent discount.

2   If the foregoing explanation is not clear and you feel that you need additional clarification, kindly advise.

3   We must know the exact size and color you desire in order to get your order to you by October 22.

4   Although I have no actual experience in writing advertising copy, my very thorough college training in advertising, plus my willingness to learn, leads me to believe I could handle your copy in a short time.

5   We cannot send the tarpaulin by parcel post as you requested since it is too bulky; instead, we are sending it by REA Express.

6   If, in the future, you will address your orders to this office instead of to the Racine office, you will not experience the delays that you complain about.

7   Because the building is over 40 years old, we could probably get no more than $75,000 for it.

8   Unfortunately, about 5 percent of our shipments in February were delayed because of a local transportation strike.

9   Are you handicapped in your business for lack of capital?

10   You may not have expected to hear from me, but I have been requested by Mr. Meell to answer the letter you wrote to him about our new discount policy.

11   Your request for additional information regarding our VOICECASTER Telephone Amplifier has been referred to me.

12   I have not heard from you, and I have begun to wonder if by any chance you did not receive my book, A Career in the Hospitality Industry.

13   Because of high printing costs, we can no longer supply these manuals free of charge but must charge 50 cents a copy.

14   It is regretted that we cannot send you the reprints you requested, promptly, since the supply is exhausted and another shipment is not due until June 12.

15   If you do not like this particular color, Miss Milne, we can supply binders in Renaissance Red and Puritan White.

16   You may not wish to keep this examination copy, in which case you may return it for full credit.

17   We should be glad if you would tell us how you are displeased with our service.

18   I cannot agree with you that untrimmed pages in a book denote a cheaply manufactured product.

B   Rewrite the following, eliminating the negative and accentuating the positive.

Dear Mrs. Goheen:

I am sorry to be so late in answering your inquiry about the availability of Monarch Cork-Prest Bulletin Boards, but because you addressed our Memphis office, your letter was delayed in reaching me. In the future, please address all such inquiries to the Neosho office, which serves your area.

The information you require is contained in a small catalog which I am sending you. Please read it carefully, and if you find that it does not contain the information you want, don't hesitate to write.

Yours very truly,

C   The following letter was received by the Monkton Falls Furniture Store.

Gentlemen:

Can you please tell me how to remove stains from marble?

About six months ago I purchased a marble-top DuBois Coffee Table (Model 661) from your store, and recently I noticed that it was stained in several places—mostly rings left by glasses and cups. Although I have tried several cleaning fluids and detergents, nothing seems to work.

I would appreciate your advice.

Sincerely yours,

Mrs. Anna Klein

Here is the response Mrs. Klein received.

Dear Madam:

Re your inquiry regarding the removal of stains from marble, we are extremely sorry about this difficulty. As you perhaps have discovered, marble stains very easily and once the stains are allowed to penetrate, they are very difficult to remove—often impossible. People should be warned not to set wet glasses or cups on marble surfaces.

I am making inquiries about methods that may be used to remove the stains, and I will let you know when I have obtained the information. In the meantime, I am sending you a copy of Caring for Your Marble, which has been recently published. I believe it will be exceedingly helpful.

Yours truly,

Criticize the response to Mrs. Klein in terms of appropriateness and helpfulness. What would you have written?

D The Lorick Manufacturing Company, manufacturers of air-conditioning and refrigeration equipment for industrial use only, received the following letter.

Gentlemen:

I am building a beach house near Red Bank, New Jersey, which I am planning to air-condition throughout. Please send me full information on your air-conditioning systems.

Sincerely yours,

Here is the response made by Lorick Manufacturing Company.

Dear Mr. Shuster:

Unfortunately, we do not distribute our products to individual consumers. We sell only to business and industrial users.

Thank you.

Very truly yours,

Rewrite the response, supplying whatever details you need to give Mr. Shuster the help he wants.

■■■■■■■■■■■■■■■■■■■■■■■■■■■■■■■■■■■■

UNIT 5 PLAN YOUR WRITING WITH A PURPOSE

If you could sample the letters and reports written every day in a typical business or government organization, you would probably say, "Why, I can do better than most of those people—and they're more experienced." The chances are you would be right. And the fact you are studying communications and acquiring a business writing skill will give you an even greater edge.

ORGANIZATION

One of the most serious flaws you would notice in your study of actual business writing would be poor organization, which is usually the result of the writer's failure to plan his message. What is "poor organization"?

1. Failure to establish the purpose of the communication and make that purpose a running thread throughout.
2. Failure to proceed along a straight throughway to the desired objective, constantly turning off the main course to follow bypaths.
3. Use of the hit-and-run technique. The writer introduces a subject; spars with it a bit; then moves on to a new subject, which he treats similarly; and later goes back to the first subject for further discussion.

PURPOSE

Planning requires deciding upon the mission you expect your communication to accomplish; thinking through, with your reader in mind, all sides of the situation; and then organizing your presentation so that the ideas you finally record flow smoothly, logically, and sequentially toward the desired goal.

True, some communications don't require much thought or planning. If you saw an advertisement in a professional management magazine inviting readers to send for a free four-color booklet, *Modern Art Miniatures for the Modern Office,* you would probably dash off something like this:

> Gentlemen:
>
> Please send me the free booklet <u>Modern Art Miniatures for the Modern Office</u>, advertised in the July 17 issue of <u>Administrative Digest</u>.
>
> Sincerely yours,

Or if you have to tell your boss in writing about your vacation preferences:

> I have chosen June 15–26 for my vacation time. Could you possibly let me know by March 1 whether these dates are OK?

You will write many letters and memos that are just as simple, and you won't spend a lot of time thinking about what you will say. On the other hand, if you have to reply to a letter from an irate customer in which he blasts you because of the mistakes your company has made at his expense, then planning, thinking through, and organizing become essential. Here the stakes are too high for you merely to dash off something.

Yet many communications concerning matters of extreme importance seem to have been dashed off. The writers do not appear to have understood the objective their letter or report is to accomplish, or to have thought through what they were going to say before they said it. The result is that they eliminate essential facts, throw in irrelevant details, zigzag from one subject to another, repeat themselves, and wind up writing too much.

Every good writer has some sort of plan in mind before he begins to write. The veteran writer may use only a "think plan." First, he has clearly in mind what he wants to accomplish—to say no without creating ill will, to say yes in a way that will bring the most benefits to him, to create interest in a product, to sell an idea to top management, to achieve agreement on a controversial matter, to obtain payment of a bill, and so on. With the objective in mind, the writer thinks through the entire message before he starts to dictate, reciting to himself the things he wants to cover and thinking hard about what the reader's reaction will be to his various points.

The novice starts with a think plan, too; but, in addition, he prepares a written outline before he starts to write. He may put his outline in the form of jottings on a sheet of scratch paper, or if he is answering a letter or memo, he may jot notes in the margins of the incoming message. Some writers plan by writing or dictating a complete rough draft, which they then edit and revise. The latter method is slow and costly, but it can be worth the time when the message is important and one's writing ability is not yet fully developed.

In any event, a plan must start with the writer's thinking through the entire message before he puts a word on paper. This may appear obvious; however, many communicators don't do it. When criticized for their efforts, they fall back on the excuse, "I never was a good writer." This is simply an alibi. A person endowed with a flair for writing can still produce unintelligible communications if he doesn't plan them; conversely, a person with only a modest talent for expressing himself can overcome his weakness by intelligent planning and organizing. "Genius is the art of taking infinite pains," said Thomas Carlyle, essayist and historian. And taking pains is perhaps the chief distinction between those who communicate effectively and those who don't.

Case Example

In the Receiving Department of Benson Plastics, Inc., one of the most important pieces of equipment is the photocopying machine. It is in constant use for making copies of purchase orders, invoices, bills of lading, receiving reports, and letters. But it is old, and you want permission to buy a new one. Requests of this type must be in writing. Look at the following memorandum.

TO: Andrew L. Harvey   FROM: J. R. Holley
SUBJECT: New Photocopier   DATE: January 16, 19—

We need a new photocopying machine in the Receiving Department. May I have your permission to purchase one?

                                                              J.R.H.

The trouble with this memo is that the writer didn't do much thinking before he wrote it. If he had, he might have asked himself, "What will my boss need to know in order to authorize this purchase?" And putting himself in the boss's position, he probably would have said, "I'd want to know what, why, when, and how much."

Before attacking even this simple communication problem, the writer ought to devise a think plan that will help him cover all the necessary points and organize these points in the right sequence.

A think plan for this situation might look like this:

1. Present machine (Tru-Copy) NG—slow, faint copies, breaks down, costly.
2. Work piling up—need dependable machine.

3. Suggest F-87 (Keen-Fax). Cost, trade-in, etc.
4. Purchase order; demonstration?

From such a think plan, the following memorandum results.

TO: Andrew L. Harvey	FROM: J. R. Holley
SUBJECT: New Photocopier	DATE: January 16, 19—

Our photocopier, Tru-Copy, is no longer adequate for our needs, and I'd like your authorization to buy a new one. The Tru-Copy is now four years old and very slow. The copies we get from it are faint (see sample attached). What's more, the machine breaks down constantly, and while we're waiting for it to be repaired, we have to use the photocopier on the 16th floor. This puts us behind in our work.

Last week the representatives from Keen-Fax demonstrated their new F-87 model to several of us, and we are very much impressed with it (a description is attached). I'm convinced that this machine would pay for itself within two or three years. During the past year we spent over $100 in repair bills on the Tru-Copy, and the wasted time, effort, and paper would probably be double that figure. The cost of the F-87 is $600, and Keen-Fax would allow us a trade-in of $50 on the Tru-Copy.

Just in case I have convinced you, I'm attaching a purchase order for your signature. If, however, you would like to see the Keen-Fax F-87 in action, I am sure I can arrange a demonstration.

                                                                J.R.H.

Case Example

You work as a customer account manager for the Drummond Supply Company. You have received a letter from Graham Matthews, manager of accounting services for Houghton, Incorporated, one of Drummond's good customers. Mr. Matthews is out of patience. He has received a statement of the amount he is said to owe Drummond, and he is sure the statement is in error. He has tried several times to straighten out this matter, exchanging several letters with various people in your company, but has received no satisfaction. He wants this matter cleared up—now—and you must respond to him. He says he owes Drummond nothing.

The mission of your response is to get the situation squared away and give Mr. Matthews the satisfaction he deserves. How will you go about achieving your objective? Obviously, the first thing you have to do is get the facts. You will get the correspondence Mr. Matthews refers to; talk to the people who keep the Houghton, Incorporated, account; study these records; discuss the situation with the salesman who calls on Houghton; and talk to anyone else in the company who might have had a hand in this particular problem. By the time you are finished with your investigation, you may have a page or two of notes. You study all the data you have collected until you know exactly what the problem is. Only after you have gathered all the facts and reached some definite conclusions about them will you be able to plan what you are going to say to Mr. Matthews when you write to him. If the story cannot be pieced together in such a way that you are sure of your ground, you may have to go back to all your sources and recheck everything. You might even have to write Mr. Matthews for clarification on certain points.

Let's say you uncover all the evidence you need to convince yourself that Mr. Matthews is right—he owes your company nothing. Now you are ready to start to plan your letter.

The plan starts with the question, What does Mr. Matthews want to know? The answer is simple: he wants to know if he is going to get what he asked for—a clean bill of health. The first item in your think plan will be something like this.

He's right on all counts. He owes us nothing.

You could stop there, of course, and write your letter. But if you do, the customer might think you look upon such mistakes as run-of-the-mill in your company and that he can expect more of the same in his future dealings. So the next item in your think plan might be this:

I should explain how these errors happened, even though some of them are minor. I won't duck the responsibility for them, but I don't want to give the impression that we do this sort of thing routinely.

Is there another point that ought to be covered? Yes. You will want to try to build goodwill and resell Mr. Matthews on your company. Your think plan continues:

Houghton is a good customer, and these people don't deserve the kind of runaround we gave them. At the same time, I hope Mr. Matthews won't hold this one experience against us and put us in bad with his purchasing office. We want their business.

If the foregoing think plan is put in the form of a written plan, it might look something like this:

1. Right--he owes us nothing. New stmt.
2. Explanation:
   #763--error in ext. (should have been $433.40).
   #877--discount of 2% ($6) should have been allowed.
   Ret'd shpmt.--Accounting not notified by whse.
3. Apologies (runaround).
4. Special attn. on next order.

Such a plan is likely to produce a letter like the following.

Dear Mr. Matthews:

You are absolutely right—you owe us nothing. I'm enclosing a new statement which provides the details, but the important thing about it is the "00" balance!

As you will see, we made an error in our extension on Invoice 763. The figure should have been $433.40 instead of $466.40. For some reason, the discount to which you were entitled on Invoice 877 wasn't given you; this amounts to $6. And credit for $888.80 for the returned shipment was not given because our warehouse didn't notify the accounting department that it had arrived.

I am very sorry about these mistakes, Mr. Matthews, and I can't imagine why they all happened to you. Nor can I explain why you got a runaround when you tried to get the matter settled.

We've made such a fuss here about the treatment you received that I think it's safe to say that your future transactions with Drummond are going to have special attention from everyone. In fact, I look forward to your next order so that I can prove that statement!

Thank you for your patience.

Sincerely yours,

Suppose the customer is right on two points but wrong on one. How will your plan differ? Probably you will take the opportunity to deliver the favorable news first, telling him where he is right and apologizing for the mistakes. Then you will gently explain where he is wrong and why; here you will offer a fuller explanation because the customer will want to know precisely how he erred.

Case Example

You are supervisor in the Order Services Department of West Fairfield Aluminum Company. You have received a letter from R. F. Follett, manager of the Lone Star Department Store, saying he is returning a shipment of lawn chairs. The manager claims that the chairs he received are not the ones he ordered, and he requests a credit memorandum for the total of the order, $477.80, plus shipping charges of $43.20.

Your investigation shows that the chairs sent to Lone Star are the ones that were ordered. Since you do accept shipments returned in good condition, there are no problems about giving Lone Star full credit. At the same time, you do not feel that it is fair for the manager of Lone Star to ask you to pay the shipping charges. It's against company policy to do so unless an error was made by West Fairfield Aluminum, and in this case the error is the customer's.

This letter requires two answers—yes on the credit memorandum for the returned chairs and no on the shipping charges. But you decide to check on that latter point; company policy is often loosely interpreted, depending on the customer and the circumstances. Lone Star happens to be a new customer—a potentially big buyer—and getting him on your side could mean several hundred thousand dollars' worth of business a year. Your boss might think $43.20 is a small price to pay for keeping a customer as large as this one.

If such a concession sounds inconsistent—and unfair to customers who do not receive such privileges—it is nevertheless realistic. Making such a decision, however, requires a thorough knowledge of one's job as well as sound business judgment.

Your think plan might be as follows.

1. *Certainly, we are willing to accept the chairs and give full credit.*
2. *But I think I should let him know that the chairs shipped were the ones he ordered; otherwise, he might think we usually get orders mixed up.*
3. *As a special favor to him, we'll pay the return shipping costs, but he ought to know that it's an exception.*
4. *I wonder why he didn't say anything about placing another order for lawn chairs? Did he forget? Does he want information about other styles? I'll try to get an order from him.*

Once you have thought through all the problems, you are ready to put your plan in writing.

1. Credit memo for $521, incl. shipping charge of $43.20.
2. Sorry about mix-up, but these appear to be chairs ordered. Copy of order encl.
3. Important thing is to place new order. Catalog section.

Here is the letter that might evolve from such a plan.

Dear Mr. Follett:

Here is our credit memorandum for $521, which covers the returned shipment of Compac lawn chairs ($477.80) and shipping charges ($43.20).

Although the chairs we sent you seem to be the ones listed in your April 7 order, perhaps they are not what you had in mind. I'm sending you a copy of your order, together with a tear sheet of the Compac line, so that you may check. Because we think there might have been some misunderstanding, we are paying the return shipping charges, which we don't ordinarily do.

The important thing, of course, is that you have a stock of lawn chairs to meet your summer needs. Be sure to place another order soon so that you may have them for the first warm day. Separately I am sending you a section from our general summer furniture catalog; you might be more interested in the new Ezy-Fold line (pages 18–22), which is fast becoming our best seller.

Let me know, please, how I can be of further help. By the way, we can ship your next order the same day it is received.

Sincerely yours,

Case Example

Assume that you are assistant to the director of public relations in the E. H. Black Pen Company. Your company receives a great many letters from organizations asking for free pens to be given away as favors at conventions and meetings. Black has a rigid policy on giving free pens; one had to be established because the company found the practice greatly abused and too costly.

The convention chairman of the Arbuckle Ski Club, A. Raymond Woolsey, has written you that the club is having its annual meeting next month in Denver and would like to give a kit of favors to each person who attends. Mr. Woolsey would like your company to contribute 500 pens for the kits.

The request cannot be granted. If you make an exception in this case (and the organization does not appear to merit an exception), you will throw the doors open to others requesting a similar favor. Your think plan will probably look like this.

1. *This is probably a worthy organization, and I wish I could give Mr. Woolsey those 500 pens he wants.*
2. *But I can't—it would be setting a dangerous precedent—and we've got to treat everybody alike.*
3. *We do give away a lot (several thousand pens a year), but we've had to confine our donations to youth groups.*
4. *Maybe I ought to suggest that he write to one of the sporting goods companies that sometimes give free pens to sports organizations.*
5. *I hope the Arbuckle Ski Club will understand why I've got to turn them down.*

Your written plan in this case is jotted in the margins of the letter from Mr. Woolsey, as illustrated on page 65.

Here is the letter you might write.

Dear Mr. Woolsey:

Thank you for thinking of Fleetmade Pens when planning your national convention in Denver in December.

I certainly wish that I could give you the 500 pens with our compliments, Mr. Woolsey; your organization is doubtless a worthy one. At one time we provided free pens for groups such as yours, but the demands became so great that we had to give up the practice. Today we limit our contributions to a group of selected youth organizations (we typically give away several thousand pens a year).

ARBUCKLE SKI CLUB

Pilgrim Bank Building

Boston, Massachusetts 02102

October 16, 19--

E. B. Black Pen Company
212 South Wabash Avenue
Chicago, Illinois 60605

Gentlemen:

The Arbuckle Ski Club, a nonprofit organization of some 1,200 *1. Appreciate*
members, is holding its annual convention in Denver December *2. Worthy org.*
28-31.   *3. Discontinued—*
                                                                   youth groups
We are preparing a kit of favors for each person who registers   *only*
for the final banquet--the kit to include toilet goods, sta-   *4. Sporting*
tionery, key chains, ball-point pens, etc. Would you supply   *goods co's*
500 pens for these kits? Other firms have generously donated   *5. Thanks,*
their products.   *etc.*

I shall look forward to hearing from you.

Very truly yours,

A. Raymond Woolsey

A. Raymond Woolsey
Convention Chairman

National sporting goods manufacturers often provide favors to sports-minded organizations. Perhaps you will want to write to one or more of these companies.

Best wishes for a successful convention.

Sincerely yours,

When you think through your communication before you reach for the typewriter or a dictating machine, you are bound to produce a more accurate, complete, and logical message. Don't, then, eliminate this step in your writing activities. Advance planning for a writer is like a rehearsal for an actor. No professional performer would dream of going before an audience without rehearsing his part. Why should a writer think he can?

■■■■■■■■■■■■■■■■■■■■■■■■■■■■■■■■■■■

PROJECTS

A The Riverhead Department Store received the following letter from Levitan-Morris Corporation. It refers to an invoice that Riverhead submitted to Levitan-Morris for an advertisement that was run in the Philadelphia *Bulletin*.

Gentlemen:

Attached please find your advertising claim, which cannot be honored and is being returned to you for the following reason:

> Your ad does not show the use of our name or trademark—as per advertising requirement shown in our catalog and like copy attached.

As this claim cannot be authorized, we suggest that you void the attached invoice so that both your records and ours can be cleared.

We also suggest that you run another ad at your convenience, using our name, and submit another claim at that time.

Thanks very much for the nice business given us. Your prompt cooperation in canceling this claim will be appreciated.

                                        Sincerely yours,

Study the above letter carefully, and then write a plan for responding to it. After you have completed your plan, write the appropriate letter.

B Rewrite the following letter. As you think about an appropriate revision, make a plan to guide you in preparing the letter.

Gentlemen:

We are pleased to enclose ten copies of our brochure on our new Model 900, 18-inch-diameter indexing table.

This model supersedes our old Model 805, and is considerably heavier duty, better engineered, and of much more rugged construction than the old Model 805—at no additional increase in price.

We will continue to supply service parts on the old 805 but wish that you would quote all your 18-inch tables as the Model 900.

We are pleased with the quality of this new brochure and feel as though it will give you an additional sales boost. We would appreciate any comments that you may have. Should you require further copies, please write us and specify your requirements.

Thanking you for your consideration in this matter, we remain,

Very truly yours,

C   Criticize the following paragraph, taken from a sales training manual, as to logic, flow, and general appropriateness.

FIRST CONSIDERATION IS THE NEW MAN. Your first goal should be to help the new man make his plans rather than to give him a crutch to lean upon. Hence, your first consideration in training is the man rather than the method. He must feel he has become one of a family instead of a cog in a selling machine. Show the new man how to prepare for each kind of prospect call he will be making, including pre-call planning. Show him how to make a good, thorough call. Teach him the right way to work with various types of prospects.

■ ■

UNIT 6   PUT IT IN PROPER FORM

Written communications tell a lot about a writer and the organization he represents just from the way they are set up. Just as a good picture can lose much of its impact on the viewer if it is improperly framed, an expertly written letter or memo can lose a great deal of its effect if it is set up badly. And, on the other hand, good form and arrangement can make a business message seem much better than it really is.

Even if the letter writer is a top executive, his responsibility extends to making sure that his letters and memos appear in attractive and appropriate form. Of course, a good secretary is half the battle. But let's take a rundown of the essentials of appropriate letter style and format.

LETTERS

Stationery. For general business use, the most popular size of stationery is $8\frac{1}{2}$ by 11 inches. The paper should be at least 20-pound bond with about 25 percent rag content to assure acceptable quality. The letterhead and the paper used for second sheets should be of the same weight and quality.

In addition to the standard $8\frac{1}{2}$-by-11 size, top executives often use a distinctive size, such as Monarch ($7\frac{1}{4}$ by $10\frac{1}{2}$ inches) or Baronial ($5\frac{1}{2}$ by $8\frac{1}{2}$ inches), for personal-business, social-business, and professional correspondence.

Letterhead. Since the company letterhead is intended to project the "company image," its design is usually entrusted to a specialist in graphic arts. The best source is usually an art agency that specializes in this kind of graphic presentation, since creating a distinctive letterhead requires a knowledge of typefaces, layout, color, and other artistic factors. In any case, unless you have your own business or are permitted your own letterhead, you won't have much to say about letterhead design or color. And if you do have the responsibility for letterhead design, we recommend you have it done by a specialist.

Letter Styles. A few companies adopt one letter style and require all the people in the company to use it. Most, however, leave the selection of format to the executive or his secretary.

The two most popular letter styles—the blocked and the semiblocked—are illustrated on pages 69 and 70.

Punctuation Patterns. The most commonly used punctuation style for letters is the *standard.* This requires a colon following the salutation and a comma following the complimentary closing. Another acceptable style is *open* punctuation. This style omits all punctuation at the ends of display lines (other than those that end with an abbreviation, of course).

The punctuation pattern used in a letter should be in harmony with the letter style. Standard punctuation is more suitable for a semiblocked letter and open punctuation for a blocked letter.

Parts of the Letter. Most business letters include at least these parts: letterhead or return address, date line, inside address, salutation, body, complimentary closing, and signature block.

Letterhead or Return Address. A printed letterhead not only contains the company name and address but it may also include telephone numbers, cable address, advertising slogan, names of major officers, and so on. The trend in letterhead design, however, is toward simplicity. Observe the uncluttered look of the letterheads illustrated on pages 69 and 70.

If a letterhead is not used, the heading consists of the writer's return address and the date. This information is usually flush with the right margin, thus:

> 1224 Gatewood Avenue, N.W.
> Washington, D.C. 20016
> July 21, 19—

Date Line. The date may be placed so that it balances the letterhead (centered under the company name, placed under the name of the city, etc.) or so that it ends even with the right margin.

Inside Address. The inside address gives the name of the person to whom you're writing and his address. The inside addresses in the letters on pages 69 and 70 are typical: the name and title on the first line, followed by the company name, the street address, and the city, state, and Zip Code.

The Art Collector's Guild

3120 Market Street · Youngstown · Ohio 44507

November 16, 19--

Miss Cynthia Russon
6020 Bannockburn Drive
Bethesda, Maryland 20034

Dear Miss Russon:

You are invited to join a small group of discriminating people who truly
appreciate fine original art. These are people who, like yourself, are
aware of its artistic and economic worth. As the accompanying folder
shows, you may acquire individually signed and numbered, authenticated,
and framed original lithographs by outstanding artists at less than half
their appraised value.

I'm sure you will also enjoy the framed original I would like to send as
a gift of membership. Each is independently appraised at between $40
and $70.

Our Board of Advisors seeks out only those living artists whose works
have already been accepted by respected critics, galleries, and museums.
Each large, original, full-color lithograph is chosen both for its
artistic beauty and for its financial potential.

Obviously, Miss Russon, The Art Collector's Guild--by its very nature--
must choose its members carefully.

Please note that you risk nothing at all by joining. You will never be
required to make a single purchase. Your $10 membership fee is a one-
time payment, for which you will be billed only after you have received
and approved your free, framed original etching or lithograph. Please
act quickly--return the enclosed postage-paid form today.

                                        Sincerely yours,

                                        Phyllis Lowe Bradshaw

                                        Mrs. Phyllis Lowe Bradshaw
                                        Membership Director

PLB/sc
Enc.

Blocked letter

Salutation. The salutation is typed two spaces below the inside address. When
addressing one person, it is traditional to include *Dear* in the salutation (*Dear
Miss Cole, Dear Henry*). Some women, regardless of marital status, prefer the
title *Ms.* and their preference should be honored. In writing to a firm or an
organization, the appropriate salutation is *Gentlemen* (not *Dear Sirs*), even

THE BELLEVUE-NETHERLANDS

360 Seventh Avenue

New York, New York 10036

April 20, 19--

Mr. Philip J. Landers, President
Larchmont Industries, Inc.
3224 16th Street, N.W.
Washington, D.C. 20010

Dear Mr. Landers:

        You will, I think, enjoy the accompanying brochure, "Fit for
a King." In the past six months every suite and room at The Bellevue-
Netherlands has been completely refurnished and redecorated in a most
elegant fashion. All our rooms and suites now have air conditioning
and television.

        Our location is second to none: We're at 59th Street and
Seventh Avenue (opposite beautiful Central Park)--close to magnificent
shops, the theater district, and the Coliseum.

        Let me assure you that even though the Bellevue-Netherlands
has a new look, our policy of superior service still prevails. I
look forward to the pleasure of welcoming you to our hotel in the near
future.

                          Cordially yours,

                          George R. Markovis

                          George R. Markovis
                          Manager

GRM:ct
Enc.

Semiblocked letter

when you know that some of the chief executives in the organization are
women. If you know, however, that all the executives are women, the correct
salutation is *Mesdames* or *Ladies*.

Body. The body is, of course, the message itself. It is usually single-spaced
with a blank line between paragraphs. Depending on letter style, paragraphs
may be indented five or ten spaces or start flush with the left margin.

Complimentary Closing. Tradition dictates that we close a letter with some kind of sign-off. Most popular are *Sincerely yours* and *Cordially yours.* When you want to be more formal, you may use *Very truly yours* or *Very cordially yours* or, more personal, *Sincerely* or *Cordially.*

Signature Block. Three typewriter spaces are left for the signature of the writer, and this space is followed by the writer's typewritten name and title. (See illustrations on pages 69 and 70.)

Reference Notations. Usually the initials of the dictator and the stenographer are shown at the bottom left, two spaces below the signature block. This practice probably sprang from a desire to fix responsibility in case someone other than the signer actually dictated the letter and also in case the stenographer needed to be identified if some question arose. At any rate, identifying the dictator and the stenographer seems to be a fixed habit in most businesses, even though its actual value is questionable. A current practice is to show only the typist's initials in small letters at the bottom left. Since the dictator's name is typed under the signature line, it does seem a bit redundant to repeat his initials a line or two below. Also, if the dictator types the letter, no initials are used.

Following the identification line are other notations that may be made to establish a record. For example, *Enclosures 2* means that the writer has enclosed two documents and the recipient should look for them in the envelope. The notation *cc: T. R. Feldon* means a copy of the letter has been sent to T. R. Feldon, and *bcc: Mrs. R. Mullins* indicates that Mrs. Mullins is getting a copy of the letter but without the knowledge of the recipient (the notation does not appear on the original).

MEMORANDUMS

The memorandum is used for interoffice letters and informal reports. On page 72 is a memorandum typical of those written in business. It is from the executive vice president of a corporation to the vice president in charge of operations.

Parts of the Memo. The stationery on which memos are written contains printed headings that eliminate the need for formal inside addresses, salutations, and closings. Although memorandum forms differ, most of them contain at least four headings: TO, FROM, SUBJECT, and DATE. Other headings are added to speed delivery or establish identification; for example, DEPARTMENT, LOCATION (branch office, for example), FLOOR, TELEPHONE EXTENSION, ROOM, and so on.

The "To" Line. The addressee is not usually given a courtesy title, such as *Mr., Miss,* or *Dr.* (It is common, however, to use *Mr.* when addressing a person of much higher rank than the writer.) The job title (*Vice President, Operations*) may be used in very formal circumstances. If there is no provision in the form

Interoffice Memorandum

TO   R. Phillip Donnelly
      cc: C. J. Moore
DEPT Operations

FROM David J. Byram
DEPT. Executive

SUBJECT Fourth Quarter Expenses

DATE November 18, 19--

I have just finished my analysis of the October operating statement
and would like to call some things to your attention.

As you have noted or will shortly note, October was somewhat disappointing. While our sales were slightly over budget, we missed our
predicted operating profit by $370,000. This underage was a result
of our going over budget by $397,000 in direct expenses and $119,000
in indirect expenses. Contrasted with October of last year, we
produced $94,000 less net profit on increased sales of $1,400,000.

Obviously, if we are to produce the profit we expect and are capable
of, we must make a special effort to hold down expenses for the
remainder of the year. I urge you to make all managers aware of the
problem, keeping in mind that next year's plans and budgets will not
be finally approved for another four to six weeks.

Would you report to me by November 25 what steps you are taking to
meet this problem.

                                        D.J.B.

DJB:am

for ''department,'' this may be indicated alongside the addressee's name; for example, *Homer R. Lee, Personnel Relations.* Such an identification may be very important in a large company.

When the memorandum is addressed to several people, the ''To'' line may appear as follows:

TO: Publications Committee

TO: See below

(and the names or initials of the individuals addressed are listed at the end of the memorandum, thus: *Distribution: WIT, MRMc, LRB, RJH, FMS, TRR, CIG.*)

Copy Notation. The name of the person receiving a copy of the memorandum may be placed below the addressee's name but more usually at the bottom left margin. If several people are to receive copies, the notation is placed at the bottom of the memorandum:

cc: C. J. Moore   Mrs. Amy Post
    Albert J. Elliott   Anthony Finletter
    G. M. Hotchkiss   Harold H. Locke

The "From" Line. Neither a courtesy title nor a job title is given to the writer of the memorandum. However, when the memorandum form does not provide for an identification of the department from which the message is sent, the writer should include this information beside or below his name; for example, *FROM: Peter A. DiSalle, Customer Relations.* This is especially important when the writer is a new employee in a large company or an employee who is not likely to be widely known in the firm.

The "Department" Line. The department from which the memorandum comes and to which it goes is usually taken for granted. There is a chance that the memo may be misdirected; therefore, it is wise to identify the department.

The "Subject" Line. Stating the subject of the memorandum enables the reader to know at a glance what the memo is about. The wording should be as short as possible but long enough to tell the reader what you're going to talk about in the memorandum.

SUBJECT: REQUEST FOR LEAVE OF ABSENCE

SUBJECT: Overpayment to Jackson Associates

SUBJECT: Comparative Study of Retirement Policies in Six Major Petroleum Companies

The Body. The body of the memorandum, like the body of a letter, is usually single-spaced, with paragraphs blocked. If the message is very short, double spacing may be appropriate.

The Signature. Many memorandum writers feel that their name on the "From" line makes a signature unnecessary, either typewritten or hand-written. Again, whether you initial or sign your memorandums is up to you. If you want to personalize your memos, either initial or sign them. The best place for a signature is at the bottom of the memo, although some people like to sign or initial below their typewritten name on the "From" line.

■■■■■■■■■■■■■■■■■■■■■■■■■■■■■■■■■■■■■

PROJECTS

A   Edit the following letter and rewrite it in proper form. The sender, Ruth P. Genesco, has no letterhead; her address is 245 Landis Lane, Deerfield, Illinois 60015. Use the current date.

Mr. Josel S. Gaines, Vice President for Market Research and Promotion, Literary Review, 4740 Earhart Blvd., New Orleans, La. 70150. Dear Sir, Did you know that your family name was recorded with a coat-of-arms in ancient heraldic archives more than 7 centuries ago. My husband and I discovered this while doing some research for some friends of ours, who have the same last name as you did. We've had an artist recreate the coat-of-arms exactly as described in the ancient records and this drawing along with other information about the name, has been printed up into an attractive one page report. The last part of the report tells the story of the very old and distinguished family name of Gaines. It tells what the name means, the origin of the name, it's place in history and famous people who share it. The first part of the report has a large, beautiful reproduction of an artist's drawing of the earliest known coat-of-arms for the name Gaines and this entire report is documented, authentic, and printed on parchment-like paper suitable for framing. This report so delighted our friends that we have had a few extra copies made in order to share this information with other people of the same name. Framed these reports make distinctive wall decorations and they are great gifts for relatives and it should be remembered that we have not traced anyones' individual family tree but have researched back through several centuries to find about the earliest people named Gaines. All we are asking for them is enough to cover the added expense of having the extra copies printed and mailed. If you are interested, please let us know right away as our supply is very limited. Just verify that we have your correct name and address and send the correct amount in cash or check for the number of reports you want and we'll send them promptly by return mail. Sincerely, P.S. If you are ordering only one report, send two dollars ($2). Additional reports ordered at the same time and sent to the same address are one dollar each. Please make checks payable to me, Ruth P. Genesco.

B   Edit the following letter and put it in proper form. Use the current date.

LAKESIDE HILLS INN
860 Lakeside Highway Northwest
Columbia, South Carolina 29202

Mr. Liborio M. Sanchez, Sales Manager, Allied Products Corporation, 1333 West 5th Ave., Columbus, O. 43212. Dear Mr. Sanchez, We would like to host your next meeting, conference, or seminar! Lakeside Hills Inn, a complete resort on blue Lake Murray, has the following attractions to accommodate your meeting: 80 luxurious sleeping rooms with private balconies (some with fireplaces) overlooking Lake Murray; 4 public meeting rooms, 3 carpeted—each with a lake view; 18 hole championship golf course, driving range; swimming pool, horseback riding, 3 tennis courts, shuffleboard; complete marina with boat rentals for fishing, skiing, sailing, and other water sports; a 3200 foot paved airstrip with Unicom communications to the Lakeside Hills Inn (122.8); the elegant Yacht Club for use of registered guests; our very capable, willing staff is another asset to Lakeside. While we want most emphatically to host you and your associates and to have you keep us on your mind, we do not want to send you unwanted literature and news of Lakeside. Thus, if you will fill in and return the enclosed self-address, postage paid postcard, we will comply with your wishes. I look forward to hearing from you in the near future and if I may be of any assistance to you or your association, please let me know. Cordially yours, (Miss) Elizabeth Newman, Seminar Sales Coordinator.

part

2

**REQUEST
LETTERS
AND
MEMOS
NEARLY
EVERYONE
WRITES**

YOUR JOB

You are assistant office services manager for the Far Western Insurance Company, San Jose, California. The Office Services Department, managed by Harold R. Prince, Jr., has the responsibility for seeing that all incoming and outgoing mail is processed quickly and efficiently, that office space in the various departments of the company is properly utilized, that furniture and equipment are adequate, that appropriate supplies are available, that interoffice communication systems are effective, and that company records are properly maintained. The department also must constantly study the flow of paper work in the company to see that it is handled with minimum cost and maximum efficiency. You and the supervisors in the department act as consultants to the managers of the other departments on such matters as dictation, typewriting, letter form, and records maintenance.

Although your responsibility for written communications is not heavy, you do write letters to suppliers and vendors and memos to Mr. Prince and others in your department as well as to people in other departments.

CASE 1 — REQUESTING FREE MATERIALS

PROBLEM: As assistant office services manager of Far Western, you must have on hand the latest catalogs, price lists, and other materials of major manufacturers and distributors of office furniture, supplies, and equipment. Since you have only a few of these items—most of them out of date—you need to write several suppliers requesting up-to-date catalogs and price lists.

BACKGROUND

Letters written by a potential customer asking suppliers for free materials, information, or routine service are among the easiest to write. Obviously he is in a position to receive what he is asking for since it is to the supplier's advantage to provide it. The potential customer needs to use little salesmanship when making his request.

Even though you are in the driver's seat when writing letters such as these, approach the task as though you were on the receiving end and think about the kind of letter *you* would like to receive if the situation were reversed. Of course you would grant the request because it is in your company's interest to do so. In fact, you would be willing to go out of your way to be helpful. You would ask only that the writer tell you everything you need to know—no more, no less. And you would prefer a letter that is courteous.

In writing routine request letters, you should plan to give all the information the supplier will need if he is to be really helpful, keep your request as brief as possible without omitting important details, and express your wishes courteously and tactfully.

SOLUTION A

Gentlemen:

In consulting my files of catalogs of equipment and supplies and checking them off against various manufacturers, it was noticed that I did not have your most current issues, which possibly were received but if so I misplaced them, and I like to keep up to date on all manufacturer's catalogs and price lists.

For this reason I would like to request that you send me your latest catalogs of equipment and supplies (plus price lists) at your earliest convenience.

Thanking you in advance, I remain,

Yours truly,

Analysis of Solution A. How many examples of the following did you spot in Solution A?

1. Incorrect grammar and punctuation
2. Misspelled words
3. Poor sentence structure
4. Circumlocutions
5. Trite expressions
6. Unnecessary words
7. Irrelevant details

In writing even the most routine letters, some people seem to want to tell their life story, wasting time for everyone and obscuring the purpose of the message. The writer did not need to go into an involved explanation of why he wants a new catalog and price list; the reader is not helped by it nor is he interested in the details.

Although this letter probably will produce the results the writer wants, it marks him as muddle-brained, incoherent, bumbling. More serious, it wastes both the writer's and the reader's time.

It is generally unwise to open a letter with an ''In'' phrase (*In consulting my files, In answer to your letter, In response to your question*) or with words ending in ''ing'' (*Replying to your letter, Acknowledging your inquiry, According to our statement, Referring to your question*). Such poor openings are equally weak closings. Don't close a letter with *thanking, hoping, or expecting,* for example. The sentence that begins with one of these words will not be complete unless you end with the old-fashioned and meaningless *I remain* (as shown in the example) or *I am.*

Too, most people consider it presumptuous to thank someone in advance. The appropriate time to thank the reader is after he has complied with your request.

SOLUTION B

Gentlemen:

Send me your latest price lists and catalogs.

Very truly yours,

Analysis of Solution B. Solution B may be perfectly satisfactory. Certainly it is brief. Yet, although the writer committed no serious faults, he might have spared a "please" or a "thank you" or some other expression of courtesy. Also, if he had thought carefully about the situation, he might have come to the conclusion that giving the purpose of the request would have been helpful (some companies, upon receiving requests for catalogs and other promotional material, are inclined to rush a salesman out with the material). And the writer might have asked, "How can I be sure of receiving all new catalogs and similar materials as they are issued? If I could get on the mailing list to receive such information automatically, I wouldn't have to worry about remembering to write for them."

SOLUTION C

Gentlemen:

May I have your latest catalog and price list? I am setting up a product information file for reference by our supervisors and managers, who often need the latest data about office equipment and supplies.

Will you please put me on your mailing list for all of your promotion and catalog material?

Sincerely yours,

Analysis of Solution C. Solution C is an effective letter for these reasons:

1. The tone is appropriate. Even though the prospective customer could say almost anything in his letter and get what he wants, the writer wisely observes the rules of good human relations. He could have said in the first paragraph, "I want your catalog" or "Send me your catalog," but those are demands. "May I have your latest catalog and price list" is a courteous request and the tone makes a world of difference. In the last paragraph, the writer could have written, "Put me on your mailing list," but asking and using the word *please* changed a demand to a polite request.
2. The letter is brief but complete. It gives only the information the reader needs in order to help.
3. The reason for the request is clearly stated, even though it is not absolutely essential in this case.

4. The letter starts with a question. Of course, this isn't the only way to begin such a letter, but it did get the writer into his subject immediately.
5. The writer obviously thought about his continuing need for new materials (last paragraph); his request can save additional letters in the future.

■ ■

PROJECTS

A   The June issue of *Modern Office Training* featured the article "Making Films for Training," by Charles E. Wirtz, which you enjoyed reading. In the article, Mr. Wirtz mentioned a booklet available from Amerigo Film Productions, Baltimore, Maryland, *The ABC's of Making Motion Pictures,* which is free to business firms. You're thinking of preparing your own motion picture films for training clerical personnel. Write for the free booklet. Make up an address.

B   About a month ago, you ordered and received from Southern Manufacturing Company, Decatur, Georgia, its latest catalog, *Functional Furniture*—an expensively produced booklet with transparent color overlays. You have made good use of the catalog and have shared it with several others. Unfortunately, the catalog has disappeared and, although you've made a thorough search, you can't find it. Write for a replacement copy.

C   The personnel training director has showed you a copy of *Tips on Telephoning* and told you the booklet is available free from the New England Telephone Company, Hartford, Connecticut. You want 12 copies by May 1 for use in a special training class that you plan to conduct for secretaries and others in the Office Services Department. Write for them.

D   Write your own version of each of the following good request letters.

1

Gentlemen:

Your advertisement in the May issue of Leisure invited readers to send for a free copy of So You've Bought a Boat. May I have one?

                              Sincerely,

2

Dear Mr. Jamison:

I certainly enjoyed reading "Business and the Ecological Movement" in July's Management Profile. Every businessman all over the country should act on your suggestion.

Please send me a copy of Are You a Dirty Business? that you mentioned. In fact, if you can spare five copies, I'd like to have them. You can be sure they'll get into the right hands.

                              Cordially yours,

■ ■

CASE 2 — REQUESTING INFORMATION

PROBLEM: The Customer Accounts Unit is planning a new office layout in order to achieve better flow of paper work, and you have been asked to help. One of the questions you must answer is, Is the available space adequate to accommodate the new layout? You know there are various devices by which the workableness of a layout can be tested without having to move furniture and equipment around to see whether it fits the space. These devices include templates, planning boards, and three-dimensional models. However, none of your catalogs contains the information you want about these devices, nor can you find what you want in nearby office supply stores. You decide to write for information to one of the large dealers with whom you occasionally place special orders, the Pioneer Office Supply Corporation, Chicago.

BACKGROUND

Often you will write for information when you aren't exactly sure what you want or what the supplier has available. In these cases, you are asking the supplier to think through a problem with you and help you solve it. Obviously, to be of any assistance, the supplier must be told exactly what your problem is.

When you request information about a puzzling problem, be very specific. The supplier can't read your mind! At the same time, your request should be reasonable. An example of an unreasonable request is that written by a youngster to a large aircraft manufacturing company:

> Gentlemen:
>
> I'm interested in planes. Please send me all the information you have about them.
>
> Very sincerely yours,

If this example strikes you as ridiculous, remember that business firms and government offices receive similar letters by the thousands every day and not just from little boys: "Please tell me all about space exploration." "I would like to know how to write a book" "I'm interested in computers. Please tell me all you know about them."

SOLUTION A

> Gentlemen:
>
> I am interested in layout devices. Please send me complete information.
>
> Yours very truly,

Analysis of Solution A. Solution A might achieve its mission. If the correspondent for Pioneer Office Supply Corporation tries to put himself in the writer's shoes, he will probably come up with some kind of solution to the problem. But his job would be a lot easier if he had more information to go on. Besides giving too little information, the writer has committed two faults:

1. He has assumed that Pioneer carries layout devices even though they're not shown in the Pioneer catalog. The recipient of the letter is likely to think, "We don't handle layout devices; I'd better set this guy straight."
2. His brevity and impersonal tone make the request seem unimportant. If Pioneer's correspondent is on his toes, however, he won't treat the request as routine (even though we tend to be influenced in what we are willing to do by the importance attached to it by the person requesting help).

SOLUTION B

Gentlemen:

Will you help me? We are planning a new layout of our Customer Accounts Unit in order to provide for a more efficient flow of work.

The various devices used for making preliminary layouts, such as templates, planning boards, and three-dimensional models, are not available in the local stores, and I haven't found any in the dealers' catalogs. If you do carry them, I would appreciate having complete information about them, including costs, delivery time, and ordering procedures.

If you don't handle layout devices, can you refer me to a company that does? You may jot the name at the bottom of the enclosed copy of this letter and return it to me.

Sincerely yours,

Analysis of Solution B. Solution B is a much better letter than A for these reasons:

1. The writer frankly asks for help, telling his reader exactly what the problem is and how he has attempted (unsuccessfully) to solve it.
2. The tone of the letter is good; the writer is businesslike and, at the same time, courteous and appreciative.
3. All necessary background information is supplied, but the writer does not bury the reader in words.
4. The writer makes it easy for the reader to respond.

■ ■

PROJECTS

A   As assistant office services manager, you are frequently asked by supervisors for advice on employee relations. You have learned that Ranier Films, Wilmington, Delaware, distributes excellent motion pictures on the subject of supervision and human relations, and you decide to write for information. Prepare the letter.

B The catalog arrives from Ranier Films and contains descriptions of several interesting films that you are considering suggesting Far Western purchase for training purposes. There is also a list of new films under the heading "In Production—Soon to Be Released," with no additional information: *Motivating Employees, Group Dynamics, Communicating With Employees, Dos and Don'ts of Employee Ratings,* and *The Human Manager.* You are interested in all these films and would like to know when they will be available, whether they will be in black and white or color, the cost, and the running time of each. Write the letter.

C You plan to set up a small reference library for the secretaries in the Office Services Department who have requested source books on English grammar and style, words, secretarial procedures, and communications. You are not certain which books would be best for the purpose, and you decide to write the business books editors of several major publishing houses for their suggestions.

1 Criticize the following as to its effectiveness in obtaining the information you want.

Dear Sir:

Please send me all the information you have about setting up a reference library for our secretaries.

                                    Yours truly,

2 Write a letter that will do the job better.

D The vice president has asked Mr. Prince, office services manager, to find out about accommodations at the Ridge Falls Hotel, near Santa Cruz, California, for a three-day conference of department managers and company executives. Mr. Prince asked an assistant to prepare a rough draft of a letter to Ridge Falls Hotel requesting the necessary information. Criticize the draft and then rewrite the letter.

Dear Sirs:

I would like to know about your facilities. Please send information about them, costs, etc.

                                    Yours sincerely,

E Write your own version of these effective letters requesting information.

1

Gentlemen:

Our company library is eager to obtain a book, published in the 1920's, about the 1894 Pullman strike. The author's name is McLean and the title is something like "Decisive Encounter" or "Encounter of Decision."

I have written to several other publishers, but none has been able to help me. Can you? You'll make me very popular with our readers if you can.

                                    Cordially yours,

2

Gentlemen:

Please give me the name of a dealer in or near Charlotte, where I might see Famous Heritage Furniture. I have not been able to locate a store that carries this line, and I am particularly eager to see "The Mariner" dining room furniture that was advertised in the July Better Homes and Gardens.

Sincerely yours,

■ ■

CASE 3 WRITING A ROUTINE REQUEST MEMO

PROBLEM: You recently received a circular announcing a two-day workshop on data processing for modern management to be held a month from now at the Century Plaza Hotel in Los Angeles. The program looks interesting to you because you are becoming more and more involved in data processing, particularly computer programming and systems analysis. You would like to go, but you must get the permission of your boss, Mr. Prince.

Of course, you could telephone Mr. Prince or see him in person to ask for permission to attend the workshop, but you know that he prefers to have this kind of request in writing.

BACKGROUND

An employee who requests something requiring a considerable expenditure of money should always make his request in writing. He may choose to "break the ice" with his superior with a verbal request; however, it should be followed up with one in writing. The person who receives the oral request may not have the final authority to approve it and need something in writing to send to *his* boss for an OK.

Before writing the request memorandum to Mr. Prince, you should consider the following think-plan questions.

1. What justification will Mr. Prince need for my spending the money and time to attend this conference?
2. What specific information will he need from me to act on the request?
3. What allowance should I make for the possibility that Mr. Prince may have to get additional approval?

SOLUTION

Following is the memo that might result from the think-plan questions.

TO: Harold R. Prince, Jr.   FROM: Jacob T. Salzbach
SUBJECT: Data Processing Workshop   DATE: July 14, 19—

The Data Processing for Modern Management Workshop described in the attached circular looks very interesting, and I would like to attend.

Note the two sessions on the ABC's of computer programming to be conducted by Dr. Leon McCambridge. As you know, I am becoming more and more involved in programming; and, according to what I have heard and read, Dr. McCambridge is one of the leading authorities on COBOL.

The fee for the workshop is $150, and travel and other expenses will amount to about $100. The week of the 16th is a good time for me in terms of my schedule. Miss Brady will be back by that time, and she can take over for me while I'm away.

Analysis of the Solution. The memo provides the essential information Mr. Prince will need to act upon the request.

1. The purpose of the memorandum—to obtain permission to attend the workshop—is expressed immediately.
2. Justification for the request is clear and persuasive; attaching the program was a good idea—it will help to sell the idea.
3. Information about the cost of the trip and how your work will be handled while you're away is provided because you know that Mr. Prince will need to know this.
4. The tone is appropriate for a top executive in case Mr. Prince wants to send the memo "upstairs."

■ ■

PROJECTS

A   You have been invited to become a member of the San Jose chapter of the National Association of Office Supervisors. The group meets monthly for dinner and a program that usually includes a speaker or a panel. You have attended three meetings during the past year as a guest and you found them interesting and helpful. The annual dues are $10, which entitles members to a free monthly magazine, *The Effective Supervisor,* and to various reports and surveys published by the Association. The cost of dinner averages $7.50.
Write a memo requesting permission to join the Association.

B   You receive an announcement (plus descriptive folder) of the Business Show to be held at the Fairmont Hotel in San Francisco. This show, which features exhibits of new office equipment, furniture, and supplies, will run for three days beginning Monday, April 11. You want to go for one day (it doesn't matter which day) and to take with you two supervisors (Miss Marple and Mr. Poirot) who have also expressed an interest in the show. You plan to drive up and return the same day, and you estimate the total cost of the trip for all three of you to be about $15.

Write the request memo.

C   You have received permission to attend the Business Show in San Francisco. Since then, you received a printed invitation to attend a special open house sponsored by Voca-Mation, Inc., a company that recently entered the dictating machine business and has caused quite a stir with its new line. You are interested in seeing this new equipment and want to go to the open house, but you would have to stay over an extra day.

Write a memo asking for permission to do so.

D   Write your own version of the following memos (all are perfectly satisfactory).

1

I'd like your permission to take two extra days off when I go on vacation July 17–31. A friend of mine is being married on August 1, and I have been asked to be in the wedding party.

If you approve, it means that I would not return to the office until August 2. Of course, I understand that I will not be paid for these two extra days.

2

For the past few years I have wanted to become a member of the Washington chapter of the Electronic Technicians Association.

Along with my application, I must submit a letter of recommendation from the chief engineering executive in the company. Would you write such a letter for me? I would certainly appreciate it.

Your letter should be addressed to Paul Lippin, 460 Fluornoy Building, Washington, D.C. 20010.

3

To: Milton Fasnacht
From: S. C. Lauder

May I be put on the list to receive the minutes of the monthly Operations Committee meetings?

I realize that these minutes are generally not distributed to those below the managerial level, but perhaps you will make an exception in my case. The warehousing and shipping group is not represented on this committee, and many decisions reached at its monthly meeting have a direct bearing on the priorities we establish.

S.C.L.

■ ■

CASE 4   REQUESTING A HOTEL RESERVATION

PROBLEM: You receive permission from Mr. Prince (Case 3) to attend the data processing workshop in Los Angeles. The meeting is to begin at nine on Monday morning, and in order not to miss the first session you will fly down Sunday afternoon. You plan to stay at the Century Plaza Hotel, the site of the workshop, if you can get a reservation.

BACKGROUND

Although some people choose to telephone a hotel for a reservation, it is generally wiser to write a letter requesting a room reservation. A letter provides a record for both you and the hotel and may encourage the hotel to send you written confirmation of your reservation. A written confirmation is often important; every day people are refused hotel rooms because they can't produce evidence of a reservation even though they were assured by telephone that a room was being held for them.

Two essentials in writing for a room reservation are these: ask for a written confirmation, although most hotels send one automatically; when you are attending a sponsored meeting at a hotel, mention the meeting and the sponsor. Often special arrangements are made with the hotel to assure accommodations for the participants and special rates for guests.

Some reservation letters are a little more complicated. If you wish a room at a certain price, will arrive late in the evening of the date of your reservation, or need special accommodations, you should say so in your letter. A typical hotel reservation letter is simple to write.

SOLUTION

> Gentlemen:
>
> Please reserve a single room for me for October 16 and 17. I will be attending the Data Processing for Modern Management Workshop at the Hotel Benson sponsored by the Computer Machinery Association.
>
> May I have a confirmation, please.
>
>   Sincerely yours,

Analysis of the Solution. The hotel reservation clerk will quickly read and understand such a letter. You will get a room if there is one, and you will receive a confirmation.

■ ■

PROJECTS

A Write a letter to Ridge Falls Motel, Santa Cruz, California, requesting three single rooms for you, Felicio Cortez, and Orin L. Farley for the night of May 16. You will arrive about 10 p.m.

B You have been invited to attend a meeting of Far Western agents in Portland, Oregon, July 17–18 to discuss new procedures for handling sales commission payments. You plan to arrive in Portland about 4 p.m. on the 17th and to leave about 3 p.m. (your presentation is at two o'clock) on the 18th. Reserve a room for yourself at the Oregonian Motel, minimum rate. Since check-out time is 1 p.m., ask for an extension to 2:30.

■ ■

CASE 5 SUBSCRIBING TO A MAGAZINE

PROBLEM: The Office Services Department subscribes to two magazines—*Management Science* and *Systems Digest*—which are circulated among those in the department who want to read them. A new magazine, *Forecast,* has come to your attention recently, and several people have said that they would like to read it regularly. Although the company library subscribes to *Forecast,* there is such a long waiting list for it that sometimes a month passes before a copy reaches your department. The magazine costs $12 a year, $20 for two years.

First, you must ask Mr. Prince for permission to subscribe to *Forcast* for departmental use. If he agrees, you must then write the publisher.

BACKGROUND: The Request Memo

We mentioned earlier that when you request permission to do something that requires spending company money, it is wise to put your request in writing. In getting ready to write the memo to Mr. Prince about subscribing to *Forecast,* you will want to consider these think-plan questions:

1. What is my purpose?
2. What background information will Mr. Prince want?
3. On what basis can I justify this request?

SOLUTION A

TO: H. R. Prince, Jr.   FROM: Paul Brown
SUBJECT: Forecast Subscription   DATE: April 24, 19—

Several people in the department want to read the new management magazine Forecast regularly. May we have your permission to subscribe to it?

Analysis of Solution A. As you undoubtedly observed, the request memo
does not contain sufficient information; the writer obviously did not think
before he wrote. Management always wants to know *why* and *how much,*
and Solution A does not provide these facts.

SOLUTION B

TO: H. R. Prince, Jr.   FROM: Paul Brown
SUBJECT: Forecast Subscription   DATE: April 24, 19—

Will you give me permission to subscribe to Forecast, a new management
magazine that you may have seen (copy accompanies this memo)?

Several people in the department have asked to see Forecast on a regular
basis. The library gets one copy each month, but often it is weeks before
we see it; and sometimes we don't get it at all. Many have said it is the
best management magazine they have read.

The subscription rate is $12 for one year and $20 for two years. I am thinking
of a two-year subscription.

Analysis of Solution B. This memo is effective because:
1. The writer indicated the purpose of the memo in the first sentence.
2. He sent a copy of the magazine to Mr. Prince. Attachments that assist
   in the selling job are always in order.
3. In the second paragraph the writer gave the necessary justification for a
   departmental subscription.
4. He stated the cost, always an important fact to the manager who has
   authority to spend company money.

BACKGROUND: The Subscription Letter

Mr. Prince writes the following on your memo and returns it to you: "OK.
Subscribe in your name. Pay for it and put it on your expense account." You
are now ready to write to the publisher, and the letter is a very simple one.

It is not always necessary to include the name and address in the body
of the letter if you are using a letterhead. Some letterhead addresses are
confusing, however; and by putting the name and address in the body, you
leave no doubt who is to receive the magazine and where it is to go.

When sending a check or money order, always mention that fact and the amount you are sending. This information is valuable for your records and for the recipient's as well.

SOLUTION C

Gentlemen:

Here is my check for $20 for a two-year subscription to Forecast. Please address the magazine as follows:

Mr. Paul Brown
Office Services Department
Far Western Insurance Company
462 El Camino Real
San Jose, California 95120

Very truly yours,

Analysis of Solution C. As you can see, the letter is:

1. *Concise.* The writer included no more and no less information than the publisher needs to process the subscription request.
2. *Straightforward.* The writer carefully avoided a long windup or dragged-out closing.
3. *Specific.* The writer included the name of the magazine, the length of the subscription desired, the form and amount of the payment enclosed, and the address for mailing the magazine. Note that the address is displayed, rather than run in with the first sentence, to make it easy to read.

■ ■

PROJECTS

A Write a letter requesting a one-year subscription to *Secretarial World,* 330 West 41 Street, New York 10036, for the department library. The subscription rate is $3.50 a year. The magazine is to be addressed to you (you are writing on the company letterhead). Request the publisher to bill you.

B Syntax, Incorporated, a large manufacturer of computers and other office equipment, publishes a magazine called *Dynamism,* 110 Fifth Avenue, New York, New York 10036, which is distributed free to large business firms on a selective basis. You would like to receive a copy for the Office Services Department library. Write the letter.

C Subscribe to *Data Management Report,* 1205 Montgomery Street, San Francisco, California 94101, for two years at the two-year rate of $14. Assume that you will enclose a company check. The magazine is to be addressed to Office Services Department.

■ ■

REQUESTING AN APPOINTMENT

PROBLEM: The Seattle branch office of Far Western Insurance Company has asked someone from the San Jose office to visit there for a few days to help straighten out a problem involving procedures for handling policyholders' changes of address. Mr. Prince has given you permission to go, and you already have your travel and hotel accommodations.

One of your equipment suppliers, VitaRecord Corporation, is located in Seattle, and while you are there, you would like to see the new line of visible indexing equipment the company has been advertising. You decide to call on some of the people at VitaRecord but need to make an appointment.

BACKGROUND

Those who "drop in" on a busy executive without an appointment are not only guilty of gross discourtesy but are likely to be disappointed because the person they want to see is not available. Just as many people resent relatives and friends who drop in for the weekend unannounced, many executives resent visitors—even potential customers—who show up without warning. Most executives operate on a tight schedule, and they like to plan their activities ahead of time. It is a good idea, then, to ask for an appointment in advance either by telephone or by letter. Letters requesting appointments should include the purpose of the visit, the date, and a suggested time. Obviously such letters are requests, not demands.

SOLUTION A

Dear Mr. Rhodes:

I expect to be in Seattle two weeks from Tuesday. I want to see your filing equipment, and I will be at your office in the afternoon.

Very truly yours,

Analysis of Solution A. Solution A violates most of the rules for effective request letters.

1. It is not specific—an exact date should have been given.
2. The purpose of the visit is not clear.
3. The time of the visit ("in the afternoon") is vague, and the writer is presumptuous if he believes Mr. Rhodes will set aside an entire afternoon on the chance he will show up.
4. The letter lacks courtesy and tact; it demands rather than requests.

SOLUTION B

Dear Mr. Rhodes:

I expect to be in Seattle on Tuesday, June 8, to meet with some of our branch office people. While in Seattle, I would like to visit VitaRecord and see your complete line of visible indexing equipment.

Would you or someone else be available to show me the new equipment from two to about four on Tuesday afternoon the 8th and, at the same time, discuss my problem of maintaining visible records of policyholders?

If Tuesday is inconvenient, I might arrange to stay over another day. Let me know, please.

Sincerely,

Analysis of Solution B. What makes the second letter better than the first?

1. The writer is specific about the reason for his visit to Seattle—"to meet with some of our branch office people"—and Mr. Rhodes will understand that the trip is not being made for the specific purpose of visiting Vita-Record. The explanation tells Mr. Rhodes that the writer's time is limited, that he doesn't have to worry about entertaining him, and that there is nothing particularly urgent about his seeing the VitaRecord equipment.
2. The writer has included complete information as to the time and the things he hopes to accomplish on his visit. This information will give Mr. Rhodes an opportunity to prepare for the visit.
3. The letter is courteous in tone and makes no unreasonable demands.

■■■■■■■■■■■■■■■■■■■■■■■■■■■■■■■■■■

PROJECTS

A You are planning to attend the western zone meeting of the National Association of Office Supervisors in Denver, October 7–10, to be held at the Brown Palace Hotel. While you are in Denver, you want to visit the showrooms of the Rocky Mountain Office Furniture Company, a large manufacturer whose catalog of office furniture and equipment you have seen. The Sales Department of Far Western is considering modular offices for the salesmen and their clerical assistants, and you want to see the equipment for yourself. (Rocky Mountain's literature carries the invitation, "Visit our showrooms when you're in Denver—an acre of new ideas in office design.") Write to the sales manager for an appointment (you don't know his name), suggesting a date and time for your visit.

B Mr. Prince is program chairman of the Western Accountants Society, which is considering holding its annual convention in Denver in December. He has had some correspondence with the Ski and Sun Motor Inn in downtown Denver and has received literature from the sales manager, Miss Claire Boudreau. Mr. Prince has asked you to visit Ski and Sun Motor Inn while you are in Denver to see its facilities and to talk with Miss Boudreau about the Society's particular needs for its convention. Write to Miss Boudreau for an appointment.

■■■■■■■■■■■■■■■■■■■■■■■■■■■■■■■■■■

PLACING AN ORDER BY LETTER

PROBLEM: The Office Services Department is setting up a small reference library, and Mr. Prince has asked you to place orders for the books that have been recommended by the people in the department.

Since you have several catalogs and price lists of publishers, you have been able to confirm the titles of the books your fellow employees would like to have. And you can obtain the names and addresses of the publishers, the names of the authors of the books, the prices of the books, and all the other information you may need from the catalogs and price lists.

BACKGROUND

Orders can be placed by phone or in several written forms:

On a purchase order form. Prepared by the company's purchasing officers, the purchase order authorizes the supplier to ship merchandise and to charge the purchaser at the quoted price.

A purchase order may or may not be accompanied by a letter. If a letter is written, it merely identifies the enclosure without repeating the information in the form.

> Dear Mr. Rhodes:
>
> Here is Purchase Order 362-18-99 for the visible indexing equipment we discussed when I was in Seattle.
>
> > Sincerely,

On an order blank. The vendor supplies printed forms for his customers' use.

By letter. Usually an order is placed by letter only when the company does not use purchase order forms or when there are no order blanks on hand from the vendor. In writing the order letter, the correspondent should first ask himself these questions:

1. What specific information (quantity, color, and size) will the vendor need to have from me about the items I want to order?
2. Will a check accompany the order or will the vendor be willing to ship the items before he asks for payment?
3. How are the items to be shipped?

Assume that Far Western does not use purchase order forms and that you do not have order blanks from the various publishers from whom you want to purchase books. You wish to place an order for six different titles from the same publishing house.

SOLUTION

Gentlemen:

Please send me 2 copies of each of the following books:

Code No.	Author	Title	Price	Extension
06012	Day	The Writer's Source Book	$11.95	$ 23.90
07630	Stein	Handbook of Management	17.50	35.00
11020	Carter	Style Reference for Stenos	6.95	13.90
17325	O'Hara and Fox	Office Cost Accounting	9.95	19.90
02111	Ortega	Computer Data Processing	11.50	23.00
83210	Pasquale	Dictionary of Business	16.95	33.90
		Total		$149.60

Our check for $149.60, plus shipping charges, will be sent to you immediately upon receipt of these books.

Very truly yours,

Analysis of the Solution. Observe these points about the foregoing order letter:

1. Complete information is given—publisher's code number, author, title, and unit price. Column headings, though not absolutely essential, guide the reader.
2. The extension figures are optional; however, they help to make it clear to the publisher that two copies of each book are being ordered.
3. No mention is made of the method of shipment. The writer assumes that the publisher will select the best method in terms of speed and economy. If, however, the books are needed at once and the writer is willing to pay extra for air express, he should mention this fact in the letter.

■ ■

PROJECTS

A   Order these three books from Acropolis Publishing Company (make up an address) for the Office Services Department library: *Complete Handbook of Personnel Management* (by E. R. Chisholm), $17.50; *Color Guide for the Professional Designer* (by Steven Hotchkiss), $47.50; and *Readings in Modern Management* (by Smith and Wesley), $12.75. Assume that your company has established credit with Acropolis and that you will be billed. You need the books within two weeks and ask that they be sent by air express, for which you will pay the charges.

B   Place an order for 50 reprints of ''Did I Say That?'' an article by E. R. Risley that appeared in the July issue of *The Administrator*. The copies are to be distributed to employees enrolled in an in-company communications course. The cost is $12.50, and you are enclosing your personal check. You need the reprints by July 10, when the class begins. Make up the address.

C   Write your own version of each of the following (they are satisfactory request letters).

1

Gentlemen:

Enclosed is my check for $5 for 50 reprints of "Say It Simply" that appeared in the October issue of Forecast.

Could you please put a special rush on the mailing? We are running a communications seminar for our secretaries November 17–19, and we would like to distribute these reprints on the opening day.

Very truly yours,

2

Dear Mr. Salten:

This is our order for 16 bowling shirts (Model K-22), for which I am enclosing our check for $176.

We have chosen white as the basic color of the shirts, and the lettering COLUMBIA STEELERS is to appear in bright green across the back. For the lettering, please use the circular arrangement shown on page 3 of your bowling supplies catalog.

The sizes are: 3 small, 6 medium, 3 large, and 4 extra large.

Cordially,

■ ■

part 3

TRANSMITTAL, CONFIRMATION, AND FOLLOW-UP LETTERS AND MEMOS

YOUR JOB

You are continuing as assistant office services manager for the Far Western Insurance Company, San Jose, California.

CASE 1 — TRANSMITTING AN IMPORTANT DOCUMENT

PROBLEM: Recently the company entered into an agreement with the local office of a computer manufacturing company for service to be provided by data processing equipment and for consulting service on programming and systems analysis. Two copies of the contract, with one slight change which was agreed upon in a telephone conversation between C. J. Webb of the computer manufacturing company and R. C. Boswell, vice president and treasurer of your firm, have been signed by Mr. Boswell. One copy has been retained for Far Western files and the other copy is to be returned to the computer manufacturing company. You are to write the letter transmitting the contract.

BACKGROUND

When you send a check, a contract, a report, or any other valuable or hard-to-replace document to someone outside your company, it is always a good idea to send a transmittal letter with it. Similarly, when you send such a document to someone within your own company, always write a transmittal memo to go with it. The main reason, of course, is to provide a record (your file copy of the letter or memo) of *when* you sent *what* to *whom* and, if appropriate, *why*. Another reason is to assure proper delivery of the document and to let the receiver know what action, if any, is expected of him.

SOLUTION

Attention: C. J. Webb

Gentlemen:

Enclosed is a copy of the signed agreement covering services to our Data Processing Department for one year. We have retained the original.

Note the change in paragraph 1 (c) relating to minimum number of hours to be delivered under this agreement. This change was agreed upon by Mr. Webb and Mr. Boswell, vice president and treasurer of Far Western, in their telephone conversation on Wednesday, the 16th.

Yours very truly,

Analysis of the Solution. This is a good transmittal letter.

1. Although the writer addressed the letter to the computer company, he directed it to the attention of the representative who negotiated the contract. This is not unusual because the contract is with the company, not with Mr. Webb. The letter could have been addressed personally to Mr. Webb, which is the more common practice.
2. The writer mentioned the subject of the contract so that it could be easily identified.
3. The writer pointed out the change that was made, citing the authority for it (''agreed upon by Mr. Webb and Mr. Boswell, vice president and treasurer of Far Western, in their telephone conversation on Wednesday, the 16th.'')

■ ■

PROJECTS

A   Mr. Prince has signed an agreement with Ski and Sun Motor Inn, Denver, for the annual convention of the Western Accountants Society, December 2–5. He has asked you to transmit the signed letter of agreement to Miss Claire Boudreau, the sales manager.

B   You have written a report, ''Clerical Personnel Requirements in the 70s,'' at the request of Mr. Prince. He has complimented you on the report and is eager for several people in other departments to read and react to it. Prepare a transmittal memorandum.

C   The accounting department has sent you the check for the Acropolis Publishing Company for $82.35, which you are to transmit. The check is in payment for books ordered for the Office Services Department library (Project A, page 93), and the vendor's invoice number is PC 41913.

■ ■

CASE 2
CONFIRMING AN IMPORTANT ORAL AGREEMENT

PROBLEM: Mr. Prince has arranged with a local firm to refinish and repair some of the office furniture in the Purchasing Department. He has had several conversations with Raymond Courtland, owner of a furniture refinishing company, and they have reached an oral agreement that you are to confirm in writing.

BACKGROUND

It makes good business sense to confirm in writing any important oral agreement. Too often people forget conversations or misunderstand the terms agreed upon and when one person doesn't live up to the agreement, problems arise. Written confirmations of oral agreements should be specific as to who is to do what, where, and when—and, if appropriate, the terms of payment.

If proof of delivery is necessary, send the letter by registered mail—and if you want to go all the way, request a return receipt of delivery. Another way in which you can make sure of delivery—as well as acceptance of the terms—is to type at the bottom of the letter "Accepted and agreed to," with space for the recipient's signature and the date. If you follow the latter procedure, you will need to send two copies of the letter and ask the recipient to sign both copies and return one to you.

SOLUTION A

Dear Mr. Courtland:

This will confirm our agreement whereby you are to refinish six executive chairs, eight double-pedestal metal desks, and six 4-drawer filing cabinets at a total of $1,320.

Very truly yours,

Analysis of Solution A. Solution A is inadequate because it describes too vaguely the work Mr. Courtland is to do. The word *refinish* could mean a number of things—simply repainting, for example. Where is the work to be done? When is it to be done? What is Mr. Courtland to supply?

SOLUTION B

Dear Mr. Courtland:

This will confirm the oral agreement we reached yesterday afternoon concerning the work you are to do on our office furniture.

1. Six Executive Chairs. You are to sand and refinish in walnut stain all exposed wood, replace all casters, and reupholster in Tufftex vinyl plastic (three in camel tan and three in blue spruce, for which you have samples). The price we agreed on is $100 for each chair, regardless of present condition.

2. Eight Double-Pedestal Metal Desks. Chips and cracks are to be smoothed out and each desk is to be painted metallic grey (two coats). No work is required on the linoleum surfaces, except that they are to be cleaned. The price we agreed on is $60 for each desk, regardless of present condition.

3. Six 4-Drawer Filing Cabinets. Chips and cracks are to be smoothed out and each cabinet is to be painted metallic grey (two coats). The stainless steel handles are not to be painted. The price we agreed on is $40 for each cabinet, regardless of present condition.

All work is to be done on your premises, and you will furnish the paint, vinyl, casters, and all other materials. At your expense, you will pick up the furniture on July 10 and return it to us on or before August 12. Payment will be made on the delivery date.

Please write to me immediately if you have any questions about this agreement.

Cordially yours,

Analysis of Solution B. Solution B provides a written confirmation of what was actually agreed upon.

1. Notice the enumeration of the three types of equipment that are to receive attention from Mr. Courtland, with a description of what is to be done to each.
2. Most controversies arise over money matters, and the agreed-upon price is put in writing so that there will be no question later.
3. The last paragraph gives Mr. Courtland a chance to take issue if he does not agree. If he does not protest, he cannot say later that he did not agree with or understand the terms.

■■■■■■■■■■■■■■■■■■■■■■■■■■■■■■■■■■■■■■

PROJECT

The Program Committee of the National Association of Office Supervisors, of which you are a member, is planning an afternoon meeting and dinner on June 12 at Morningside Manor in Carmel, about sixty miles away. The committee chairman has asked you to make reservations. You talked to the assistant manager of Morningside Manor by telephone and made tentative reservations for (1) a private meeting room for ten people, (2) single sleeping rooms for six (yourself, Rudy Patterson, Leo Frailey, Peter Musette, Jane Logan, and Morris Haritan) for one night, and (3) dinner (to be selected from the menu) for ten in a private dining room. The hotel is to supply the meeting room without charge and is to bill NAOS for the dinner. Each person staying overnight is to pay for his own room. Confirm your reservation request by letter.

■■■■■■■■■■■■■■■■■■■■■■■■■■■■■■■■■■■■■■

CASE 3   FOLLOWING UP ON A REQUEST

PROBLEM: It has been over a month since you asked Steelway Equipment Company to send you a price list on the Rock-a-Way Filing Cabinet line, and you haven't received either the price list or a letter of explanation. A letter from you asking for action is in order.

BACKGROUND

Follow-up letters and memos are commonplace in business. People fail to respond to communications for a number of reasons. They don't realize they are supposed to respond. They lose or misplace requests. They fall behind in their work and don't get around to writing. They simply ignore requests. Or they must give a "no" answer and don't know how to say it. There are any number of reasons and excuses—all of which lead to follow-up letters and memos.

Secretaries often keep a tickler file of requests their bosses have made (oral as well as written, and in-company as well as out-of-company requests). At the appropriate time, the secretary either follows up on the request or reminds her boss to do so.

SOLUTION A

Gentlemen:

I can't understand why you didn't respond to my request for a new price list on your Rock-a-Way line of filing cabinets. It has been over a month. Obviously, we're not going to place any orders with you until we can compare your prices with those of other manufacturers (all the others responded).

I hope you will be courteous enough to reply this time.

Very truly yours,

Analysis of Solution A. It is readily apparent, of course, that Solution A reflects the writer's anger. Certainly it is annoying when your requests seem to be ignored, but a "mad" letter is not the answer. Threats and insults are unlikely to produce the desired results.

Such statements as "I can't understand why," "Obviously, we're not going to place any orders with you," "all the others responded," and "I hope you will be courteous enough to reply this time" are particularly offensive.

SOLUTION B

Gentlemen:

On August 12 I wrote asking for a new price list on your Rock-a-Way line of filing cabinets. I suspect that my letter did not reach you because I haven't received the materials or an acknowledgment.

We are getting together comparative prices on new filing equipment, and I don't want to place an order until I have prices of all leading manufacturers. May I have yours by September 20 at the latest?

Sincerely yours,

Analysis of Solution B. Solution B is a better letter than A because it creates a desire on the part of the manufacturer to do the right thing and do it quickly. Note these features of Solution B.

1. The letter gives the recipient the benefit of the doubt insofar as the first request is concerned.
2. The second paragraph says in effect, "If you want a chance at getting our business, you had better give us the information we need," but of course the statement is much more tactful.
3. The specific response date should be a red flag to the manufacturer if he is on his toes.

■ ■

PROJECTS

A Last month you filled out an advertising coupon from *The Administrator* in which readers were invited to send for a free booklet, *Communicating With Employees*. You affixed the coupon to the company letterhead and sent it to Lathrop Paper Company. The materials have not arrived, and you would like to have them for a report you are preparing on management-employee communications. Write a follow-up letter.

B You received a printed card from Lathop Paper Company, as follows. (It is common practice for advertisers to acknowledge requests by means of printed cards and letters.)

Dear Sir:

We are out of stock on Communicating With Employees. Thank you for your inquiry.

LATHROP PAPER COMPANY

Criticize the tone, completeness, and other aspects of the message and then rewrite it.

C About three months ago you wrote the following letter to Tele-Media Communications Systems.

Gentlemen:

Please send me descriptive literature on your Speedi-Com Interoffice Communication Systems. We are considering installing an audio system sometime this year, and I am interested in Speedi-Com.

Do you also handle signaling devices? If so, I should like information about them as well.

Sincerely yours,

You received the following response.

Dear Miss Carpenter:

I am delighted to send you our most recent catalog describing our Speedi-Com Communication Systems. I think you will find among these various systems precisely the one that fits your special needs.

If you need further help, why not telephone or write our San Francisco distributor, Golden State Electronics Corporation. They'll be glad to send someone to talk with you at your convenience.

Yours sincerely,

The catalog describing Speedi-Com Systems arrived very shortly after you received the letter; however, no information was supplied concerning the signaling devices you asked about. Follow up.

■ ■

part

4

**SPECIAL
REQUEST
LETTERS,
ACKNOWLEDGMENTS,
AND
MEMOS**

You are continuing as assistant office services manager for Far Western Insurance Company, San Jose, California.

CASE 1

ASKING FOR AND ACKNOWLEDGING SPECIAL HELP

PROBLEM: Mr. Prince feels that there are too many different forms in use in the company. No one has made an effort to control the output of forms—in fact, anybody can make up his own forms and duplicate them in large quantity. The result is that supply rooms are overstocked with unused forms and files are bulging with duplicate records. Obviously, time and money are being spent foolishly. Mr. Prince is considering appointing one person, or perhaps a committee, to act as a clearinghouse for all new forms. He has asked you to make a study of practices concerning forms design and control in some of the leading firms in the country. You decide to write to office managers in 25 companies in various parts of the United States and to prepare an acknowledgment letter for all responses.

BACKGROUND: Requesting Special Help

The letters we have been talking about up to this point concerned requests for materials and information from people who find it to their advantage to grant the requests. Such letters require no particular persuasion or salesmanship to get what is wanted.

Some asking letters, however, require a little different approach. These are the letters asking for favors that will benefit the writer more than the recipient. In writing such letters, keep in mind that the people with whom you correspond have little to gain from cooperating with you; thus you have a selling job to do.

When you write a letter asking for special help, make sure your letter measures up to these requirements: (1) Gives complete information about what is wanted and why it is wanted. (2) Makes it easy for the recipient to respond with a minimum of effort. (3) Is tactful, reasonable, and extremely courteous. (4) Conveys appreciation for assistance.

SOLUTION A

Dear Mr. Cortez:

Would you please tell me how you handle forms design, standardization, and control in your company. I would appreciate all the information I can get.

Sincerely,

Analysis of Solution A. Solution A is courteous and tactful and appreciative in tone. But it is not a good letter for these reasons:

1. It does not provide enough information. Mr. Cortez might understand what the writer wants to know, but there is a risk that he will not.
2. The response to such a letter will require much time and thought, and the writer has not made it easy for Mr. Cortez to respond. Thus, the request borders on the unreasonable. The person making a request of this kind should put himself in the recipient's shoes and think hard about the difficulty he may be causing.

SOLUTION B

Dear Mr. Cortez:

Would you take just a few minutes to give me the benefit of your experience?

Our company is making a study of forms design, standardization, and control, and we are asking 25 top organizations to tell us how they handle the problem. I would be very grateful if you would answer the following questions in the space provided.

1. Is the responsibility for forms design, standardization, and control centralized in your company? Yes _____ No _____

    a. If your answer is Yes, what is the title of the person who has this responsibility? _____

    b. Does this person have management authority to approve or disapprove all forms used in the organization? Yes _____ No _____
Exceptions: _____

_____

2. Are most of your forms:

    a. Reproduced in the office? _____

    b. Done by a printer? _____

3. Have you used committees (representatives of various departments) to control forms usage? Yes _____ No _____ If your answer is Yes, was the plan:

    a. Satisfactory? _____
    b. Excellent? _____
    c. Unworkable? _____

4. What is the title of the person in your organization who is responsible for designing forms?

_____

5. For which types of forms do you use sulphite paper stock?

_____

6. For which types of forms do you feel that rag stock is required?

_____

If you care to make additional comments, I would be very pleased to have them.

An extra copy of this questionnaire is enclosed for your records. Please use the enclosed addressed envelope for returning the questionnaire to me.

Sincerely yours,

P.S. Would you like to have a copy of the results of this study?
Yes _____ No _____

Analysis of Solution B. Observe the following characteristics of the letter to Mr. Cortez.

1. The purpose for which the information is needed is clearly stated.
2. The letter is complimentary to the reader ("benefit of your experience," "25 top organizations," etc.), but it is not effusive.
3. The questions are easy to answer; Mr. Cortez will not need to compose a letter.
4. A summary of the results of the study is offered. This courtesy is customarily extended to those who give such assistance.
5. An addressed envelope is enclosed. More often than not, a stamp is affixed to the return envelope; however, it is not necessary in correspondence between large companies where postage-meter equipment is likely to be used.

BACKGROUND: Acknowledging Special Help

Courtesy demands that each response to a request for a special favor be acknowledged as soon as it is received.

The letter may be short; however, the writer should not try to lengthen a short, sincere message with a trite and stereotyped "Thanks again" in an effort to add another sentence or paragraph. If the writer can honestly and sincerely state how the reply has helped him, he should do so and end the letter.

SOLUTION

> Dear Mr. Cortez:
>
> Thank you for completing the questionnaire concerning forms design, standardization, and control. I especially appreciate your added comments.
>
> Just as soon as I have tabulated the results of the study, I shall see that you get a copy.
>
> Sincerely yours,

Analysis of the Solution. The solution is courteous and appreciative in tone. It tells what the writer will do with the information and says that he will send the reader a copy of the results of the study.

■■■■■■■■■■■■■■■■■■■■■■■■■■■■■■■■■■■■■

PROJECTS

A You are a member of the Employee Relations Committee. One of your assignments on this committee is to study the feasibility of developing a house organ for company employees. You need to find out what type of magazine would be most suitable, how large it should be, how often it should be published, how much it will cost, and so forth.

   You decide to write to 100 different companies throughout the country for help. You want sample issues from them (two or three different ones, if possible). You would like to know how often the magazine is published, whether the company has a professional staff of editors whose sole job is to publish the magazine, employee reaction to the magazine, the number of copies printed, and whether the magazine is restricted to employees or is available to others. You would also like a statement from each company as to the main purpose of the magazine (some magazines feature management information, others emphasize employee activities, and so on). And you'd like to know the annual cost of publishing the magazine.

   Prepare a letter to send to the 100 companies you have selected, making it as easy as possible for each recipient to respond.

B Several companies respond to your request (Project A) with very helpful comments, supplying much more information than you asked for. Write a special thank-you letter to send each of these companies.

C Mr. Prince has asked you to lead a management seminar, a monthly meeting of department heads at which company policies and practices are discussed. The theme of your meeting is "Simplification of Personnel Procedures."

   The February meeting of the National Association of Office Supervisors featured Neil Reiff, of Management Consultants, Inc., a firm in Stockton, California. In making his presentation, Mr. Reiff used a set of flip charts showing, by means of diagrams and cartoon drawings, the process of recruiting, hiring, placing, training, and promoting personnel. You would like to use these charts in your meeting. Write Mr. Reiff (you met him after the NAOS meeting and learned that his firm has done consulting work for Far Western) asking if the flip charts might be made available to you.

D   Mr. Reiff (Project C) sends the charts and tells you that you may keep them; he has several sets. Write the appropriate letter to Mr. Reiff, assuming that the charts were used with great success in your presentation and will be very useful in future management meetings.

E   Your company is considering overhauling its pension plan for employees, and you have been asked to study the problem and prepare a preliminary set of recommendations by June 11. In a recent issue of *Employee Relations* there is an excellent article entitled ''Trends in Pension Plans.'' You would like to quote from this article in your report. Write to Miss Aileen Engle, the editor, for permission.

■ ■

CASE 2 REQUESTING A SPECIAL-FAVOR APPOINTMENT

PROBLEM: You have just read an article in *Management Science* about information storage and retrieval systems. The author, Dr. John Dyson, a vice president of McLuen and Morris, Sacramento, California, described the new electronic data system in his firm and told how it is solving many of his company's communications problems. You are going to be in Sacramento for a three-day conference this month, and you would like to visit McLuen and Morris and have a look at the system Dr. Dyson described. You decide to write to Dr. Dyson for an appointment.

BACKGROUND

As in the letter to Mr. Cortez about forms design and control (Case 1), this one will require some persuasion because the appointment is more to your advantage than to Dr. Dyson's. Obviously, Dr. Dyson is the buyer, and you are the seller. The only benefit he could gain from showing you through his company is the satisfaction of doing a favor for a fellow businessman; he has nothing to sell you and probably little to gain from you.

What is your mission? It is to get inside the firm of McLuen and Morris to learn all you can.

SOLUTION A

Dear Mr. Dyson:

I find that I am going to be in Sacramento on July 11–14, and I would like to have a look at your information storage and retrieval system.

My best time is Tuesday, the 12th, and I look forward to seeing you then.

Sincerely yours,

Analysis of Solution A. Solution A is an awkward, ineffective letter for several reasons:

1. The recipient should be addressed as ''Dr.'' since he has earned that privilege.
2. Probably Dr. Dyson would be pleased to know that his article in *Management Science* was read and enjoyed, and the writer missed an easy chance to score on this point.
3. Dr. Dyson doesn't know who the writer is or what his motives are. He's probably a busy man who can't take time to show every Tom, Dick, and Harry around his company.
4. The letter is completely lacking in courtesy and tact.
5. ''Have a look'' seems to be a flippant expression to a stranger.
6. The writer is overbearing and presumptuous. He takes for granted that he will be welcomed and at a time that is convenient to *him* rather than to Dr. Dyson. He has forgotten that he is in no position to demand.
7. The letter emphasizes the writer—*I want, my best time,* and so on. Letters asking for special favors should emphasize *you,* the reader.

SOLUTION B

> Dear Dr. Dyson:
>
> Your article, "Information and Retrieval Systems," in the June issue of *Management Science* is one of the best I have ever read on the subject. The system you have established at McLuen and Morris sounds as though it would have direct application to the company in which I work (an important part of my job is improving communications systems).
>
> Would it be possible for me to visit your office and see the system in operation? I am attending a conference in Sacramento July 11–14, and I would enjoy very much spending a little time with you or one of your associates.
>
> Your time is the important thing, and I can adjust my schedule to your convenience. If you can't spare an hour, I would appreciate whatever time you can give me.
>
> Sincerely yours,

Analysis of Solution B. Solution B is better than A for the following reasons.

1. It establishes a point of contact (the magazine article); then tells who the writer is and what his motives are.
2. The writer compliments but does not flatter Dr. Dyson. Here we have to assume that the writer really feels that Dr. Dyson's article is the best he has ever read on the subject. If he doesn't believe it is, he shouldn't have said so.
3. The request is persuasive in that the writer shows Dr. Dyson how he might be helpful to the profession (a person who writes professional articles is assumed to be proud of what he has to say and flattered to think his profession will benefit from it).

4. The letter is not presumptuous. The writer doesn't make Dr. Dyson feel that an invitation is automatically deserved.

■■■■■■■■■■■■■■■■■■■■■■■■■■■■■■■■■■■■■■

PROJECTS

A   Miss Rita Philbin, training director for Mountain States Casualty Company, Boulder, Colorado, was a guest speaker at a recent office management seminar that you attended. In her remarks, Miss Philbin mentioned that the best collection of books, articles, reports, and monographs on employee motivation that she has seen is in the company library of Creative Systems, Incorporated, Spokane, Washington, which she recently visited.

   You are planning to be in Spokane the week of August 11, and you would like to spend two or three hours in the library of Creative Systems. Write to the director of public relations, asking for permission.

B   Assume that your visit to the library of Creative Systems was very profitable. The librarian, Mrs. Cynthia Halver, was very helpful and made sure you had access to all the materials you wanted to see. Write a thank-you letter to Mrs. Halver and another one to Paul G. Farquahar, director of public relations, who arranged for your visit.

■■■■■■■■■■■■■■■■■■■■■■■■■■■■■■■■■■■■■

CASE 3   INVITING AND THANKING A SPEAKER

PROBLEM: You are program chairman of the Western States Management Conference, which will hold its spring meeting at the St. Francis Hotel in San Francisco, March 25 and 26. The theme of the convention is "Management *Is* Communication," and you are looking for a keynote speaker—one who can open the meeting dynamically and set the stage for the rest of the program.

   Auren Pulver, of Portland, Oregon, is a nationally known authority in management. He has written several books in the field, has spoken all over the world, and is a consultant to many large organizations. Your committee has selected Mr. Pulver as the keynote speaker, and you are to write asking him if he will accept the assignment.

   Immediately after his presentation, you are to prepare a letter thanking him. Draft one letter assuming he did an outstanding job and another assuming he did a poor job.

BACKGROUND: Asking Someone to Give a Speech

Letters asking someone to give a speech, write an article, or perform some other special service are of the persuasive type. Although outstanding speakers and writers usually receive a fee for their work, often they are very busy or the fee offered is so low that they can't afford to take on the assignment. In writing such letters, you should emphasize the importance of the assignment and make an acceptance of it seem worthwhile.

SOLUTION

Dear Mr. Pulver:

The theme of the Western States Management Conference this spring is "Management Is Communication." Our members would be honored if you would give the keynote address.

Your pioneering work in employee communication and your excellent writings on the subject—plus your ability to capture and hold an audience—make you the unanimous choice of our program committee.

The conference will be at the St. Francis Hotel in San Francisco on March 25 and 26. The keynote address is scheduled for 7:30 on Friday evening, the 25th. We are allowing 30 to 40 minutes for it and are prepared to offer you an honorarium of $300, plus all expenses.

Can you be with us? All of us certainly hope you can. Just as soon as I hear from you, I will telephone and give you complete details. We expect an audience of about 300 from eleven western states.

Please let me know as quickly as you can. If you prefer, you can telephone me at (415) 766-4190.

Sincerely yours,

Analysis of Solution. You probably have already spotted the things that make the letter to Mr. Pulver an effective one.

1. It is persuasive. Mr. Pulver should feel that he has an important contribution to make to this conference.
2. It is friendly.
3. It supplies all the information Mr. Pulver needs to either accept or refuse the invitation.

BACKGROUND: Thanking a Speaker

The quality of the speech given will, of course, determine the content of the thank-you. If the talk was well given and well received, the letter should be courteous, sincere, and appreciative. Any complimentary remarks made regarding the talk can be honestly stated.

SOLUTION A

Dear Mr. Pulver:

Your keynote talk, "What Is Your Communication IQ?" set exactly the right tone for our conference. You will be pleased to know that your remarks were referred to time and again by the speakers in the various group meetings, leaving no doubt at all that your message reached home.

I am sure you know from your long experience that a good keynote speech can make or break a convention. The fact that this was the most successful conference we have ever had should be ample evidence of the effectiveness of your presentation.

Thank you.

Sincerely yours,

Analysis of Solution A. The letter is effective because it is courteous, sincere, and appreciative. The writer's comment regarding the speaker's ability to "reach home" is important because speakers recognize that their audience's understanding is important to their success.

SOLUTION B

If, however, the keynote talk was disappointing, the speaker still deserves a letter of appreciation for making the trip and participating in the program. Such a letter is tricky to write. You do not want to tell Mr. Pulver he was great when he was a flop, but on the other hand, there is nothing to gain by telling him he had little to contribute.

Dear Mr. Pulver:

You will be pleased to know that our Western States Management Conference went very well. The reaction of the various audiences was generally enthusiastic, and the conference members are already talking about another convention next year—possibly even this fall.

I hope your trip back to Portland was a pleasant one and that you made your early Saturday morning appointment without difficulty.

Thank you for your participation in our conference. I enjoyed meeting you, and I was greatly interested in your provocative remarks.

Sincerely yours,

Analysis of Solution B. This letter shows appreciation to the speaker for making the trip and assisting in the program. It is honest in that it doesn't say that the talk was well given or well received—simply that the reaction to it was generally enthusiastic. All in all, this letter is a tactful, effective thank-you message to a speaker who, at least in the writer's opinion, did somewhat less than an outstanding job.

■ ■

PROJECTS

A Recently you read a *Personnel Weekly* article by Mrs. Phyllis Larsen of Permutit Corporation in Phoenix, Arizona, about an unusual wage-incentive plan. The biographical sketch that accompanied the article mentioned that Mrs. Larsen travels widely speaking to various personnel groups. As program chairman of the National Association of Office Supervisors, you would like to "book" Mrs. Larsen for the evening meeting three months from now. The Association has authorized you to offer her an honorarium of $250 plus travel expense. The NAOS meets once a month for dinner (beginning at 6:30) at the Golden Crest Motel. The speaker is given about 40 minutes after dinner for his presentation, which is followed by a discussion period of about 20 to 30 minutes. Write the letter to Mrs. Larsen.

B Mrs. Larsen's speech before the NAOS (Project A) was very well received. Although several people took issue with her ideas on wage incentives, the discussion following her presentation was very lively and ran twice as long as usual. Several told you it was the best meeting of the year, even though they didn't necessarily agree with Mrs. Larsen's views. Write Mrs. Larsen an appropriate letter, enclosing a check for $250.

C Mrs. Larsen has not submitted a report of her travel expenses, even though in a previous letter you had asked her to do so. She responds, returning the honorarium and saying that company policy prevents her accepting honorariums or travel expenses and thanking you for your thoughtfulness. Upon informing the president of the NAOS, you are told that the $250 check will go into the Association's scholarship fund for outstanding local high school students. Write Mrs. Larsen to this effect.

D In a course that you are conducting for supervisors in Far Western Insurance you have scheduled several guest speakers—men and women from the San Francisco–Oakland Bay Area who have achieved distinction in their various specialities.

   At last week's session, you had invited Reginald Bedell, vice president of California Consultants, Inc., to speak on the subject "Evaluating Employee Performance." However, Mr. Bedell was called out of town at the last minute and sent in his place Joseph Zincus, a member of Mr. Bedell's firm. Unfortunately, Mr. Zincus had virtually no time to prepare for his presentation, and the result was disappointing. Several people in the course came to you later to say that the evening was a waste of time.

   You must write an appreciative note to Mr. Zincus, however. After all, he gave up an evening for you and did the best he could under very difficult circumstances. Prepare the letter.

■ ■

part

5

HUMAN RELATIONS
LETTERS AND MEMOS

You are supervisor of the Records Management Department of Keystone Designs, Incorporated, Chicago, specialists in modern office furniture and interiors. You are responsible for seeing that the company's records are properly maintained, which means that you establish records systems, select equipment and supplies, maintain check-out and safekeeping procedures, determine when inactive materials are to be transferred or disposed of, and so on.

CASE 1 — EXPRESSING APPRECIATION FOR A FAVOR

PROBLEM: Recently you were asked to speak at the Tri-State Conference of the National Records Management Association on "Legal Implications of Records Disposition." Although your job requires a general knowledge of statutory requirements for certain records, you do not feel that you are an authority on the subject. You had to read as much as you could, therefore, in order to get ready to write your speech. Mrs. Abigail Parkington, assistant librarian of the company, helped you find materials on your subject and came up with several reports, reprints, and clippings that were extremely helpful to you. Your talk was enthusiastically received by those at the meeting. You feel that you should write to Mrs. Parkington and thank her for her help.

BACKGROUND

We mentioned earlier that many business letters become personal letters when they are exchanged between friends, even though the letters pertain to business transactions. The next several cases emphasize business communications that are the most personal of all—those written to express appreciation for favors, to congratulate others on their achievements, to extend and accept invitations, and to express sympathy, for example.

Nearly everyone writes—or should write—personal-business letters when the occasion is appropriate. Aside from making the occupational journey a little more rewarding for everyone, such messages are simply good business. Some typical occasions for letters of this type might include the following:

1. Mr. Steinkraus, your boss, has just received word that his son has won a National Merit Scholarship Award.
2. The woman in the travel agency who has taken care of the transportation arrangements for all your recent business trips was elected to the local school board, according to the papers.
3. A fellow member of the Filing Supervisors Association was selected by the organization to represent the local chapter at the international convention in Düsseldorf, Germany.
4. A firm that has been trying to win your printing business (forms, letter-heads, pads, etc.) has sent you a set of Audubon bird prints suitable for framing.
5. The purchasing manager in a firm whose business your company has been trying to win was awarded a certificate of merit by the Kiwanis Club.
6. The woman who supervises employee benefits in Keystone Designs, Incorporated, and with whom you work very closely, has just lost her father.
7. The manager of computer services in your company has resigned to accept a job as financial vice president in another organization.
8. A co-worker who entered the company the same day you did, went through the orientation program with you, and later became a fairly good friend has been appointed director of advertising research.
9. You were among the guests who attended a dinner party given by Mr. and Mrs. Steinkraus in their home.

You may write personal-business letters on company stationery or on plain stationery, depending on the occasion and the persons to whom they are addressed. For example, as an executive, you would use company letterhead to congratulate a member of your department on her fifteenth anniversary with the company. For the occasions listed above, the following should *not* be written on company letterhead: numbers 1, 6, 7, 8, 9. Very close friends will expect personal letters. In these cases use plain bond paper or social stationery, because company stationery takes away some of your individuality.

Some people write personal-business messages to fellow employees on the company's interoffice memo form. Although the memo form is perfectly acceptable for these messages, plain paper or a letterhead is better because it is less "mechanical" looking.

Although rules for writing personal-business letters are not rigid, one principle that should guide you in composing messages of this type is: be yourself but don't get carried away. The use of superlatives, such as in the following examples, has a tendency to destroy believability.

> Your promotion to director of advertising research is the greatest thing that ever happened.
>
> The set of Audubon prints is the handsomest present I ever received.
>
> The dinner you prepared was just about the tastiest I have ever eaten. How did you do it?

Of course, if you are honest when you use words like *greatest, handsomest,* and *tastiest,* go ahead. Chances are, though, that in your eagerness to say the right thing you are overdoing it.

On the other hand, it is possible to pass over too lightly the occasion your personal-business letter is honoring, and the result can be worse than going overboard.

> Allow me to congratulate you on your promotion to director of advertising research.
>
> This will acknowledge the set of Audubon prints that I received recently.
>
> I had never eaten a real Armenian dinner before; so it was a new experience for me.

Somewhere between the two extremes lies the appropriate tone for personal-business letters.

> I was delighted to learn that you have been promoted to the position of director of advertising research. Congratulations!
>
> The Audubon prints are beautiful, and I can think of a dozen places where they will look mighty handsome on the wall.
>
> The Armenian dinner was a "first" for me, and I enjoyed it immensely.

SOLUTION

> Dear Mrs. Parkington:
>
> You'll be pleased to know, I think, that "our" speech at the National Records Management Association meeting in Omaha went over quite well. In fact, I had nine requests for copies of it—so somebody was listening!
>
> Thank you for all your help, Mrs. Parkington—I would have been practically lost without you. The Keystone librarians, particularly you, have won an ardent supporter.
>
> Sincerely yours,
>
> cc: Miss Grace Garvin
> Head Librarian

Analysis of the Solution. This letter is a good one.

1. The tone of the letter is friendly, conversational, believable. The writer expresses appreciation without becoming effusive.
2. Note the use of Mrs. Parkington's name in the body of the letter. Using the reader's name adds a personal touch as long as it isn't overdone.
3. Observe that a carbon copy of the letter was sent to Mrs. Parkington's immediate superior. This courtesy is always in order. Often this gesture means more to the recipient of the letter than the letter itself.

■■■■■■■■■■■■■■■■■■■■■■■■■■■■■■■■■■

PROJECTS

A Some of the people who heard the talk (''Legal Implications of Records Disposition'') you gave at the National Records Management Association meeting feel
that it should be published, and you have decided to submit it to *Records
Management Journal.* Before doing so, however, you asked R. C. Garrison, the
attorney for Keystone Designs, to read the manuscript. He agreed, and in his
review he corrected a few minor factual errors and offered several good ideas
for improving the material. Write an appropriate thank-you letter or memo to
Mr. Garrison.

B Recently you were at a luncheon in one of the private dining rooms of Keystone
for several people, most of whom were out-of-town guests. The food and the
service provided by the dining room staff were excellent, and you decide to drop
a note to the manager, Larry Barstow, expressing your appreciation. Write the
letter or memo, supplying details about the menu, special services, and so on.

C Professor Ernest Wilford, of Northhampton University, recently spoke to a
management training class in Keystone on the subject of organization planning.
As a member of the class, you found the talk very helpful. For the first time
you understood the need for clear lines of organization, delegation of responsibility, and individual authority to exercise assigned duties. Write Professor
Wilford a letter of appreciation.

■■■■■■■■■■■■■■■■■■■■■■■■■■■■■■■■■■

CASE 2

EXPRESSING APPRECIATION FOR A GIFT

PROBLEM: Paul Whitcomb, sales representative for Westline Lithographers,
a company from whom you purchase printing, has sent you a beautiful
lithograph of Wyeth's famous painting, ''Christina's World,'' suitable for
framing. You plan to write Mr. Whitcomb to thank him for the gift.

BACKGROUND

The gift from Paul Whitcomb (actually a gift from the company for which he
works) deserves a letter expressing appreciation. Such gestures have a commercial flavor, of course; a business organization that bestows favors on its
customers and potential customers is obviously mindful of the promotional
advantages. Some organizations (particularly government) have established
strict policies against accepting gifts from suppliers. But where the gift is

permitted, the donor is entitled to a thank-you letter even though both the giver and the recipient know that the transaction is more business than personal.

SOLUTION A

Dear Paul:

The print you presented to us is very much appreciated, and on behalf of Keystone Designs, Incorporated, I want to express our gratitude.

Sincerely yours,

Analysis of Solution A. One might admire the writer's restraint, but the letter is too cautious, too impersonal. There is no warmth, no friendliness—all in all, it is a poor expression of appreciation.

SOLUTION B

Dear Paul:

The beautiful lithograph of "Christina's World" came today, and I am delighted with it. How did you find out that I like pictures with people in them? You know, I think this is Wyeth's best.

As much as I hate to give Christina up, I think our department's reception room is the best place for her. At any rate, when you next visit us, you will find this beautiful reproduction in a prominent place.

Thank you, Paul, for this thoughtful and generous gift.

Sincerely,

Analysis of Solution B. Unlike Solution A, this letter shows genuine appreciation, friendliness, and personality. Paul Whitcomb is certain to get the feeling that he has done the writer a favor that will be remembered.

Note that the writer makes clear that he considers this gift a business, rather than a personal, one by stating that the lithograph will be placed in the department's reception room. Many people feel it is unwise to accept gifts for their personal use only because they are in a position to buy the donors' products or services.

■ ■

PROJECTS

A   In today's mail you received a copy of a 270-page book, *Office Guidebook,* published by Walsh–Hiller, manufacturers of office equipment. Attached to the front cover is a card which reads "Compliments of Norman Morrison." Mr. Morrison is the local representative of Walsh–Hiller, and he has apparently submitted your name as one who should receive this book, which contains facts and ideas about modern office equipment and its efficient use. Write a letter to Mr. Morrison expressing your gratitude.

B   Nancy Wicker, manager of Career Personnel Agency, sent you a desk calendar at Christmas. The calendar is handsomely bound in imitation leather and your name has been stamped in gold on the cover. Write an appropriate thank-you letter. (You use the Career Personnel Agency often when you need temporary and full-time office help, and you have found the agency, especially Nancy Wicker, extremely efficient. Assume that you are on a first-name basis with Miss Wicker.)

■ ■

CASE 3
EXPRESSING APPRECIATION FOR SPECIAL SERVICE

PROBLEM: You have been asked to speak at Creighton University, Omaha, Nebraska, on new developments in records management. One of your suppliers of filing systems has produced a film, *Filing and Finding,* which you would like to show during your talk. You find, however, that all copies of the film, except the reserve copy in the company's library, are out and none will be available in time for your presentation. In fact, you got your request in so late it is doubtful that the film could have been delivered in time even if it had been available.

Although the supplier has a rule of not releasing its library copy of a film, he has made an exception for you. In fact, he is sending it to you by air express to make sure you get it in time. You receive the film, make effective use of it, and now must write the supplier expressing your appreciation for this special service.

BACKGROUND

Customers expect to receive efficient service from those with whom they do business. The old saying "The customer is king" is as true today as it ever was. Now and then, however, a supplier will go considerably beyond the call of duty for a customer, and when he does, it is appropriate and thoughtful to express written appreciation for the service.

SOLUTION A

Dear Mr. Norton:

The film Filing and Finding arrived in plenty of time for my guest appearance at the Management Institute of Creighton University. You would have been pleased by the reaction of the audience to the film; as I explained, my entire talk was built around it.

You went to a lot of trouble in order to get this film to me—even to the extent of robbing your library of its last copy—and I appreciate your help more than I can express.

The film has already been mailed back to you, and you should receive it this week.

Thank you very much.

Sincerely yours,

Analysis of Solution A. The letter illustrated is only one version, since there is no one best solution to a letter problem. Note how the writer has stressed four points that he knows the reader is interested in:

1. The film arrived in time.
2. The audience reacted favorably to the film.
3. The writer appreciates what the supplier went through to get the film to him.
4. The film has been returned promptly.

SOLUTION B

Dear Mr. Norton:

Filing and Finding was sent this morning by air express. With it goes my gratitude to you for getting it to me in time for my talk at Creighton University.

My presentation was extremely well received, and a number of people praised the high quality of the film. It certainly added drama and excitement to my talk.

Thank you, Mr. Norton, for going out of your way to help me. I'm deeply grateful.

Sincerely yours,

Analysis of Solution B. There is no particular order in which points to be discussed must appear. Solution B, which covers the same points, is as effective as Solution A.

■ ■

PROJECTS

A   On October 13, you placed an order for a Peerless C.O.M. (Computer Output to Microfilm) Reader with Micro Line, Inc., Benton Harbor, Michigan. You were in a special rush for this reader and asked for delivery by October 20, even though the advertising literature mentioned that purchasers should allow at least 30 days for delivery. The reader arrived on October 19, and you realize that your order must have been given special attention. Write to the president (you don't know his name), expressing appreciation for this special service.

B About a week ago you wrote to View Gems Corporation asking for information about the cost of making color transparencies that you need for training new file clerks in the Records Management Department. You received a letter from Miss Bess Sarazen telling you that View Gems does not make transparencies. In her letter, however, Miss Sarazen listed the names and addresses of several companies that do this kind of work. She also enclosed a reprint of a magazine article, ''Preparing Art Work for Color Transparencies,'' that she happened to see the same day your letter arrived. Write Miss Sarazen an appropriate letter of appreciation.

■ ■

CASE 4 EXPRESSING CONGRATULATIONS AND APPRECIATION

PROBLEM: The training director of Keystone Designs, Incorporated, recently ran a week-long seminar on human relations for supervisors. As supervisor of the Records Management Department, you felt that it was a profitable conference. You want to express your appreciation for the seminar and, at the same time, congratulate Mr. Breir, the training director, on the way it was conducted.

BACKGROUND

In the typical business firm hardly a day goes by that somebody doesn't receive a promotion or an honor or do something worthy of favorable comment. To write or not to write, as far as you are concerned, depends entirely on how you feel about a particular event. It is neither necessary nor appropriate to write congratulatory messages to people whom you've never seen and have no particular association with. In some companies, one could spend a considerable amount of time composing letters of congratulation. There is no rule either that says you have to write to people you do know but don't get along with very well or have no particular liking for. Some people write letters to all their business associates who have been cited for one thing or another, but you must decide whether you can do so without sounding forced.

The number of letters you write to people outside the company depends on your job and your own inclinations. If you work in advertising, sales, public relations, or publicity, you will probably write more congratulatory letters to customers, potential customers, and the general public than you would if you worked in the tax, accounting, insurance, production, or data processing department. Many such letters written to people outside the firm create goodwill. Even though they may also have a sales mission, they must be genuine. A congratulatory letter to a potential customer that smacks of commercialism is worse than no letter at all.

SOLUTION

Dear Mr. Breir:

Last week's seminar, "Human Relations in Management," was the best I have ever attended, and I want you to know how much I enjoyed it. Congratulations to you and those who assisted you in planning and staging the conference.

There were many highlights, but the things that helped me most were the "T" sessions run by Mr. Praeger, the group dynamics program you and Mrs. McNally conducted, and the play "Ishmael's Day in Court." The luncheon and dinner speakers were outstanding.

I sincerely hope we'll have more seminars along the same line. I'm already trying to put into practice what I learned last week, and a refresher course from time to time would be valuable to me.

Sincerely,

Analysis of Solution. When you are congratulating someone for an outstanding achievement, make sure you are specific about what you are congratulating that person for. In the solution above, the writer not only expressed his appreciation but also cited a number of things that merited special mention.

■ ■

PROJECT

You have just returned from a two-day conference on work measurement held at O'Hare Inn and sponsored by the Chicago chapter of the National Records Management Association. The chairman of the conference was Miss Elaine O'Donnell, of Kemper Insurance Company, with whom you've had a close professional association for several months through the NRMA's activities.

The conference was a huge success as far as you are concerned, and you know how hard Miss O'Donnell worked to make it so. Write her a letter expressing your appreciation and congratulations. Supply your own details about the program, speakers, and so on.

■ ■

CASE 5 CONGRATULATING THE BOSS

PROBLEM: Your boss, Hans Steinkraus, has just been elected president of the local chapter of the Society for the Advancement of Management. You are a new member of this group. The announcement of Mr. Steinkraus's election was made at last night's meeting.

BACKGROUND

No matter who they are, people appreciate letters of congratulation when they have achieved something important. Your boss is no exception. Although you may congratulate him in person, you might write him because a written message is much more meaningful and enduring. You will probably do both.

The main danger in writing such a letter is that you could give the impression that you are politicking. A few bosses will have this feeling no matter what your intentions are or what you say in your letter. Most, however, will appreciate your thoughtfulness. The tone of your letter will depend, of course, on how friendly you are with your boss.

SOLUTION

Dear Mr. Steinkraus:

Congratulations on your being elected president of the Chicago chapter of the Society for the Advancement of Management and to the Society for its splendid choice.

As a new member of SAM, I look forward to the year ahead under your leadership. Now, more than ever, I am pleased that I decided to join this group.

Sincerely,

Analysis of Solution. If the writer of the above letter is sincere in his statements, it is an entirely appropriate message. As you will observe, it is a rather personal letter: *Congratulations on your being elected . . . . I look forward to the year ahead . . . . Now, more than ever, I am pleased that I decided to join this group.*

■ ■

PROJECTS

A   A good friend and fellow member of the National Records Management Association, Miss Frances Parks, who works for another company in Chicago, has just

125

been elected second vice president of the local chapter. This office carries the responsibility for planning the Association's annual programs. You learned about the appointment in the Association's monthly newsletter, *NRMA-Chicago* (you missed the dinner meeting at which the news was announced). Write a letter of congratulation.

B   You read in last night's paper that Dr. E. L. Williams, a former professor under whom you studied psychology and with whom you had a special rapport, was selected to attend a White House conference on higher education. This is a great honor, and you know that Dr. Williams must be pleased. Write a letter of congratulation. Assume that although you have not seen Professor Williams for about a year, he will remember you well. Supply any personal details that you think would be appropriate.

■ ■

CASE 6 CONGRATULATING AN EMPLOYEE UPON AN ANNIVERSARY

PROBLEM: The Personnel Department of Keystone Designs, Incorporated, keeps a record of the anniversary dates of all employees. The personnel manual recommends that supervisors acknowledge anniversary dates upon completion of the first, fifth, tenth, fifteenth, etc., year of employment.

Miss Millie Cox is celebrating ten years with Keystone. She began as a file clerk in the Contracts Department and, through a series of promotions, is now section supervisor, Central Files. She is a most valuable employee—hardworking, pleasant, dependable. Although you are now her boss, she has been at Keystone several years more than you have. You are to write the congratulatory message to Miss Cox.

BACKGROUND

It is customary to acknowledge an employment anniversary by letter, even though older employees may have special luncheons and banquets given to them to celebrate a fifteen- or twenty-year anniversary. Of course, in such a letter, the emphasis is on the employee's contributions to the company; and, depending upon the rapport between the writer and the employee, a bit of reminiscing may be in order.

SOLUTION A

In the following solution, we are assuming that the writer and the employee enjoy a good rapport and have become friends.

Dear Millie:

You must know how much I value you and your work. I couldn't supervise this department without you.

On the occasion of your tenth anniversary, I want to pay special tribute to you—for your support of my efforts, your efficiency, your cooperation, your dependability. No one has contributed more to this department than you have.

Personally, I hope we'll be working together for many more years to come.

Sincerely,

Analysis of Solution A. Solution A may strike you as an effusive—at least overgenerous—letter. In some instances it would be. As mentioned earlier, whether or not this is a good letter depends on the kind of person the writer is and the feelings he has about the employee.

SOLUTION B

Dear Miss Cox:

Congratulations on your tenth anniversary with Keystone.

In one way, it seems unbelievable that you could have been with us that long—unbelievable because I prefer not to admit that time can fly that quickly. On the other hand, when I look at the many important things you have done, I wonder if it hasn't really been longer.

On this occasion, one is tempted to reminisce about the past ten years and what they have brought in the way of progress, pleasure, and satisfaction. But I'd rather think about the future and the mountains we have yet to climb. I just hope you'll be here, doing your usual fine job, prodding us on, and helping the department reach the top.

Sincerely yours,

Analysis of Solution B. Some executives could not write a letter like Solution A because they prefer a more formal relationship between themselves and their employees. They would write a letter similar to Solution B, which is quite all right if it reflects the personality and feelings of the writer.

■ ■

PROJECTS

A   Loraine Carlson, a clerk-typist in your department, is celebrating her first anniversary with Keystone. As her supervisor, you must write the customary letter of congratulation. Assume that Loraine is a personable, hard-working, efficient, and popular employee. You value her highly; in fact, you are thinking about promoting her to an assistant supervisor's job, but you are not yet ready to announce the fact. Write the letter, supplying your own personal details.

B   Jack Kiley, a messenger in the Records Management Department, has just completed his fifth year with Keystone. Jack does not take his job very seriously (although he has had modest annual salary increases, he has never received a promotion), but he manages to do it just well enough to keep it. Jack is one of those people who do no more than they have to; yet he is agreeable and accepted by other employees, who refer to him as a "pretty good guy." Write an appropriate letter acknowledging Jack's anniversary.

■ ■

CASE 7 CONGRATULATING AN EMPLOYEE UPON RETIREMENT

PROBLEM: The chief design engineer of Keystone Designs, Incorporated, Blake Baumgartner, is responsible for the company's design of office furniture and interiors. One of the most gifted of his furniture designers—the veteran of the department—is William Osler, who is retiring after forty years with the company. During this period, Mr. Baumgartner has seen the company grow from a small manufacturer of advertising-promotion novelties to one of the leading designers and manufacturers of office interiors in the industry.

Although Mr. Osler will be honored at special department luncheons and a company banquet, he will receive letters of congratulation when the story of his retirement is published in the company newspaper.

BACKGROUND

Letters to those who are retiring probably fall in the congratulations category, though to some retirement is not a particularly joyous occasion. In writing such letters, however, you must assume that the retiree is looking forward to the new leisure time and freedom to do what he has always promised himself he would do if he had the time.

To many people who reach retirement age, letters of congratulation naturally are extremely important, particularly if the retiree's worth is emphasized. When one has devoted many years of his life to his job and is proud of his record, letters are evidence that his efforts were appreciated.

SOLUTION A

Dear Bill:

Congratulations on your retirement after forty years of service at Keystone. I am sure this is a happy occasion for you.

Best wishes for many successful retirement years.

Cordially yours,

Analysis of Solution A. The letter says nothing and will probably have very little meaning to Mr. Osler. Nothing is said about his achievements, and there is no indication he will be missed—only that "I am sure this is a happy occasion for you," which it may not be. There is very little here that Mr. Osler can look at in his retirement with any pride or satisfaction.

SOLUTION B

Dear Bill:

As I look around my office, I can see the hand of Bill Osler everywhere. It should be a great source of satisfaction to you, as it is to me, that you have left so many magnificent creations for all to see and admire for years to come.

It is impossible to begin to count all the contributions you have made to our growth and prestige. Let's just say that I give you credit for putting us on the map and making our name favorably known throughout the country. That's a pretty sizable achievement when one considers that we could claim neither distinction until you came along.

May the years ahead bring rich and satisfying rewards to you—and all the fishing you have planned. But if I know you as well as I think I do, you will find time to continue your professional associations too.

Good luck, Bill. And come to see us often.

Sincerely,

Analysis of Solution B. Solution B is much better than A for these reasons:

1. Mr. Osler is reminded that his contributions will be long remembered in tangible form ("As I look around my office, I can see the hand of Bill Osler everywhere").
2. Mr. Osler's impressive record as a designer is emphasized, a fitting tribute to a valuable employee.
3. A salute to the retiree's future and an invitation to come back for a visit put a personal capstone on the letter.

■ ■

PROJECTS

A   Homer Ault, supervisor of the Archives Section of the Records Management Department for the past fifteen years and a thirty-five-year employee of Keystone, is retiring this week at the age of sixty-five. Mr. Ault is practically an "institution" at Keystone—highly regarded by everyone for his knowledge, effectiveness on the job, and personableness. Although you are relatively new as Mr. Ault's boss, he has never resented you; indeed he has been your good friend and confidant. Mr. Ault has many hobbies, but the one that occupies most of his free time is stamp collecting. He and Mrs. Ault plan to move to Southern California later in the year and eventually to establish a small business, buying and selling rare stamps. Write an appropriate letter of congratulations.

B   Miss Grace Holden, manager of the Payroll Department, is a casual friend of yours (she serves on several committees of which you are a member). It has just been announced in the company newspaper that Miss Holden is retiring next month for reasons of health and is moving to Arizona. Miss Holden, sixty, has been with Keystone for thirty-three years and is highly regarded in the company. Write a suitable letter to her.

■ ■

CASE 8   EXPRESSING SYMPATHY

PROBLEM: During the past week, death has touched the lives of two of your friends. The mother of Miss Millie Cox (Case 6) passed away. Although you had not met Mrs. Cox, she was spoken of often by those in your department who had. You feel that an appropriate letter to Millie is in order.

The wife of one of your college professors also passed away during the week. Professor Gudonov became a very close friend while you were a student, and you were in his home many times. Mrs. Gudonov was hostess at a number of informal advanced Russian literature seminars.

BACKGROUND

Perhaps the most difficult of all letters are those expressing sympathy to those who have suffered personal losses. These letters deserve very careful thought; their only mission is to bring a bit of comfort to their recipients. Some people find such letters so hard to write that they prefer to send a printed sympathy card to which they add a short personal note. Yet nothing is perhaps so effective on these occasions as a handwritten letter on plain personal stationery.

Letters of condolence are usually brief, expressing sympathy without being maudlin.

SOLUTION (Millie Cox)

Dear Millie:

Please accept my sincerest sympathy in your great loss.

Although I had never met your mother, I felt that I knew her because so many spoke of her often and affectionately.

Sincerely,

SOLUTION (Professor Gudonov)

Dear Professor Gudonov:

The news of Mrs. Gudonov's death has just reached me, and I want to extend to you my deepest sympathy.

I count those evenings in the Gudonov home as among the highlights of my college career. She was certainly a friend to the advanced Russian lit crowd; I shall never forget her warmth, cheerfulness, and unselfishness.

I hope that I shall see you before long. Is there a chance that you will be in Chicago this fall? Ruth and I would like very much to have you come out to the house on your next trip.

Sincerely,

Analysis of the Solutions. Both the letter to Millie Cox and the letter to Professor Gudonov are simple, short, sincere expressions of sympathy. While the letter to Professor Gudonov does include a bit of reminiscing (the second paragraph), neither it nor the letter to Millie Cox dwells excessively on the reader's loss of a relative.

■ ■

PROJECT

You have just learned of the tragic death of Paul LaFitte, a fellow member of the National Records Management Association, as the result of an automobile accident. Paul, a former president of the Chicago chapter of the Association, was a good friend of yours; in fact, he sponsored you for membership in the organization and introduced you to the members. The two of you worked together on several committees. You think it would be appropriate to write a letter of condolence to Mrs. LaFitte, Paul's mother (he was not married), whom you have met on two or three occasions.

■ ■

part

6

**LETTERS
TO
CUSTOMERS
AND
PROSPECTIVE
CUSTOMERS**

YOUR JOB

You are assistant manager of Pickwick Manor, a large hotel in Pompano Beach, Florida. Although the hotel provides accommodations by the week to individuals, its principal business comes from firms, organizations, and associations who use it for meetings and conferences. The hotel provides regular room accommodations for the conference participants, meals, meeting rooms, and banquet facilities. Various recreational opportunities are available—swimming, golf, tennis, boating, surfing, and so on. Your job involves not only management of the daily activities of Pickwick Manor but also advertising and promotion, customer services and relations, and general public relations.

CASE 1

SUPPLYING INFORMATION TO A PROSPECTIVE CUSTOMER

PROBLEM: You receive the following letter from the Marlow Cement Manufacturing Company, signed by Carl E. Bigelow, executive vice president.

Gentlemen:

We are planning a conference of our regional managers December 3–7 and are considering the Pompano Beach area. Your place has been recommended to us by several people who have had successful meetings there.

We will need 12 double rooms and 6 single rooms to accommodate a total of 30 people (including the wives of 12 managers).

Would you please supply information about your facilities and rates and let me know whether you could accommodate us on the dates indicated.

Sincerely yours,

BACKGROUND

The request from Mr. Bigelow illustrates the type that every business depends on to survive. Such requests are the result of the expenditure of a great deal of money for advertising, salesmen, and good service. And speaking of good service, the greatest compliment a business can receive is the recommendation of a satisfied customer.

Business spends millions upon millions of dollars every year on direct mail and other forms of advertising, sales personnel, and various types of promotion in order to attract letters such as the one illustrated. Unfortunately, many of the people who handle such inquiries do not realize the effort and money that have been expended to generate these sales opportunities, and they make the mistake of treating them routinely.

To supply information to prospective customers, most commercial firms prepare special booklets, often printed in color. Depending upon the number of inquiries they receive, they send the booklets to prospective customers with a personal letter, a form letter, or a printed acknowledgment memo or card. Obviously, a well-written personal letter is most effective, but when hundreds of responses to inquiries must be prepared each month, the cost of such personal messages is usually prohibitive.

Pickwick Manor is a relatively small enterprise, however, and its staff answers every inquiry with a personal letter.

SOLUTION A

Dear Mr. Bigelow:

Enclosed is our colorful brochure describing the facilities of Pickwick Manor. We can accommodate your group nicely December 3–7.

Sincerely,

Analysis of Solution A. Solution A may do the job if the brochure accompanying it is sufficiently impressive. But the writer has obviously treated the request routinely, saying in effect, "We don't care whether you choose Pickwick Manor or not." And when one thinks of all the effort that has been expended to generate this kind of sales lead, such a response seems a very feeble effort at this "moment of truth."

SOLUTION B

Dear Mr. Bigelow:

It's good to know that you are thinking of Pickwick Manor for your regional managers conference December 3–7. We will be very glad to have you.

The enclosed brochure was prepared especially to give you the information you will want. Please note that you will be entitled to our summer rates (the winter rates, which are considerably higher, go into effect December 15).

Although Pickwick realizes the importance of your conference and makes sure you have the best possible facilities for that purpose, we expect you will find time for relaxation, too. Our tennis courts, golf course, swimming facilities, and indoor game rooms are the finest in this area (we can arrange for deep-sea fishing expeditions, too!).

Our social director, Miss Mary Glendenning, considers it an essential part of her job to see that wives of conference participants are happily occupied during the day. Mary arranges for sight-seeing tours, boat trips, fashion shows, and bargain-hunting excursions for those who want to be on the go; but she realizes that some ladies want no more than a beach chair, a book, and someone to bring them a cool drink from time to time.

With the hope you will choose Pickwick Manor for your conference, Mr. Bigelow, I am tentatively holding accommodations for you. May I suggest that you let me know your plans by September 14—reservations for December are filling up rapidly.

Sincerely yours,

Analysis of Solution B. Solution B will do a better job than A for these reasons:

1. The letter is personal. Although many business firms prepare form letters for the purpose of answering inquiries, such letters can, with only slight adaptation, be individualized. In solution B, for example, note:
    a. The specific reference in the first paragraph to the date of the conference and the group (regional managers).
    b. The description of special activities for wives of conference participants (Mr. Bigelow's letter mentioned that wives would be included).
2. The writer does not repeat the information contained in the accompanying brochure but merely emphasizes some of the important points described in it—special rates, meeting facilities, and recreational opportunities.
3. The writer asks for action (last paragraph). One of the cardinal rules of good salesmanship is: Try to get the prospect to make a favorable decision—ask for the business.

■■■■■■■■■■■■■■■■■■■■■■■■■■■■■■■■■■■■■

PROJECTS

A The following letter from Arthur O. Lasser, executive secretary of the United Air Conditioning Institute, is on your desk.

Gentlemen:

The United Air Conditioning Institute is conducting a three-day meeting March 16–18, and we are looking for an appropriate site. Your hotel has been recommended to us.

Do you have accommodations on those dates? We are expecting about 300 people to attend. We will need ten separate conference rooms for our section meetings, an auditorium for our general meetings, luncheon and dinner facilities (two luncheon and two dinner affairs are scheduled), and, of course, adequate sleeping accommodations.

Please send details, including prices. Incidentally, we are allowing a half day for recreation. Would it be possible to reserve exclusive golf accommodations for our party one afternoon? What arrangements can be made to transport some of our people to Miami on that day?

Yours very truly,

Prepare a response to this inquiry letter, assuming that (1) you can accommodate Mr. Lasser's group on the dates mentioned, (2) you will accompany your letter with a colorful brochure describing Pickwick Manor's facilities, and (3) you can take care of the special needs mentioned in the last paragraph. Provide any details you think would be appropriate.

B   Shortly after you wrote to Mr. Lasser, you received the following letter.

Thank you for the information concerning Pickwick Manor. We are studying the materials you sent and will let you know our decision as quickly as possible.

I forgot to ask about the availability of audiovisual equipment for our meetings, and I did not find mention of them in your materials. We will need a 16mm motion picture projector, two or three cassette playback units, two carousel slide projectors, screens, and perhaps other equipment. Will you be able to supply this equipment, or must we arrange for it ourselves?

Respond to the letter. Assume that you have the equipment he needs (or can obtain it locally) but that you would like to have a specific list so that you can make sure there will be no slipup.

■ ■

CASE 2
FOLLOWING UP AN INQUIRY

PROBLEM: Mr. Bigelow has not responded to the letter you wrote him about his December 3–7 conference (Case 1). It is now September 15 and you had asked for a reply by the 14th. You decide to write a follow-up letter.

BACKGROUND

Business firms are not satisfied when their first response to an inquiry produces no results, and they set up a system for follow-up. Some organizations write as many as four letters to the prospect in hopes of getting a favorable response. Others send telegrams (indicating urgency) to encourage response to an inquiry.

SOLUTION A

Dear Mr. Bigelow:

I cannot hold the tentative reservation I made for your group beyond September 25. Please let me know at once whether you intend to be with us.

Sincerely,

Analysis of Solution A. Solution A will only annoy Mr. Bigelow. He did not ask that facilities be reserved—he merely inquired about them—and the writer seems miffed that he has not received a confirmation.

SOLUTION B (Telegram)

Hope you can still be with us for December regional managers conference. Reservations filling up. Urge you make yours right away.

Analysis of Solution B. Telegrams may attract more than routine attention. On the other hand, a telegram used as a promotion device may nettle those who associate telegrams with crisis situations; they may consider it a false alarm, a hard sell. The sales correspondent, therefore, must weigh the telegram's merits against its shortcomings.

SOLUTION C

Dear Mr. Bigelow:

Your reservations at Pickwick Manor for your December 3–7 conference for 12 double rooms and 6 single rooms to accommodate a total of 30 people are still being held. Although you did not ask me to, I wanted to make sure we could accommodate you when you have made your final plans. Unfortunately, Mr. Bigelow, I won't be able to guarantee accommodations for you beyond September 25. May I please know your plans by that date.

You will be interested to know that we have recently added a solarium with indoor pool at Pickwick. Now, no matter what the weather outside, you can always be assured of good swimming every day.

Sincerely yours,

Analysis of Solution C. Solution C is a tactful and persuasive follow-up letter. Note that the writer mentions a new attraction at Pickwick Manor (the solarium with swimming pool), an effective method of reawakening interest in a cooled-off prospect.

■■■■■■■■■■■■■■■■■■■■■■■■■■■■■■■■■■■■■■■

PROJECTS

A   Mr. Lasser (Project B, page 137) has not responded to your letter. Write an appropriate follow-up letter, reinforcing Pickwick Manor's advantages and hinting that reservations should be made now while there is still space available.

B   Two weeks have gone by since you wrote your follow-up letter to Mr. Lasser. Compose a telegram that you might now send as a last-ditch effort to get the business.

C Mr. Lasser responds at last, telling you that the membership has voted to hold its convention in the Pocono Mountains of Pennsylvania. He expresses his appreciation for your help and the hope that at a future date the United Air Conditioning Institute will come to Pickwick Manor. Write an appropriate response.

■■■■■■■■■■■■■■■■■■■■■■■■■■■■■■■■■■■

CASE 3

TURNING DOWN A REQUEST FOR SERVICES

PROBLEM: Mrs. Rhoda Leavitt has written asking for accommodations at Pickwick Manor for 20 members of the Northeastern Antique Collectors Association for November 7–10. Pickwick Manor is sold out for those dates (her request for reservations arrived much too late), and you must tell her so.

BACKGROUND

Even though a request for a product or a service must be denied (the product is temporarily out of stock or is no longer being carried, or the service is not available on the dates requested), the letter writer must remember that the inquirer is still a prospect for a different product or for the same product or service at another date. He keeps in mind the advertising money and effort expended to generate interest in his product or service, and once he has a live candidate he doesn't let him go without a struggle. Even if there is no chance to land the prospect immediately, he keeps the prospect's name in an active file and sends him letters and other promotional literature for several months—perhaps a year or more—until all hope is gone.

SOLUTION A

Dear Mrs. Leavitt:

You waited much too late to make reservations at Pickwick Manor, and we are filled up for November 7–10. If you had written a month earlier, we might have been able to help you.

I am sorry.

                    Yours very truly,

Analysis of Solution A. Solution A is obviously a very poor letter, totally negative. If we want to get a prospective customer on our side, we don't start off with an accusation ("You waited much too late") and then tell him what he should have done ("If you had written a month earlier").

Although the writer could not provide the services requested, he could have tried to build goodwill so that Mrs. Leavitt might want to consider Pickwick Manor some other time. Solution A will succeed only in eliminating Pickwick Manor as a future meeting place for the organization Mrs. Leavitt represents.

SOLUTION B

Dear Mrs. Leavitt:

I wish it were possible for me to reserve accommodations for the Northeastern Antique Collectors Association for November 7–10. Unfortunately, Mrs. Leavitt, our facilities have been taken for those dates.

The only available openings in November to accommodate a group your size at the Pickwick Manor are from the 16th to the 20th. If you would like to consider this date, please let us know by October 2.

In any event, thank you for considering Pickwick Manor. Perhaps before too long we may have the pleasure of being your hosts.

Sincerely yours,

Analysis of Solution B. Solution B employs an effective technique for saying no to a customer: state your desire to provide the requested product or service before delivering the unpleasant news that you can't.

Observe that the writer has made an attempt to save the sale, even though he knows that the chances of Mrs. Leavitt's changing her meeting date are very slim.

The closing is friendly and persuasive.

■■■■■■■■■■■■■■■■■■■■■■■■■■■■■■■■■■■■

PROJECTS

A   Basil Milne, associate secretary of the Automotive Equipment Manufacturers Association of the U.S.A., has written the following letter:

Gentlemen:

The Automotive Equipment Manufacturers Association of the U.S.A. is looking for accommodations for its annual convention April 12–16.

An important part of this convention is the display of equipment of the various manufacturers, which requires considerable space and special platforms on which to display very heavy machinery. It is estimated that about 2,500 square feet of space will be needed for this purpose.

Buyers as well as Association members will be attending the convention. We estimate that approximately 1,500 will register. We will, of course, require an auditorium large enough for this group as well as about 20 private meeting rooms to accommodate 75 in each room. Most people will want to stay at the hotel for the week.

Will you please send complete information about your facilities, including prices. Also, are we correct in assuming that luncheon and banquet arrangements can be made to accommodate our group?

Very truly yours,

You must turn down this proposal. Your facilities are not suitable for displaying heavy equipment, and you're afraid damage might result from moving, setting in place, and housing such equipment. Also, the group is too large for your hotel; you can accommodate only about 500 comfortably. Write the letter, choosing the reason you think most appropriate for turning down the request. Suggest an alternative to Mr. Milne.

B   You received a letter from P. R. Lorenz, of Dynamic Mail Promotion, Inc., asking you for the list of registrants who attended a recent convention of purchasing agents. You must refuse because you don't have an official register; besides, it is not wise to give out this information (Mr. Lorenz obviously wants the list for promotion purposes) even if you had it. Suggest that he write the Commonwealth Association of Purchasing Agents, in Boston, for the information he desires.

■■■■■■■■■■■■■■■■■■■■■■■■■■■■■■■■■■■■■

CASE 4   THANKING A CUSTOMER FOR PATRONAGE

PROBLEM: The Marlow Cement Manufacturing Company held its meeting at Pickwick Manor on December 3–7, and the participants have returned home. You decide to write Mr. Bigelow to thank him for his business and to express the hope that he will use your hotel for such meetings again.

BACKGROUND

Often a businessman will write a letter to a customer to thank him for his patronage. Many firms make it a practice to thank those who have placed their order or used a service for the first time, as well as those who have placed unusually large orders. The message may be a printed card or a form letter— not as good as a personal letter but better than nothing. The intent of such follow-up letters is, of course, to encourage the customers to return.

SOLUTION A

```
Dear Sir:

    Pickwick Manor is pleased that you chose us as your
hosts for your recent meeting.  We enjoyed having you--
and we hope you will come again.

                              Sincerely yours,

                              PICKWICK MANOR
```

Analysis of Solution A. The postcard in Solution A is obviously a form message without individuality. If a businessman has thousands of active customers, he would find it too expensive to write each of them a personal letter every time he receives an order. In these cases, a postcard, printed memo, or processed letter is better than nothing at all. However, it is unlikely that Pickwick Manor, which is in the hospitality business and has a relatively small number of customers, could not afford a personal letter.

SOLUTION B

Dear Mr. Bigelow:

All of us at Pickwick Manor are delighted that you chose us as your hosts for your recent meeting. It was a pleasure having you. Mary Glendenning told me this morning she has never had a more enthusiastic group for the various social and recreational activities!

Please come back soon, Mr. Bigelow. Last week we had the pleasure of having 300 doctors at a medical convention. As you know, our main auditorium, the Beachcomber Room, seats 500 people comfortably.

Warm holiday greetings to you and your associates.

                              Sincerely,

Analysis of Solution B. Solution B is an appropriate thank-you letter. It was obviously written especially for Mr. Bigelow and has no to-whom-it-may-concern flavor. Note that the writer has taken advantage of the occasion to do some subtle selling for the future.

■■■■■■■■■■■■■■■■■■■■■■■■■■■■■■■■■■■■

PROJECTS

A   The Association of American Women Composers has just completed a three-day convention at Pickwick Manor. Write to Miss Emily Shoreham, president, expressing your pleasure in serving this group. Supply any details you believe appropriate.

B   Prepare a form letter or postcard that may be sent to all guests of the hotel, thanking them for choosing Pickwick Manor.

■■■■■■■■■■■■■■■■■■■■■■■■■■■■■■■■■■■■

CASE 5 RESPONDING TO A CUSTOMER'S COMPLAINT

PROBLEM: You received the following letter from C. H. Thompson, president of the Capitol City Personnel Directors Association, whose members recently concluded a three-day meeting at Pickwick Manor.

> Dear Sir:
>
> Thanks to the inefficiency of your staff, the fall meeting of the Capitol City Personnel Directors Association was a big disappointment. As you know, the materials that were shipped to your hotel two weeks in advance for use in our group sessions were misplaced by someone there and were never found (they arrived here today from your hotel). The entire program was built around these materials; and, as a result, we had to improvise, which proved to be a sorry mess.
>
> Your statement for $988.65 arrived today, and I am tempted not to pay it. In any event, it would seem that we are entitled to some kind of discount for the inconvenience we were caused by your staff.
>
> I expect an explanation from you before I make payment.
>
>   Yours truly,

You must, of course, answer Mr. Thompson's letter.

BACKGROUND

Every business receives letters resembling the one illustrated. No matter how hard a business tries to satisfy its customers, mistakes are made. Orders are delayed, wrong merchandise is sent, errors are made in customer billings, a customer is offended by a salesman, and so on.

Most businesses take the attitude that the customer is right—until proven wrong, but they carefully investigate each complaint before responding. If the customer is right, an apology is in order, along with the necessary adjustment. If the customer is wrong, he is usually told so gently and given a full explanation of the circumstances.

In the case of Mr. Thompson's complaint, investigation showed that the materials in question arrived at the hotel several days before the meeting. A part-time janitor received the materials (they arrived in the middle of the night) and, not knowing where to put them, locked them up in the Lost and Found room. He left the hotel to go on vacation the following day and his whereabouts were unknown. Later, someone piled several pieces of luggage on top of the carton so that it was hidden from sight. Although the Lost and Found room was searched at the time people were looking for the Thompson materials, no one thought to lift the luggage to see if there was anything underneath it.

Although you are willing to offer Mr. Thompson your sincere apologies, you are not authorized to give him a discount on his statement. The challenge, then, is to write a letter that will pacify Mr. Thompson and at the same time induce him to pay the bill in full.

SOLUTION A

Dear Mr. Thompson:

I am very sorry that the materials you say were sent here were not available for your meeting, but I do not believe this fact is justification for giving you a discount on your bill. We supplied you with meeting rooms, meals, and sleeping accommodations for your group, which is what we contracted to do, and you made use of our services. Therefore, I expect full payment of our invoice for $988.65.

Sincerely yours,

Analysis of Solution A. You don't have to be told that Solution A is an atrocious letter. The following errors are nearly unforgivable.

1. The writer, even though he knew that Pickwick Manor was at fault, failed to admit the hotel's error. Doing so was dishonest. In the first sentence, ''you say'' implies that Mr. Thompson did not tell the truth.
2. The tone of the letter is sarcastic, rude. There is no excuse for the writer's assuming this defensive, officious attitude.

Although Mr. Thompson will undoubtedly pay the bill after he licks his wounds for a time, he certainly will not return to Pickwick Manor—and what's worse, he will tell his associates to stay away too.

SOLUTION B

Dear Mr. Thompson:

All of us are terribly embarrassed that the materials for your meeting were misplaced by a member of our staff and were not available to you.

Let me tell you what happened. A part-time janitor signed for the carton when it was delivered late at night and, not knowing what to do with it, placed it in our Lost and Found room for safekeeping. Later, several pieces of luggage were piled on top of the carton, hiding it from view. We tried in vain to locate the janitor, but he left on vacation the day after the materials arrived and could not be reached. Although several people searched the Lost and Found room, no one thought to look under the luggage that obscured the carton from view.

What can I say? If you are thinking that this mishap borders on the incredible, I would have to agree with you. But if you have had something similar happen in your company—something that really defies explanation—then you may know how I feel and can appreciate my deep embarrassment.

After such an experience here, it may be presumptuous of me to suggest that you give us another opportunity to show you that we really are experts in the hospitality business, even though now and then it "doesn't show!"

                                        Sincerely yours,

Analysis of Solution B. The writer of Solution B handled this difficult situation about as tactfully as it could have been done. He apologized, explained, and made the assumption that Mr. Thompson is human enough to understand his position. If Mr. Thompson does not understand or pretends not to (every company, including Mr. Thompson's, experiences such moments of extreme embarrassment), there isn't much that can be done. Observe that the letter ends on a positive note—the give-us-another-chance theme. This is good psychology because it implies that Mr. Thompson is big enough to forgive an unintentional mistake.

Should the writer have asked that the invoice be paid in full? Probably he was wise not to, letting Mr. Thompson assume that he isn't going to get a discount. Leaving something unsaid is often stronger than an out-and-out "No."

■■

PROJECTS

A Mr. and Mrs. Eugene Byram were recent guests of Pickwick Manor for three days. An unfortunate series of mishaps marred their stay. Their room, which had been reserved weeks before their arrival, was not ready, and they had to wait in the lobby for two hours until it was ready. Although they had specifically asked for and been promised an ocean-front room above the tenth floor, the one they were given was on the third floor facing the street. A switch was made, but not until late afternoon of the second day. Finally, when Mr. Byram received his statement (he had asked to be billed), he found an error. Because he was attending a convention, he was to receive the special daily rate of $30 for the ocean-front room but he was billed at the rate of $40.

When sending his check (on which he made the adjustment for the room rate he was promised), he wrote that he had never seen such a "comedy of errors" and was bitterly critical of the hotel. Your investigation revealed that all the errors referred to by Mr. Byram were actually made and that he is due an apology. Write the letter. Assume that the street-front room, which the Byrams occupied the first night, was specially priced for the convention at $25 but that Mr. Byram made no mention of this in his letter.

B Miss Dianne Madison, who recently spent a week at Pickwick Manor and paid her bill in full when she checked out, wrote that upon examining the statement she found an error. She was charged for a dinner in the King Arthur Room for which she paid cash. According to Miss Madison, she signed the dining room check and entered her name and room number on it (which is the hotel's signal to place the amount on her bill). As she left the dining room, however, she decided to pay cash ($10.70) for the dinner. Upon investigation, you find that she is right. Write her, enclosing your check and apologizing for the error.

■ ■

CASE 6   RESPONDING TO A REQUEST FOR AN ADJUSTMENT

PROBLEM: You received the following letter from Cynthia Gabrini, treasurer of Quill, International, a group of amateur writers who recently held a conference at Pickwick Manor.

Dear Sir:

I have received your invoice for expenses of our Board of Directors during our recent convention at your hotel, and I believe there is an error. The rooms for these six people are charged at the rate of $30 a day on December 15 and 16; the amount should have been $18 a day, as it was for December 13 and 14.

I am enclosing our check for $432, although your invoice is for $576.

Very truly yours,

BACKGROUND

Misunderstandings about prices often arise between customers and suppliers. In the case problem, the letter confirming the reservations of Quill, International (addressed to Simon Hawkins, president), specifically mentioned that winter rates of $30 per room a day would go into effect December 15 (the daily rate up to that time was $18). Possibly the treasurer, Miss Gabrini, was not aware of the letter to Mr. Hawkins. In any event, Miss Gabrini's request must be refused.

SOLUTION A

Dear Miss Gabrini:

Thank you for your check for $432 in payment of the rooms for the six board members of Quill, International.

When your president, Mr. Simon Hawkins, originally made the reservations, I wrote him that on December 15 the winter rate of $30 a day a room would go into effect. He signed the agreement to that effect, and a copy is enclosed.

My calculations are as follows:

$$6 \text{ rooms at } \$18 \text{ a day for December } 13, 14 = \$216$$
$$6 \text{ rooms at } \$30 \text{ a day for December } 15, 16 = \underline{360}$$
$$\text{Total} \qquad \$576$$

Would you prefer to issue a new check for $576 or to prepare an additional check for $144?

Sincerely yours,

P.S. It was a pleasure having Quill, International, at Pickwick Manor, and we hope that you will come to see us again.

Analysis of Solution A. Note the tactful manner in which this transaction was handled:

1. An expression of appreciation for the check, even though it was the wrong amount.
2. An explanation of a possible misunderstanding, including a copy of the agreement as evidence.
3. A detailed calculation of how the invoice was figured.
4. A subtle reminder (last paragraph) that the full amount of the invoice is due without the writer's actually asking for the money.
5. A friendly P.S. which says, in effect, ''Let's still be friends.''

SOLUTION B

Assume that there was a misunderstanding about the bill, and that special summer rates were extended to Quill, International, for December 15 and 16 but that this information somehow was not communicated to Pickwick Manor's billing clerk. Here's the letter you might write.

Dear Miss Gabrini:

You are absolutely right—you owe us exactly what you paid us—$432. Although winter rates went into effect December 15, we gave Quill, International, special summer rates for December 15 and 16. This fact was not taken into account, however, when the invoice was prepared. Please accept my personal apology.

It was a pleasure to serve you and we thank you for choosing us as your conference headquarters. I hope you had a good meeting and that you will return to Pickwick Manor before too long.

Sincerely,

Analysis of Solution B. Solution B is an effective response to a customer who was overcharged in error. When you are wrong, it is best to admit it immediately and say what you are going to do about it. It is important, however, not to overstress your error. You are not expected to go down on bended knee. And never say that such a mistake will not happen again. Everyone knows that an occasional error is inevitable. Observe the friendly closing which ends the transaction on a positive note.

■■

PROJECTS

A   S. P. Cleveland, representing the Danforth Hog Breeders Association, objects to the gratuity charge of 15 percent that was added to the cost of the Association's banquet held recently at Pickwick Manor. In fact, Mr. Cleveland deducts the 15 percent ($108) from the total bill of $828, sending his check for $720.

Your contract with the Association specifically provided that a 15 percent gratuity charge would be made for the banquet, and Mr. Cleveland signed it. Respond to Mr. Cleveland, explaining that you cannot allow the deduction of the gratuity (such a charge is customary).

B   Three weeks have gone by, and you have had no response to your letter to Mr. Cleveland (Project A). Write a follow-up letter.

■■

CASE 7 RESPONDING TO A CUSTOMER'S COMPLIMENT

PROBLEM: You received a very warm thank-you letter from Mrs. Rachel Ericksen, president of the Duluth chapter of the Association of Women in Banking, which concluded a two-day convention at Pickwick Manor about ten days ago. Mrs. Ericksen expressed gratitude for the excellent rooms, meeting facilities, food, social activities, and the friendly atmosphere. She said it was the best convention her chapter has ever had, and she gave Pickwick Manor a large share of the credit.

BACKGROUND

Letters complimenting a business for outstanding service are relatively rare—not because outstanding service is rare but because it is expected as a matter of course. When a business firm receives a letter of commendation, a response is a must. In replying to these letters, be careful not to be overly modest but at the same time do not display undue vanity.

SOLUTION A

Dear Mrs. Ericksen:

How very nice of you to compliment us as you did for our part in the success of your meeting. Although you may have thought we went out of our way to serve you, we simply extended to you the Pickwick hospitality which all our guests learn to expect.

Please come again.

Cordially,

Analysis of Solution A. Although the tone of Solution A is generally good, the writer is guilty of smugness—indeed, of ''putting down'' Mrs. Ericksen for her well-intended compliment. The letter is not likely to achieve its mission: to reinforce a good feeling on the part of the customer.

SOLUTION B

Dear Mrs. Ericksen:

You were very thoughtful to compliment us for our part in the success of your meeting.

It was our pleasure to have you with us. Our people here who had a hand in providing service to the Duluth chapter of the Association of Women in Banking will be happy to know their efforts were appreciated. You may be sure that I will share your generous letter with them.

We hope you will come to Pickwick Manor again—soon.

Sincerely,

Analysis of Solution B. The writer of Solution B is neither too modest nor too vain. The letter is what it should be: a straightforward expression of gratitude for a compliment. Is the letter too brief? No. What is important is that everything that needs to be said is said.

■ ■

PROJECTS

A You received the following letter from Mrs. Mary K. Bonwit:

Gentlemen:

Enclosed is my check for $294 in payment of my bill.

Thank you for a lovely week at Pickwick Manor—one of the most delightful vacations I have ever had. The people were extremely friendly and helpful; the room, quiet and comfortable; and the food, superb. I can't think of anything I could have wanted that was not provided.

Appreciatively,

Respond to Mrs. Bonwit's letter.

B Develop a form letter that can be used as a general response to letters of commendation received by Pickwick Manor.

■ ■

CASE 8 COLLECTING AN OVERDUE ACCOUNT

PROBLEM: Mr. and Mrs. Arleigh Trumbull, of Decatur, Georgia, engaged the Ponce de Leon Room on October 7 for a wedding reception for their daughter Alice. The cost of the reception, including dinner for 200 people, was $4,500. Mr. Trumbull signed a contract for this amount and was to pay for the reception within ten days. On October 17, an invoice was sent to Mr. Trumbull and on October 25, a second statement (along with a printed reminder) was mailed. It is now November 3 and you have had no response from Mr. Trumbull. You must write to him to collect the amount due.

BACKGROUND

Most people pay their bills promptly. If this were not true, businesses couldn't afford to be as generous as they are about offering credit. When one considers that out of the millions of people who buy "on time" only a small percentage do not honor their bills, he must conclude that the majority are honest when it comes to credit. Yet, the small percentage of those who must be needled into paying represents a great deal of money, and credit managers in all commercial enterprises must everlastingly keep at them. Bad debts, even though they may represent but a fraction of the total sales, have sunk many a business.

Experience has proved that there are six basic reasons why people don't pay their bills:

1. *Overbuying.* Buyers have overextended themselves and don't have enough money to meet their obligations.
2. *Oversight.* People forget their bills or mislay them.
3. *Bad paying habits.* Some people apparently don't think it's important to settle their obligations promptly and relax into a you-can-wait attitude.
4. *Laziness.* A surprising number of customers think it too much of a chore to sit down and write a check.
5. *Personal misfortune or disaster.* Fires, hurricanes, illnesses, accidents, and other misfortunes sap the resources of some charge customers.
6. *Customer dissatisfaction.* The customer didn't like the product or service and decided not to pay for it.

Collection Letter Series. Every organization goes about the task of collecting overdue bills in its own fashion. For example, firms that do considerable selling on credit, such as large department stores, furniture stores, appliance stores, and jewelry stores, may develop several different series which they use over and over, constantly testing different combinations. Most businesses, however, develop a series along the following lines:

1. A statement which is sent at the end of the billing period.
2. A second statement, 20 to 30 days later, to which might be affixed a sticker with a message such as *Did you forget?*
3. One or two reminders, which are form letters, obviously duplicated so that they will appear to be routine and impersonal.
4. A personalized form letter, which is more urgent in tone than previous reminders. Three or four of these, each with a different appeal, may be sent. Four basic types of appeals are used to persuade people to pay:

Sympathy. Generally recognized as the weakest appeal, this one says in effect, ''We need the money because we have to pay our bills,'' or ''The company has put the blame on me for not having collected from you.''

Justice. This appeal is to one's sense of fair play and duty. (''We did right by you; now you do right by us.'')

Pride. Most people don't want to have their reputation tarnished, and an appeal to vanity is often very effective. (''A good credit reputation is a valuable asset; don't risk losing it.'')

Fear. The appeal to fear is the strongest of all, and it is used only when all other appeals fail. (''We are considering placing your account in the hands of our attorney. Don't force us to do this.'')

Practice varies from one business to another concerning collection procedures. Where one company will demand its money when a bill is not paid promptly on the due date, another will ''baby'' the customer along for months before getting hard-nosed. More often than not, the importance of a particular customer or his record of meeting his obligations determines the collection procedures. Charge customers are often inconsistent; one customer will pay his bill with Company X but neglect Company Z; another will maintain a flawless credit record for years and suddenly default. Generally speaking, the ability to pay one's bills is no guarantee that one will pay—many people on a very tight budget are more reliable than others who are affluent. Thus collecting money from customers is a genuine art; credit managers must constantly study people and develop an extra sense that tells them when a person is or is not a good credit risk.

In any event, the purpose of all collection letters is to get the money and to do so without causing ill will—a big challenge to the collection-letter writer. Nobody likes to be dunned, and the typical recipient of a persuasive collection letter will cry ''Foul!'' automatically.

Following is a typical series of collection letters that a customer might receive after he has received one or two statements of his account.

First Letter—Gentle Reminder. The following is a form letter, obviously duplicated, with blank spaces for fill-ins.

> Your account in the amount of $77.40 is now overdue. Perhaps your check is already in the mail; if so, please disregard this reminder.

Second Letter—Stronger Reminder. The following letter may also be a form letter similar to the first one.

> Perhaps you did not receive the previous reminders about the outstanding balance of your account. Otherwise, I believe you would have sent us your check for $77.40 by this time. Your account is now 30 days overdue.

Third Letter—Appeal to Justice. As you will notice, the following letter is a personalized, individually typed—rather than duplicated—letter.

> If a friend of yours borrowed money from you, promising to pay it back in 30 days, you'd expect him to keep his side of the bargain, wouldn't you? Or if he couldn't, you would expect him at least to tell you why, wouldn't you?
>
> That's the situation we are in. You bought a rug from us on credit, which is the same as borrowing money, and agreed to pay us $77.40 for it in 30 days. Those 30 days have come and gone and we still haven't received payment, nor have you told us why.
>
> Please use the stamped envelope to mail us your check for $77.40 right away.

Fourth Letter—Appeal to Pride. If the customer still hasn't paid his account, he would receive another personalized letter similar to this one.

> This morning I asked to see your account, and I have it before me right now. You have done business with us for over three years, and you have a fine credit record. Until now.

I say "until now" because your good credit reputation is in danger of being damaged. And all for the small amount of $77.40, which you've owed us for six weeks.

Probably you meant to settle your account long before this, but you simply have not got around to it. Or maybe there is another reason. Whatever it is, please take care of this obligation immediately. I don't want to see you labeled "Bad Credit Risk"—and this could happen if you delay longer. Please send me your check at once. Before it is too late.

Fifth Letter—Appeal to Fear. A letter similar to the following one gives the customer "one last chance" to avoid the unpleasantness and expense of having his account put in the hands of a lawyer or a collection agency.

The last thing I want to do is to put your account in the hands of a collection agency. It's unpleasant business—unpleasant for us and unpleasant for you. But I will be forced to take this action unless I have the $77.40 in payment of your account by July 10.

Help me to avoid this step by at least getting in touch with me and discussing your intentions. This is the last opportunity I can give you—the next move is yours.

What will you say in your letter to Mr. Trumbull about the bill for his daughter's wedding reception? Here are four variations of the first letter you might write (the previous communications were printed reminders). Note that none is demanding or threatening); yet each is a straightforward request for payment.

SOLUTION A

Dear Mr. Trumbull:

Funny how people forget.

No doubt, before your daughter Alice's wedding all that you (and especially Mrs. Trumbull) could think of was getting everything done properly that had to be done. And if you're like most parents-of-the-bride, you often wondered if you'd hold up under the strain. Everything centered on giving the bride a wedding she would never forget.

We were glad to have had a part in that memorable occasion, and we hope we were able to take some worries off your shoulders and help you to forget your responsibilities. It was, you'll agree, a beautiful reception.

Now that it's all over and, I hope, the bride and groom are happily settled, you have possibly forgotten the agonies of planning and the worries about whether everything would go off as you wished. That's only natural. But in the process have you forgotten us too?

Your payment for the reception at Pickwick Manor has not been received, and we're betting that it slipped your mind. Unfortunately, it is something we can't forget. Won't you send us your check for $4,500 right away—today?

Sincerely yours,

Analysis of Solution A. Solution A emphasizes a central theme (forgetting) throughout quite effectively. It is a tactful, reasonable appeal to Mr. Trumbull's sense of fair play. It should not offend the Trumbulls, and it should produce results—if the Trumbulls have a conscience (and the money!).

SOLUTION B

Dear Mr. Trumbull:

Your check for $4,500 is two weeks overdue now. It is very difficult for me to understand why it has not arrived.

I remember your saying to me that the reception for Alice's wedding was "beautiful" and "perfect"—we think it was one of the nicest affairs ever held here at Pickwick Manor. The orchestra, the florist, the caterers—all have been paid, but we haven't received our check.

Mr. Trumball, please don't let this matter ride any longer. Mail us your check in the enclosed envelope today.

Sincerely yours,

Analysis of Solution B. Solution B also emphasizes the fair-play appeal. It is an effective letter, and because the writer was more direct in asking for payment and stated his position in fewer words, some would choose it over Solution A. Which do you think will achieve its mission better?

SOLUTION C

Dear Mr. Trumbull:

Here's the situation as I see it.

ONE: We provided a lovely reception for your daughter Alice's wedding, which your guests described variously as "superb," "elegant," "stunning" (you said "beautiful," "perfect").

TWO: We paid the orchestra, florist, caterer, and all the others who assisted.

THREE: We asked you for payment of the contract on October 17 and again on October 25.

FOUR: We have not received payment (the amount is $4,500).

FIVE: May we have your check by November 8.

Sincerely yours,

Analysis of Solution C. Solution C reviews the history of the transaction, and the writer displays his points tactfully and convincingly. Although the letter is not a hard demand, the writer makes his point clear that he expects payment by November 8.

SOLUTION D

Dear Mr. Trumbull:

On October 17, I sent you a statement of your account ($4,500) to which I received no response.

On October 25, I wrote you again reminding you that this bill had not been paid. Still no answer.

This is November 3, and I still have not received a check or an explanation from you.

Don't you think, Mr. Trumbull, that this account should be paid in full at once? Certainly I see no reason why it should not be, and I expect to have your check by November 8.

Sincerely yours,

Analysis of Solution D. This is a variation of the history of the transaction used in Solution C. The writer is a little more demanding (last sentence), but the letter is still not harsh.

■■■■■■■■■■■■■■■■■■■■■■■■■■■■■■■■■■■■■■■

PROJECTS

A   Edward Jefferson, representing Party Time Novelties, was a recent guest of Pickwick Manor. He stayed two days and during that time incurred a bill of $275.70. At the time of check-out, he paid his bill by check. However, the bank on which the check was drawn returned the check to you stamped "Insufficient Funds." Write Mr. Jefferson, asking for payment.

B   Two weeks have gone by and you have not heard from Mr. Jefferson (Project A). Write a follow-up communication that you think is appropriate.

C   Develop a series of four to six letters, from routine reminder to final notice, that might be used by Pickwick Manor to collect overdue accounts of individual guests who have been given credit privileges.

■■■■■■■■■■■■■■■■■■■■■■■■■■■■■■■■■■■■■■■

CASE 9   RESPONDING TO A CREDIT RISK

PROBLEM: The Indian River Trotters, a folk-dance organization, held a three-day festival at Pickwick Manor two years ago. When a bill was submitted to the treasurer, Minnie Caldwell, for $1,240 for hotel services provided the group, there was considerable haggling over the amount. Although Pickwick Manor finally collected in full, the bill was not paid for over four months.

You have received a letter from Miss Caldwell requesting a reservation for the group's semiannual meeting. She asks whether payment for the services can be postponed for 60 days after the meeting. Although you have space available on the requested dates and would be pleased to have the Indian River Trotters as guests of Pickwick Manor, you do not consider the organization a good credit risk and you feel you must deny the request for an extension.

BACKGROUND

Refusing credit is one of the most ticklish, if not *the* most ticklish, of all challenges to the letter writer. When you have to say no to a credit applicant, you are in effect saying that he is not to be trusted, that you don't think he can or will pay his debts. Such a serious indictment of a person or an organization must be handled with great delicacy and tact.

Some professional credit men believe that a poor risk who must be refused credit need not be told directly that he is being turned down (''We lack sufficient information necessary to grant your request for credit''); others think it best to come right out with a no and give the reasons. Most agree, however, that if at all possible the customer should be ''saved'' and encouraged to buy on a cash basis. Obviously, this is quite a challenge, and the person who can bring off that kind of challenge is rare.

SOLUTION A

Dear Miss Caldwell:

I am sorry we cannot extend the 60-day credit privileges you asked for in connection with the fall meeting of the Indian River Trotters. We had an unfortunate experience with your group when you were here two years ago. You did not pay us for over four months, and we had to get very unpleasant about it before we collected. I am sure you will understand why we think you are not a good credit risk.

Very truly yours,

Analysis of Solution A. You will quickly agree that this is a wholly negative response. It is honest, and the writer may feel perfectly justified in stating his position in such hard terms. However, if he wants the Indian River Trotters to patronize Pickwick Manor on a cash-only basis, he has destroyed that possibility. The question that every credit man must ponder is: Is the customer worth the effort to try to retain him as a cash-only patron? Even if the writer of this letter felt that the customer was not worth the effort, he could have been more tactful.

SOLUTION B

Dear Miss Caldwell:

Thank you and your fellow members of Indian River Trotters for thinking of Pickwick Manor for your fall meeting.

Although it would be a pleasure to have you, I am afraid I cannot extend payment to 60 days. In other words, we would have to ask for full settlement at the time of check-out. This is our standard arrangement with similar organizations.

If you find it possible to accept these conditions, Miss Caldwell, you may be sure that we at Pickwick Manor will see to it that your group is extended every courtesy and service. Please make your reservations early so that you may be assured of getting the exact accommodations you want.

Sincerely yours,

Analysis of Solution B. The writer of Solution B, although straightforward, is tactful and sales-minded. Note there is no mention of the previous unpleasant experience with the Indian River Trotters. It is not necessary since the refusal itself implies a lack of trust. Note that the writer uses the last paragraph to soften his refusal of the request for credit by suggesting an alternative for Miss Caldwell's consideration.

■ ■

PROJECTS

A   Mr. and Mrs. Howard Kronefeld wrote for reservations for the week beginning December 20. They asked whether Pickwick Manor accepts U-Charge-It credit cards. You can accommodate Mr. and Mrs. Kronefeld for the week of December 20, but you will require a $50 deposit in order to hold the reservation. Although Pickwick Manor accepts Diners Club and American Express credit cards, it does not accept U-Charge-It. Write the letter.

B   John C. Helms, sales promotion manager of Pierson Camera Manufacturing Company, has written to reserve exhibit space at the November 16–20 convention of the American Photographers Association. The rental cost for the space Mr. Helms requested is $300.

  Your records show that you are still trying to collect $120 from Pierson Camera for exhibit space rented at last year's convention (Pierson was billed for $280 but sent their check for $160, claiming they were overcharged). After numerous letters to the treasurer of the company, L. T. Mace, you have not settled the matter, and Pickwick Manor has threatened to sue.

  The space Mr. Helms wants is available. However, you have been directed to ask for advance payment in full—no credit this time. Write the letter.

■ ■

CASE 10 WINNING BACK A FORMER CUSTOMER

PROBLEM: Until two years ago, The Montrose Food Corporation had held its annual sales meeting at Pickwick Manor every March for five years in a row. Although you sent your usual promotional literature during the past two years, the company did not choose Pickwick Manor for its headquarters. You have decided to write a special letter to try to win them back.

BACKGROUND

''Once a customer, always a customer'' is an axiom every business would like to make a reality. But in our competitive world, customers do stray. Sometimes they are lured away because a competitor offers better prices or service, or because his location is more convenient. Sometimes a customer strays because of downright dissatisfaction with the product or rude treatment at the hands of sales or service personnel. Whatever the reason, most businesses keep the names of their former customers and from time to time attempt to lure them back into the fold.

Many different promotional ideas are used to win back old customers: more generous credit terms, discount prices for a limited time, advance information about new styles and new merchandise, gifts, special buying assistance, and so on. One method is to write customers, inviting them to tell what went wrong and caused them to transfer their business elsewhere; another is to stress new products, new services, or a new appearance.

SOLUTION A

Dear Miss Joplin:

You're missed, you know.

For five years in a row Pickwick Manor had the pleasure of being your hosts at your annual sales meeting in March. For this reason we had begun to think of you as partners of ours—we liked you and we think you liked us.

But for two years now you haven't called upon us. And frankly we miss you. In a situation like this, it is only natural for us to ask ourselves, What did we do to those Montrose folks that would cause them to stay away? But we can't come up with a reason.

If there was something at Pickwick Manor that did not measure up to your expectations, we'd like to know about it. Honestly. And while you're at it, look over our enclosed new brochure. We hope it will persuade you to come back.

Sincerely yours,

Analysis of Solution A. Some promotion people object to the what-did-we-do-wrong theme because it is somewhat negative. There is no question but that the writer invites criticism, encouraging the recipient to think of something wrong whether there is or not. Others believe such negativism builds a little sympathy for the company that has been spurned and at least gives the former customer a chance to blow off steam.

The writer of this letter obviously feels that at least some of the additions to the hotel's accommodations will appeal to the reader (note the display arrangement that highlights each of them). And, like the writer of Solution A, he closes with a request for action.

SOLUTION B

Dear Miss Joplin:

You wouldn't recognize us! Since you were here last, we've added:

- 40 new luxurious sleeping rooms with private balconies overlooking the ocean
- 4 meeting rooms—all carpeted—each with an ocean view
- A 9-hole par-36 golf course and a driving range
- A complete marina with boat rentals for fishing, skiing, sailing, and other water sports
- A solarium with swimming pool

But there is one thing that hasn't changed: our friendly, superb service (except maybe it's better than ever!).

Why not make a reservation for your March sales conference right now while there's still unlimited choice of facilities? We want you back at Pickwick Manor. Let us show you we mean it!

Cordially yours,

Analysis of Solution B. This letter stresses the look-how-we've-changed theme in an effort to win back a former customer. It is a more positive but not necessarily a more persuasive letter than A. Such a letter is usually accompanied by a colorful folder or brochure that illustrates the "new look" talked about in the letter.

■ ■

PROJECT

Write two letters, each with a different theme, attempting to win back customers (organizations) who, after having been good customers for several years in a row, have not returned to Pickwick Manor for the past two years. Use your imagination in making the invitation attractive.

■ ■

CASE 11 WRITING A SALES LETTER

PROBLEM: You have obtained a copy of the *Directory of Under-40 Presidents Association*—a list of 1,520 men and women who became the chief executive officers of their companies before reaching the age of 40. This is a new organization, and your boss at Pickwick Manor has asked you to prepare a letter that will sell these young executives on using Pickwick Manor for their away-from-home company conferences and meetings.

BACKGROUND

Every letter we write sells something, even if it's only a point of view or idea. But the true sales letter has the primary objective of convincing someone that he should spend money for a product or a service immediately or put him in the mood to do so later.

Letters that attempt to make immediate sales, to get inquiries that may lead to sales, to determine interest in a new product or service, or to support other promotion efforts (for example, to "soften up" a prospect for a salesman's call), all come under the heading of direct-mail promotion. Perhaps you have often wondered (as you threw away, unopened or unread, sales letters that you received) whether direct mail really pays off. It does—for certain organizations and products. You wouldn't use a sales letter to sell a package of gum or a tube of toothpaste because the letter would cost more than the profit on the item. But direct mail is used extensively to sell magazine subscriptions, life insurance, stocks and bonds, luggage, appliances, air travel, and other higher-priced goods and services. Every year many dollars are spent on sales letters of one sort or another because through direct mail you can *select* your audience and often get the most for each dollar spent.

In most organizations, sales letters are written by people who are responsible for advertising and promotion, which is where the responsibility belongs. Sales letters are a specialty all their own. Even an experienced promotion man often turns to advertising agency people and direct-mail specialists for help with his sales letters. Since letters can be extremely costly, the advertising manager seeks to make his carefully budgeted advertising dollar count by reducing the odds of producing a loser. When he has a large mailing list, he may attempt to reduce the risk of wasting money by preparing two or three different sales letters and testing the pulling power of each by mailing them to small segments of the complete list. The one that gets the best response in the test mailing is chosen for the larger mailing.

What will be your responsibility for writing sales letters? If you work in the sales promotion department of a company or in the general field of advertising,

160

you're likely to write many sales letters and other direct-mail pieces. Or if you manage a small business where you have to do a little bit of everything, you'll probably write some sales letters. If you become a sales manager or marketing director, you will have to evaluate the sales letters that others write. Chances are, however, that you won't be handed many sales letter assignments. Even so, you should know something about how sales letters are constructed if only for the reason that the principles apply to all business letters. Besides, it will be fun to evaluate the sales letters you receive.

Preliminary Planning. Before you attempt to write a sales letter, you must be prepared to answer the inevitable questions a prospect will ask: Why should I buy a product like this? Why specifically *your* product? If you don't know everything there is to know about the item you are attempting to sell, you simply can't answer those two questions satisfactorily. Your product may be better-looking, lower-priced, sturdier, simpler and more economical to operate, easier to service, or better-known than that of your competitors. You may think your product is superior in some ways to your competitor's, and you may spend a lot of money researching the differences. You can be sure that the sales department of any successful enterprise can supply ''reams'' of evidence to support your claims of product superiority.

Once you know everything about your product, you must select a particular feature that you want to emphasize in your letter. You can't emphasize them all; most readers won't wade through endless ''puffing,'' no matter how strongly you feel about the merits of your product. Besides, in putting down in a letter every detail about your product, you draw attention from the *principal* points that are most likely to convince your reader he should buy. It's a good idea, then, to select one main feature of your product and pin your sales message on it. This is called the *central theme,* and it will vary according to what you can offer your readers and who your readers are. Generally, you have a special purpose for writing the sales letter (indeed, you may *create* a purpose for the occasion)—a big price reduction, a service never provided before, a special bonus offer, a new feature of an existing product, the introduction of an entirely new product—and you can use that as your central theme.

The kind of audience you are addressing will also have a bearing on your choice of a central theme. If you want to sell a house to young, middle-income couples, you're likely to emphasize economy, play space for children, ease of commuting to work, or quality and nearness of schools. If your list is made up of elderly people, however, your theme is bound to be different—convenient medical facilities or the fact that there is a minimum of walking, for example.

Mailing lists can be purchased from companies that specialize in compiling them; you can find their names in the Yellow Pages in all large cities. And, of course, you will have your own, developed from sales records, responses to advertising, salesmen's reports, business directories, club and association rosters, and so on.

Wherever your list comes from, try to learn as much as you can about your readers so that you can choose the theme for your letter that is most likely to strike a responsive chord. You can't, of course, know precisely the key that will turn on *everybody's* buying mechanism, but you can reduce your chances of being locked out if you know such things about your readers as approximate age, income level, educational achievement, sex, professional status, and general interests. Even if you know only one or two of these things, you can select an appropriate central theme much more intelligently.

A list of members of a local parent-teacher organization will, of course, include people whose interests, income, and assets vary widely, but you can be pretty sure they share one thing in common: the education of their children. Thus, if you're selling encyclopedias to parents, your central theme could logically be the value of your encyclopedias in helping children do better in school. If, however, your list is made up of socially prominent people, your theme is likely to be quite different—the craftsmanship and beauty of the volumes, for example. A letter selling a new typewriter to office managers will probably emphasize speed, economy, or quality (possibly all three). But if your list is made up of executive secretaries, you're more likely to talk about ease of operation ("Don't be all tired-out at the end of the day"), beauty ("You can choose any color to match your office decor"), and/or performance ("Earn praise—and maybe a raise—from your boss").

Once you have selected your central selling theme, based upon a thorough knowledge of your product and as much information as you can get about your audience, you are ready to construct your letter.

Structure of a Sales Letter. Let's admit at the outset that no one knows when he sits down to write a sales letter exactly how it should be put together. Of course, one must have an opinion, but the only way he will really know whether it is the *correct* opinion is when he gets the responses from his readers, in the form of a reply card, a coupon, an order, a letter asking for more information, and so on. If we knew precisely how to write a sales letter that would pull a 100 percent response, then just about everyone would use that letter. We don't know. Given the same product and the same list of prospects, two different people will write entirely different letters. Each of us has his own idea as to what is most likely to "turn on" our readers. Sales letter writing is not an exact science. Most organizations are satisfied if they get a 10 percent return on their sales letters, ecstatic if they can get 20 percent or higher. You have to figure out beforehand the kind of response you are willing to accept in order to justify the expense of the mailing.

Yet there are common elements of all successful sales letters. Common sense tells us that if we want to sell a prospect we must first get his attention. Then we must whet his appetite for the product by building his interest. We convince him that he should have the product. And finally we get him to take favorable action. A sales letter, then, should do four things:

1. Gain the prospect's *attention*.
2. Build the prospect's *interest*.
3. Create a *desire* for the product.
4. Get the prospect to take favorable *action*.

Attracting Attention. The wastebasket is the archenemy of every sales letter writer. His first objective is to catch the reader's eye and cause him to want to read the message rather than toss the letter in the wastebasket. You can attract attention in various ways. The color and shape of the stationery itself can be an attention-getter. A coin, stamp, miniature art reproduction, swatch of fabric, gift certificate, facsimile check, film negative, plastic miniature musical instrument, mirror, key, pencil, dice, and so on—affixed to the letter— can be attention-getters. Admittedly, they are gimmicks. They attract attention only because people hate to throw anything away that looks the least bit valuable. But you have to accept the possibility that your readers will associate such razzle-dazzle devices with the hard-sell, and you must decide whether it's worth the risk.

Above all, an attention-getting opening must be believable. Don't try to trick your reader with such an absurd statement as:

> CONGRATULATIONS! You've just won $5,000!
> Wouldn't you like to have someone tell you that?
> Well, we can't promise that you will win $5,000, but . . .

Many different types of openings may be used to attract the attention of your reader; we will mention only a few.

A SPECIAL OFFER

TWO FULL WEEKS TO ENJOY
   THE BEST OF IOWA'S DAILY NEWSPAPERS
      WITH OUR COMPLIMENTS

You'll save $26.50 if you order
Art Treasures of the Ancient World
before December 1 . . .

WITHOUT ONE CENT OF COST TO YOU
We will mail you one of these
SPECIAL 7" BLACK FOREST CLOCKS
Direct from Rotterdam, Holland

A QUOTATION OR AN ANECDOTE

Somebody once said, "The Greeks had a word for it," and I'm just beginning to understand what he meant.

May I borrow from an unknown author who wrote, "Though I have a thousand friends, I have not one to spare."

I WAS SITTING IN OUR SHOWROOM . . .
. . . the other morning when BANG, a firecracker exploded, a big puff of pink smoke appeared, and there stood a fellow with a rabbit in his hand.

It was Tuesday, May 12, when John and Sarah Beadling first came to see me. I remember it because it was a fateful day for me—and, as it turned out, for them.

A PROVOCATIVE STATEMENT OR QUESTION

Blackboards should be seen and not heard.

Did you ever split an axiom?

There is an "underground" in this country of about 20,000 men who use neither a safety razor nor an electric shaver. Yet they're the cleanest-shaven men in America.

Have you heard your baby cry since you left the hospital?

May we stick our nose in your business?

You are one in 60,000!

Let's look at a letter from a large investment firm, the purpose of which is to induce readers to send for a free booklet and eventually to buy their investment services from Breen.

Length of Sales Letters. Throughout this book we've emphasized keeping your communications as brief as you can without risking confusion and mis-understanding. That advice does not necessarily hold for sales letters. Some of the most successful sales letters written today run from four to six pages in length. Although we may argue that most people won't read such long messages, the companies that use them have discovered, through various tests, that they pull better for them than briefer letters. No doubt, readers take the position that if it takes six or eight pages to extol the many virtues of a product, it must be worth investigating—whether or not they actually read all those pages!

The Breen letter was processed—that is, duplicated rather than individually typed. Generally, you can afford to type individual sales letters—even by means of automatic typewriters—only when your list is small and the chances of getting a good return are very good.

When your mailing list is large, you also will usually find it too costly to insert the reader's name and address and a salutation (to say nothing of the problem of matching the typewriter type with the printed message). Many writers like to "fake" an inside address by means of a short message like this:

We pay the shipping costs
on any order
anywhere
Yes, we're so certain that you . . .

Breen & Company

Incorporated

Members
Central Stock Exchange

As an Investor . . .

Do you remember when ABC was selling for $120 a share . . . back in 1968?
Since then the stock has split 4 times. And an original $120 invested is
now worth about $1,000.

Or how about Zero, whose stock has split 15 for 1 since 1968, giving its
shareholders a profit of 50 times their original investment in 10 years?

Why have companies like ABC and Zero been so profitable for investors?
Because our rapidly changing world demands a new technology to solve
problems faster and more efficiently, and companies like ABC and Zero,
which provide industry with these new products and services, are riding
the crest of what can only be described as a technological revolution.

We're not trying to imply that an investor buying these stocks today
would realize similar results in the future.

The main point of this letter is this . . . Would you like to know more
about the technological changes that professional investors are watching
so closely today . . . the changes they feel will cause the greatest
impact in the years ahead?

If you would, just mail the enclosed card and we will send you a copy of
our new study The Technological Revolution. We think it is required
reading for any investor who wants to make his capital grow.

Very sincerely yours,

Leland Russell
Investment Counselor

Preparing the "Under-40 Presidents" Letter. We come now to the
preparation of the sales letter to the Under-40 Presidents Association. Before
you begin to structure the letter, you must first decide what you expect your
reader to do. Is he to request a free booklet? supply information about himself?
send a check? invite a salesman to call? In other words, you must decide what
action you want the reader to take so that, in your sales message, you can

lead up to it effectively. Let's assume that we are going to ask him to send for a free booklet, *Pickwick Plans a Meeting*.

In our letter to the Under-40 Presidents Association, what will be our central theme? How will we open? What ways will we choose to develop interest, build desire, and induce action? Before we try to answer these questions, let's try to determine what the members of the association are like. We know they are relatively young, reasonably affluent, probably physically active, dynamic, and aggressive. Probably, too, they are good businessmen and women, cost-conscious, eager to get their dollar's worth in behalf of their companies.

The purpose of our letter is to induce these young presidents to select Pickwick Manor as the headquarters for their various away-from-home meetings and conferences. In selecting a central theme, we have several choices: luxuriousness of the accommodations, beauty of the surroundings, warm climate, superb cuisine, big-name entertainers, convenience to air transportation, complete sports and recreational programs, outstanding facilities for meetings, friendly atmosphere, fast and courteous service, and so forth. All of these things are important, but if you were to select one of them as a theme, which would you choose? We would guess that these men and women would be interested, most of all, in making the most productive use of their time at a conference. Conferences away from home can be very expensive, and although most of them allow time for relaxation and fun, their main purpose is to transact business. We think the members of the Under-40 Presidents Association will insist on a place that can provide the facilities and services required for a productive conference. Certainly, such facilities will include some for fun and relaxation, but they become incidental to the primary purpose of the meeting. Our theme, then, would be the competence of Pickwick Manor to put on the best meeting possible in terms of facilities and services.

How would you open such a letter to attract the attention of your readers? Following are some ideas.

"Thank you—

for helping us put on the best conference we have ever had. Your superb facilities, the service, the know-how and helpful attitude of your staff—all add up to one word: Professionalism."

Pardon us for crowing just a bit, but the above message was received a few days ago from the vice president of one of . . . .

KNOW-HOW

That simple word is the difference between an outstanding company meeting and a merely passable one. That difference is Pickwick Manor. We know how.

18 spacious, carpeted meeting rooms, each seating 25+ people; 2 large auditoriums, 1 seating 150 and the other 350 people; 3 special banquet rooms accommodating from 160 to 300 guests; 1,200 guest rooms, each sleeping two comfortably . . . .

These are only a few of the <u>physical</u> facilities Pickwick Manor can offer you for your company meetings. You see, PM was designed expressly to handle meetings and conferences . . . .

Let's take the opening used in the first example and develop the theme.

SOLUTION

"Thank you—

for helping us put on the best conference we have ever had. Your superb facilities, the service, the know-how and helpful attitude of your staff—all add up to one word: Professionalism."

Pardon us for crowing just a bit, but the above message was received a few days ago from the vice president of one of the country's largest manufacturing firms. And it's typical of many we get from top executives who choose Pickwick Manor as their host for a meeting, conference, seminar, or convention.

At Pickwick Manor we know how to help you make your meetings really successful. It's what we were designed to do, what we're still in business for, the reason we're beginning to be known as "convention host to the nation." Pickwick Manor is not just another magnificent resort center that offers everything any famous resort hotel boasts about (all sports, including a challenging 9-hole par-36 golf course; a private beach plus two giant freshwater pools; outstanding cuisine; big-name entertainers; a climate that practically guarantees year-round "sun fun"; elegant shopping malls; horse racing; deep-sea fishing—you name it). We're all those things, of course, but we are more. We're professionals when it comes to arranging space for your specific needs and providing every personal service you require to make it the best meeting you have ever had. You'll find that we know what you expect to get from your meetings and conferences, and our entire staff is dedicated to seeing that you get it.

Skeptical? Do you think I may be promising more than we can deliver? Let me prove what I have been saying about our expertise in hosting successful meetings. First, look over the enclosed folder which tells something of our size and the beauty of our accommodations. Then, to learn more about our professional side—the <u>heart</u> of Pickwick Manor—mail the card for your free copy of <u>Pickwick Plans a Meeting</u>. This is all you'll have to do.

Sincerely yours,

Analysis of the Solution. As you can see, the central theme is ''getting the most from your meeting dollar,' '' and that idea is a running thread throughout the letter. Attention is obtained by the testimonial excerpt. Interest is achieved by expanding on the excerpt and the idea that such letters are almost routine. We build desire by emphasizing that although Pickwick is a great resort hotel—with all the facilities anyone would need or want—it is a *professional* host to convention- and meeting-goers. We try to convince the reader that we know what he expects from his meetings and conferences and we will go all-out to deliver. The final paragraph induces action, inviting the reader to make Pickwick Manor prove its claims.

We cannot say that the above will be an enormously successful letter, only that it has the ingredients. Assume that the letter costs about 50 cents to put in the mail; that's about $760. If you receive a 10 percent response (152) and 10 percent of them (15) eventually patronize Pickwick Manor at an average expenditure of $5,000 (a modest figure for most meetings), you've produced sales amounting to $75,000. Almost any businessman is happy to spend $760 for $75,000 worth of business!

■ ■

PROJECTS

A The Southern States Kindergarten Teachers Association is holding its annual meeting at the Pompano Beach Civic Auditorium from August 11 to 14. You have obtained a membership roster of this group and plan to write a sales letter to the members encouraging them to stay at Pickwick Manor during the convention. Your special summer rates are in effect. Plan and write the letter.

B A new organization, the American Association of Administrative Assistants, has just been formed. It is made up principally of women who are essentially executive secretaries but have earned executive rank. Write a letter to the new president, Miss Jennifer Webster, inviting the group to consider Pickwick Manor as a place for their annual meetings. Assume that you can use this same letter for other similar groups.

■ ■

part

7

ADMINISTRATIVE AND
PR COMMUNICATIONS

You are assistant to the president of Peerless Publishing Company, Paul J. Weinberger. The company, located in Des Moines, Iowa, publishes professional and reference books, encyclopedias, trade books (fiction and biography, for example), textbooks for schools and colleges, and so on. You handle much of the correspondence addressed to Mr. Weinberger, preparing some letters for his signature and others for your own.

CASE 1

RESPONDING TO AN INVITATION TO THE EXECUTIVE

PROBLEM: Mr. Weinberger has received information that a small trade publisher in Orlando, Florida, is interested in selling his business to a major publishing house. Mr. Weinberger is eager to acquire this company because of its distinguished religious-books list, an area Peerless has long been interested in. He telephoned the Orlando publisher, who invited him to come to Florida to discuss terms. While Mr. Weinberger is away, you are handling his mail and now have the following letter from an executive in a large Chicago printing firm which manufactures books for many major publishers.

> Dear Paul:
>
> Would you be willing to act as chairman of the panel "The Publisher Speaks" at the National Book Manufacturers Association conference? As you know, this one-day conference is being held in Dayton on April 16; the panel is scheduled for 2:30 to 3:30.
>
> You are the ideal man to do this job for us. You have spoken very frankly and sensibly about the publisher's own responsibilities for good bookmaking, and I know most of our members would turn out for a panel discussion of this subject if you are the chairman. For the other panel members, I think we should have a manufacturer or two, a production manager, an editor, and possibly a marketing person. But you would decide what panel makeup would be best and the people you would like to work with.
>
> As soon as you accept this invitation, Paul, I will supply more details. Please say that you can find time to be with us.
>
> Sincerely,

BACKGROUND

The principal function of an "assistant to" is to relieve a top executive of certain daily responsibilities. The assistant-to answers routine letters, sees visitors to the office and screens out those whom the executive shouldn't take the time to see, arranges and reports on meetings, and so on. The little word *to* in the title has a special meaning. An assistant general manager has direct responsibility for people, performance, and profits; but an assistant *to* a general manager usually has none of these responsibilities. He is the manager's eyes, ears, and right arm and speaks not so much for himself as for the executive for whom he works.

The man or woman who is assistant-to often walks a tightrope. Although he can make certain decisions for his boss, it is not always clear *which* decision it is safe for him to make. Thus he has the task of doing everything he can to relieve the executive of detail without appearing to usurp the executive's authority. And he must always be discreet, always be on guard against revealing confidential information, always careful not to put the executive in an embarrassing position.

SOLUTION A

Dear Mr. Wolff:

Mr. Weinberger is in Orlando, Florida, talking with the Bennington Press people about a possible merger. He will return on February 16.

Although I cannot assure you that Mr. Weinberger will be able to accept your invitation to chair a panel at the NBMA conference, his calendar seems to be relatively uncluttered in mid-April, and I expect that he will be delighted to participate.

Very truly yours,

Analysis of Solution A. You will agree immediately that Solution A is unacceptable.

1. It reveals information that should be kept confidential. When the boss is away, it is wise to simply tell outsiders he is away from the office, revealing nothing about where he is or what he is doing. Even though Mr. Weinberger and Mr. Wolff are friends, Mr. Wolff may have an even closer friend in another publishing house who would like to know about the Peerless negotiations with Bennington Press.

2. The writer practically commits Mr. Weinberger to accepting an invitation which, for any number of reasons, he may not be able to accept. Of course, we would have to know more about this particular situation before we could say definitely that the writer is in error. As a general rule, however, the executive himself should make a decision of this nature.

SOLUTION B

Dear Mr. Wolff:

Mr. Weinberger is away from the office for about ten days. He will, I am sure, let you know about chairing the panel at the NBMA conference at his first opportunity. In fact, I will be in touch with him by telephone late this week, and I will see if I can get an answer for you then.

                                        Sincerely yours,

Analysis of Solution B. Solution B is much more effective than Solution A. Solution B reveals no confidential information nor does it commit Mr. Weinberger to a speaking assignment or put him in a situation that would be hard to get out of. The writer, however, shows a can-do attitude, going the extra distance to be helpful.

■ ■

PROJECTS

A During your telephone conversation with Mr. Weinberger, he asked you to write to Mr. Wolff accepting the panel assignment at the April 16 conference of the National Book Manufacturers Association in Dayton (Case 1). Prepare the letter for your signature.

B The following is among the letters received in Mr. Weinberger's absence.

Dear Mr. Weinberger:

The Sioux City Uptown Association cordially invites you to be the luncheon speaker at our April 16 meeting.

The SCUA is a group whose aim is to promote the commercial and civic advantages of this community. Although our principal objective is to boost Sioux City, we also engage in a number of philanthropic activities in the community.

As head of a national publishing house located in Iowa, you would be an ideal speaker on the topic "Iowa Industry." We have featured this theme at this year's meetings because presidents of nationally known Iowa firms will talk about the advantages of having their headquarters in Iowa.

We would be happy to pay all of your expenses in addition to an honorarium of $100.

                                        Cordially yours,

Obviously, there is a conflict—Mr. Weinberger has already accepted an invitation to appear on the book manufacturers' panel in Dayton on April 16. You happen to know, however, that Mr. Weinberger likes to accept such invitations as the one from the Sioux City Uptown Association and that if a later date could be arranged, he would undoubtedly want to accommodate this group. Write an appropriate response for your signature.

C   Following is another letter that arrived in Mr. Weinberger's absence (he is still in Florida for discussions with Bennington Press).

Dear Sir:

We would like you to appear on a panel at our Spring Career Conference on March 24 at Maryville High School. This city-wide conference is held each year to acquaint high school students with career opportunities in various fields. Publishing is an area in which many of our students are interested.

Will you accept?

Very truly yours,

Although Mr. Weinberger feels that Peerless should participate in as many such conferences as possible, he obviously cannot appear personally on all the programs to which he is invited. You are quite sure that he will decline this invitation but will recommend the Missouri sales representative, Arnold Lorenz, for the assignment. Mr. Lorenz has participated successfully in several similar conferences. Respond to the invitation for your own signature.

D   Comment on the following response to an invitation to Mr. Weinberger, and then write one—for your own signature—that you feel is more appropriate.

Dear Miss Phineas:

Your letter to Mr. Weinberger arrived while he is on a business trip to Florida.

As Mr. Weinberger's assistant, I must decline in his behalf your invitation for him to be a judge in the annual Mt. Tabor Mystery Writers Contest. Mr. Weinberger does not have time to participate in events of this nature. As president of Peerless Publishing Company, he is a very busy man; every week he receives dozens of letters inviting him to do this or that, and he must turn down most of them.

I am sure you understand the position Mr. Weinberger must take on such matters. Thank you, however, for writing.

Very sincerely yours,

■ ■

CASE 2
USING DISCRETION IN EXECUTIVE CORRESPONDENCE

PROBLEM: Peerless is considering establishing a branch office which will include a book distribution center in the south Atlantic area. Executives are studying the advantages of each proposed site—Atlanta, Charlotte, Jacksonville, and Charleston—and the availability of suitable office and other facilities.

Until they have reached a decision, the subject is not to be discussed openly, particularly with people outside the company.

While Mr. Weinberger is out of the office, the following telegram arrives:

> Have ideal warehouse and office space for south Atlantic branch in Brunswick, Georgia. Available immediately. Low, low price. Several prospective buyers, so you must act quickly. Prefer Peerless.
>
> S. K. Vandergrift

As assistant to the president, you are to respond to the telegram.

BACKGROUND

When the boss is to be away for any length of time, it is generally understood that all important mail will be taken care of in his absence. If there are important decisions that only he can make, the mail is at least acknowledged and the writer told approximately when he can expect to receive an answer.

The assistant-to must make decisions about responding to incoming letters. Some of the correspondence will be urgent enough to trigger a telephone call or a telegram to the boss, some will be handled directly by the assistant-to, and some will be referred to others to handle.

Unless he has specific instructions, the assistant-to must exercise his own judgment, making sure that nothing important is left up in the air. Failure to keep on top of things while the executive is away can be very costly in sales and public relations.

Some executives want to keep in constant touch with the goings-on back home, especially when their trips keep them away for several weeks. They may leave instructions with the assistant-to to send them a daily log of events as well as copies or digests (extracts of important points and the action taken) of important letters. Here are a few items that such a log might include.

February 10

1. Telegram from Holyoke Printers about quantity on reprint of This Is Peerless brochure. Checked with Mrs. Norris and confirmed 120M. Wire sent.

2. Memo from Mr. Granville asking for preliminary estimate of administrative personnel needs for next year; he needs it this week for space planning. Have sent your preliminary draft, explaining you would bring it up to date when you return.

3. Letter from Crofton Office Supplies, Inc., reminding us that our rental agreement expires 4/1. They sent new contract for your signature. Wrote that you would communicate with them in March.

4. Telephone call from Mr. Abel (Gaslight Restaurant) about menu selection for April meeting of Franklin Book Group. I specified lobster as main course. OK? Also arranged for Davy Jones Room, microphone, raised dais, and photographer.

5. Proposal from Mid-America Advertising Agency saying how they would handle our advertising if they had the account. Acknowledged.

6. Miss Crowley's retirement luncheon to be held the 20th. Mr. Jacobs will present a cassette tape recorder and several operas on tape. Have drafted letter of congratulation from you (attached); they're putting all letters in a morocco-bound portfolio.

In the case problem, the writer must decide whether he will respond to the telegram for his own signature or for Mr. Weinberger's. Here we will assume that he will write for himself.

SOLUTION A

Dear Mr. Vandergrift:

Your telegram arrived while Mr. Weinberger is in Orlando, Florida. He will return on February 16.

Although Peerless is considering establishing a branch office (including a book distribution center) in the south Atlantic area, there has been no mention of Brunswick, Georgia, as a possible site. Locations being considered are Charlotte, Atlanta, Jacksonville, and Charleston. However, I will let Mr. Weinberger know about your proposal at the first opportunity.

Cordially yours,

Analysis of Solution A. You have already spotted the glaring mistake the writer made: he has revealed information that should not be revealed. Mr. Vandergrift should not be told where Mr. Weinberger is, and he is not entitled to know the locations Peerless is studying as possible branch office sites.

SOLUTION B

Dear Mr. Vandergrift:

Thank you for your telegram about the availability of your building in Brunswick, Georgia.

Mr. Weinberger is on a business trip until the middle of the month, but I shall let him know about your proposal when I next communicate with him. In any event, you may be sure that Mr. Weinberger will respond at the first opportunity.

Sincerely yours,

Analysis of Solution B. Solution B requires no comment. Although the tone is courteous and the writer offers help, the letter reveals no confidential information.

■■■■■■■■■■■■■■■■■■■■■■■■■■■■■■■■■■■■■■■

PROJECTS

A   The following letter, addressed to The President, Peerless Publishing Company, arrived during Mr. Weinberger's absence.

Dear Sir:

Through a business associate in France I have learned that Peerless Publishing Company is negotiating with Bouchard Press, in Paris, for the purpose of purchasing this French publisher.

I am acquainted with all the major publishing houses in Europe, and I consider Bouchard one of the weakest. Although this house has built a good reputation over the years, it has slipped badly during the past two years. I can bring to your attention a number of much better publishing firms that it would be to your advantage to investigate.

You may wish to have me come to Des Moines around the 15th to talk with you regarding this matter since I plan to be in the United States in May. May I hear from you—before you make any further moves.

                                        Yours very truly,

It is true that Mr. Weinberger and others in Peerless have discussed a possible merger with the Bouchard people, but they have made no decision. Respond to the above letter (it is signed by Charles Lecquex).

B   Refer to the daily log illustrated on pages 174–175 and prepare the communications required in items 1, 2, 3, and 5.

C   The consulting firm of Ferris and Borichaud, employed to design a new corporate symbol ("logo") for Peerless, has sent a rough sketch to Mr. Weinberger for his comments. Since Mr. Weinberger will be out of the office for another two weeks, you decide to make a photocopy of the sketch for your records and send the original on to him since the matter is of some urgency.

You strongly dislike the symbol that Ferris and Borichaud has come up with, and you are convinced that Mr. Weinberger will not approve it. Acknowledge the materials in Mr. Weinberger's absence.

D   While Mr. Weinberger is away, Miss Sigrid Untermeyer writes to complain about the paucity of advertising and promotion of her new book, *A Fool's Folly,* which Peerless recently published. Miss Untermeyer, an important new author who left her previous publisher to publish with Peerless, requests an appointment "right away" to discuss the matter.

You decided to telephone Earl Bamberger, manager of the department that published Miss Untermeyer's book, and he told you that she had been in to see him several times about this matter. Although he tried to pacify her by showing her the extensive advertising and promotion that has been done, she left him, saying, "I'll write to Mr. Weinberger about this."

Acknowledge the letter from Miss Untermeyer.

■■■■■■■■■■■■■■■■■■■■■■■■■■■■■■■■■■■■■■■

CASE 3 — REFERRING A LETTER TO ANOTHER PERSON TO ANSWER

PROBLEM: Here is a letter in the morning mail from Julio Gomez, a principal manufacturer for Peerless, that must be acknowledged in Mr. Weinberger's absence.

> Dear Mr. Weinberger:
>
> Have you reached a decision about the new shipping carton Frank Newhouse and I left with you on January 11? Our supply of the cartons you are now using is getting low, but before we put an order into our factory for an additional quantity, I want to make sure that you plan to continue to use it.
>
> Please let me know by February 14; I need to give our factory superintendent the decision within a couple of weeks.
>
> Cordially yours,

You know that when the new shipping carton was left with Mr. Weinberger, he said he thought it was fine but that approval would have to come from Leo Currie, manager of the Shipping Department. Mr. Currie would have to compare costs, see whether the size is appropriate for the various books Peerless publishes, and so on.

This situation calls for two communications: an acknowledgment of the letter from Mr. Gomez and a memo to Mr. Currie.

BACKGROUND

A letter acknowledging correspondence that must be referred to another person within the company is prompt and courteous. It should not, however, commit the person who is to handle the matter to a specific course of action or time limit. Above all, it should not contain direct or implied criticism of a fellow employee.

It's a good idea to telephone in advance the individual to whom a letter is being referred so that he will know it's coming and can begin immediately to gather the information he will need in order to respond.

SOLUTION A: Letter to Mr. Gomez

> Dear Mr. Gomez:
>
> Mr. Weinberger is out of the office this week, and I am handling his routine correspondence in his absence.
>
> I am sorry you have not had an answer before this time to your question about the new shipping carton. Mr. Weinberger approved it at least two

weeks ago and asked our Shipping Department manager, Leo Currie, to follow up with you. I am surprised that this matter was not settled.

You may be sure, Mr. Gomez, that you will have a decision from us this week. Mr. Currie is attending to the matter at my instructions.

Yours very truly,

SOLUTION A: Memo to Mr. Currie

TO: Leo P. Currie   FROM: Ralph G. McClain
SUBJECT: New Shipping Carton   DATE: February 11, 19—

Will you please attend to the enclosed letter right away. Apparently there was some kind of slipup. Note that the matter is somewhat urgent.

Analysis of Solution A. The letter to Mr. Gomez is faulty in several respects.

1. Although the statement, ''Mr. Weinberger is out of the office this week,'' is entirely appropriate, referring to Mr. Gomez's letter as ''routine correspondence'' is very tactless. Beware of attaching labels, even though in your own mind they may be accurate.
2. The second paragraph implies some infighting in Peerless; the writer expresses open annoyance with a fellow employee for not doing what he was supposed to do. Although he may be put out with Mr. Currie about his shortcomings, he should not express his feelings to an outsider. Mr. Currie will feel degraded, the writer will have made an enemy, and Mr. Gomez's problem will still be unsolved.
3. The statement, ''Mr. Currie is attending to the matter at my instructions,'' is officious. Flaunting authority, even when you have it, is in very poor taste.

The memorandum to Mr. Currie will further annoy him and widen the human relations gap. It is abrupt and officious in tone.

SOLUTION B: Letter to Mr. Gomez

Dear Mr. Gomez:

Mr. Weinberger is not in the office this week, and I want to give you some assurance about the new shipping carton you wrote about.

I talked this morning with Leo Currie, our Shipping Department manager, who is doing some research on the new carton. He told me he plans to write you this week. I know that some of the information he requested from the various publishing departments about the size of the carton was late getting to him because a number of people have been out of the office.

Cordially yours,

SOLUTION B: Memo to Mr. Currie

TO: Leo P. Currie   FROM: Ralph G. McClain

SUBJECT: New Shipping Carton   DATE: February 11, 19—

Here is a copy of the letter from Mr. Gomez that I spoke to you about this morning, along with my reply. Let me know if I need to do anything further on this.

Analysis of Solution B. The Solution B letter to Mr. Gomez is appropriate. The writer did what he should have done—telephoned Mr. Currie for up-to-date information before attempting to answer the letter. And rather than condemning Mr. Currie, the writer explained the delay in a way that takes Mr. Currie off the hook.

The memo is excellent for the purpose. The tone is businesslike but not officious, and the writer offers to cooperate if he is needed for anything else.

■ ■

PROJECTS

A   The following letter, along with a manuscript, arrives while Mr. Weinberger is away.

Dear Sir:

I am sending you a collection of poems that I wrote in memory of my mother. Many people who have seen these poems, including a professor of English at Pythagoras College, have told me they ought to be published. I think Peerless would be a good publisher.

Please tell me how much I will be paid. I would also like a $3,500 cash advance. Please acknowledge this manuscript (it is the only copy I have), and let me know when you will publish my poems. I am thinking of the title "A Girl and Her Mother." What is your opinion?

Yours truly,

Several things about the letter concern you. The most important is that the author sent the only existing copy of her manuscript—a dangerous thing to do because manuscripts are sometimes lost in the mails or in the files of publishers. Also, you happen to know that Peerless does not publish poetry (except for the works of a few nationally known poets). In fact, there is very little market for poetry.

If Peerless were interested in this author's manuscript, which is highly unlikely, the Trade Department (Earl Bamberger is manager) would publish it. Write the response (the letter is signed by Myrtle Parsons) and any additional communications that may be required.

B   Dale R. Badham, a graduate student at Forseti University, has written to Mr. Weinberger, requesting an interview. He is preparing a thesis on "The Economics of the Publishing Industry'' and wants to get Mr. Weinberger's view of the subject.

Mr. Weinberger is often asked to participate in studies of this nature, and when he can find the time, he accepts. When he is especially busy, however, he refers the requests to John W. Zeigler, vice president for manufacturing of Peerless. You feel that he will want to have Mr. Badham talk to Mr. Zeigler. Write the appropriate communications.

C   Mrs. Sadie Warren, an important stockholder in Peerless Publishing Company, has written Mr. Weinberger about a biography she is having prepared about her father, R. D. VanSant, who was a pioneer in bridge construction. In her letter, Mrs. Warren states that she knows such a biography will not sell enough copies to justify its publication but expresses her willingness to subsidize the cost—that is, she will pay for all editorial, manufacturing, and promotion costs. She does, however, want the Peerless "imprint" on the book.

You do not know what Mr. Weinberger's reaction will be to such a proposal (Peerless does very little of this type of subsidized publishing). In any event, the matter would come under the jurisdiction of Miss Charlotte Reichard, assistant manager of the Trade Department. Prepare the appropriate communications.

■■■■■■■■■■■■■■■■■■■■■■■■■■■■■■■■■■■■■■

CASE 4   WRITING AND SIGNING FOR THE EXECUTIVE

PROBLEM: Before Mr. Weinberger left on his trip, he said to you, "Write to Professor Peter Himmel at the University of Houston, asking him if he would be willing to act as one of our consultants on the new ecology series. Since I know Professor Himmel pretty well, probably you ought to prepare the letter for my signature and sign it for me."

You know that the consultants on the ecology series usually receive a royalty of one-fourth of 1 percent on each book sold. You also know that Professor Himmel is one of several distinguished professors being asked to serve as consultants. Your search of files shows that there has been previous correspondence with Professor Himmel and that he and Mr. Weinberger are on a first-name basis.

BACKGROUND

The assistant-to often writes communications that he signs with his boss's signature. Therefore, he quickly learns to make his letters sound as though the executive wrote them. To do this, he must know how the boss reacts to situations, his style of expression (which can be learned by studying samples of his writing), and his relationship with his correspondents. The most important of these, of course, is the executive's relationship with his correspondents, for it determines the tone of the letters.

Writing *in behalf* of the boss is not the same as writing *for* him. Note that in the first example below, the assistant is signing the letter although it is written in behalf of the executive.

Dear Mr. Frantz:

Before Mr. Caine left for Amarillo this morning, he asked me to find out whether you have completed the tests you are making on tire mileage. He especially wanted to know how Super-Ms compared with the competing brands and whether you are planning further tests.

Mr. Caine spoke enthusiastically about his trip to El Paso. He was especially impressed with the new warehouse.

Cordially yours,

Now notice how different the tone is when the assistant writes about the same situation in the name of the executive and for his signature.

Dear Charlie:

When I was in El Paso, I forgot to ask you about the results of that tire mileage test you are making. How did our Super-Ms stand up against the competition? Are you planning more tests, or do you feel that you have all the evidence you need?

It was great being with you last week. Your new warehouse looks like a winner, and I hope we can automate the Duluth and Richmond warehouses to the same extent. With nothing to do but punch buttons, you're obviously planning to get in a lot of golf from now on.

Cordially,

SOLUTION A

Dear Peter:

Would you be willing to serve as a consultant on the new ecology series we are planning? We would be willing to pay you one-fourth of 1 percent royalty on each copy of the books that we sell.

I would appreciate your prompt reply.

Sincerely yours,

Analysis of Solution A. Solution A is not an effective letter for the purpose.

1. The writer knows that Mr. Weinberger and Professor Himmel are on a first-name basis and have corresponded before, but the tone of the letter gives no evidence that they have ever met.
2. The letter is so lacking in necessary details that Professor Himmel will undoubtedly have to respond by asking for more information.

3. If Professor Himmel is worthy of being asked to serve in a consulting capacity, something should have been said about why he was chosen.
4. The mention of money is too abrupt. Although Professor Himmel would be interested in the financial aspects of the assignment, he will want to know more about the series that is being planned, the names of others who are being considered as consultants, and other details.

SOLUTION B

Dear Peter:

When I talked with you at the American Geographical Society convention in Denver last November, I mentioned that we were thinking about publishing a new series of books for the ecology curriculum in colleges and universities. Since we have decided to go ahead with this series, we are now ready to engage several consultants to assist us in planning the materials, selecting the authors, and producing the books.

Naturally, you are one of the first people I thought of as those of us here talked about this project. Would you be willing to serve as a member of our consulting board? You're our first choice because I believe that once I have your acceptance, I'll have no difficulty in getting other distinguished scientists to join the board.

We are offering one-fourth of 1 percent royalty to each consultant on all the materials developed and sold in this series. If our projections hold up, you should receive from $2,500 to $4,000 a year for the life of the series.

Let me have your reactions, Peter. We are thinking about inviting Professor J. R. Hamm, of Stanford, and Professor A. N. Matisse, of Duke, to act as consultants, but we will await your decision because we want your suggestions. At the moment, we're planning to have eight books in the series (each accompanied by laboratory manuals, films, slides, and so forth), but we can talk about this later.

Cordially,

Analysis of Solution B. Solution B is an effective letter for these reasons:
1. The writer provides background information (previous conversation about the ecology series) so that Professor Himmel can quickly understand the purpose of the letter.
2. The writer acknowledges Professor Himmel as a distinguished scholar and indicates that is why he is inviting him to serve as a consultant.
3. The financial arrangements are explicit. (By mentioning them after issuing the invitation, the writer implies that Professor Himmel is more interested in educational leadership than in money. He may actually be more interested in the money, but it is better not to imply it.)
4. The tone of the letter, although professional, is friendly and personal.
5. The writer does not try to cover everything in one letter. He mentions decisions that can be deferred as points of reference only.

■ ■

PROJECT

Refer to the following projects and prepare responses for Mr. Weinberger's signature rather than your own:

1   Project B, page 172.

2   Project A, page 176. Assume that Mr. Weinberger will be willing to see Mr. Lecquex when he comes to the United States but has no particular enthusiasm for a meeting.

3   Project C, page 180. Assume that Mr. Weinberger feels that Mrs. Warren's biography of her father is not suitable for Peerless. A small publisher, Bo-Peep Press, specializes in this type of publishing and would be a much better house for Mrs. Warren's book. Mr. Weinberger has telephoned the president, Clifton Bergstrand, and he would be pleased to hear from Mrs. Warren about the book.

■ ■

CASE 5   TURNING DOWN AN APPLICATION FOR EMPLOYMENT

PROBLEM: For several weeks Mr. Weinberger has been looking for a person to represent Peerless Publishing Company in Washington, D.C. This representative, who would be called "assistant to the president for Washington affairs," would have the responsibility for keeping in touch with important federal agencies, with the activities in Congress as they relate to budget appropriations for education, with the U.S. Copyright Office, trade associations, and with VIPs in general. The job calls for someone with heavy experience in publicity and public relations, in education, and in publishing. Although the position has not been advertised (Mr. Weinberger is leaning toward selecting a person from within the company rather than going outside), word has gotten around and several applications have been received. Following is one of them.

Dear Mr. Weinberger:

I understand that you are looking for a man to represent Peerless Publishing Company in Washington, and I would like to make application for the position.

For 12 years I have been a free-lance journalist in Washington and have had my articles published by several of the country's leading newspapers. I have also sold material to Life, Esquire, Business Week, Reader's Digest, and many other magazines. Naturally, with my 12 years' experience, I have become acquainted with most of the "shakers and movers" on the Washington scene, and I am convinced that I can make this experience pay off handsomely for Peerless.

Details are given in the enclosed résumé. May I come to Des Moines to talk with you? You can reach me at (202) 966-4343.

Sincerely yours,

Donald McNair

Mr. Weinberger, as mentioned, is responding directly to inquiries about the position in Washington. He is not impressed with the applicant whose letter appears above. The applicant is essentially a journalist, and he lacks the necessary experience in book publishing and education.

What response would be appropriate? Should Mr. Weinberger (or you, who must write the letter) tell the applicant about his shortcomings? Or should the response be simply "No," without giving reasons?

BACKGROUND

Company presidents receive many letters from people who believe they can get special attention and faster action by going straight to the top. Most executives acknowledge all mail addressed to them, but they often pass correspondence along to someone else in the company to handle. They generally refer applications for employment, particularly for other than top executive posts, to the personnel department, but the practice varies. If an executive refers the letter to someone, he usually simply expresses appreciation for the application and mentions that he is referring it to someone else; he does not offer an opinion about the applicant's qualifications or his chances of getting a position. For example:

Dear Mr. Platt:

Thank you for your interest in a position as accountant with our firm.

I am forwarding your letter to Mrs. Gretchen Simms, our personnel placement specialist for accounting and data processing positions. You should hear from Mrs. Simms shortly.

Sincerely yours,

SOLUTION A

Dear Mr. McNair:

This will acknowledge your letter in which you apply for a position as our Washington representative.

I am sorry that we cannot consider you for this position, but I appreciate your interest.

Very truly yours,

Analysis of Solution A. Solution A, as you have observed, is a tactless and rude letter. Mr. McNair might be left with the impression that his character is in question. A flat turndown like this is unnecessary.

SOLUTION B

Dear Mr. McNair:

Thank you for your interest in representing Peerless in Washington.

We are considering a number of applicants for this position, Mr. McNair, and certainly are glad to have your résumé in our hands. If we require additional information or think it would be to our mutual advantage to meet with you personally, you will hear from me or one of my associates by April 12.

Sincerely yours,

Analysis of Solution B. Solution B says no without bluntness or insult. Yet the writer has not played with the truth—everything he says is accurate. At the same time, Mr. McNair will notice that he has been given no encouragement—and he probably will not expect to hear again from Peerless.

SOLUTION C

Dear Mr. McNair:

Thank you for applying for the positon as our representative in Washington.

The person hired for this job must have a great deal more experience in book publishing and in education than you have. Therefore, we consider you unqualified.

Your letter and résumé are enclosed.

Very truly yours,

Analysis of Solution C. This solution, although honest, is too blunt. The use of the term *unqualified* is totally unnecessary, and the return of the letter and résumé is insulting.

SOLUTION D

Dear Mr. McNair:

Thank you for applying for a job as a Peerless representative.

For this position, Mr. McNair, we are searching for a person with heavy experience in book publishing and in education. Although your qualifications in publicity and public relations are superb, we think your experience is light in these other important areas.

However, we certainly will give consideration to your application, along with the many others we have received. You may expect to hear from me by May 1 if we feel that there is an opportunity here for you.

Sincerely yours,

Analysis of Solution D. Solution D is the most effective because it tells the applicant that he lacks the desired qualifications without insulting him in the process. The final paragraph implies a ''no,'' but that unpleasant and harsh word is avoided—and Mr. McNair will understand what is meant.

■■■■■■■■■■■■■■■■■■■■■■■■■■■■■■■■■■■■■

PROJECTS

A The following letter, addressed to Mr. Weinberger, is referred to you for reply.

Dear Sir:

I am writing to inquire about a summer job at Peerless Publishing Company.

At the present time I am a student at Brill College, where I am majoring in English. Upon graduation I hope to enter the field of book publishing as an editor, and I want to acquire as much experience as possible while I am still studying.

I would especially like to work on encyclopedias but would be willing to accept any editorial job that may be available.

A brief résumé is enclosed. May I hear from you?

Sincerely yours,

Nancy Rafferty

It is too early in the year to predict the need for editorial help during the summer months. However, each department is estimating its requirements for temporary people for the summer, and this information will be available about April 15—two months from now. You are impressed with Nancy Rafferty's qualifications. Write the letter for your own signature.

B Respond to the following letter for Mr. Weinberger's signature. There are no openings in the accounting and financial departments, but even if there were, Mr. Moore seems to you (and Mr. Weinberger) to be an unlikely candidate.

Dear Mr. Weinberger:

I am offering you the opportunity to put on your staff the most knowledgefull financial man in the country today. I am throughly experienced in acct'g, finance, systems, and edp. I can begin work at anytime, and I will expect to hear from you very quickly that you won't me to go to work for you. I have had many offers, so you must act fast.

Yours truly,

L. Harvey Moore

C Peerless hires several college graduates each year as editorial trainees. That is, ten to fifteen graduates with English majors are accepted and placed in a training program at a fairly good salary. Upon successful completion of training, they are eligible for promotion to the job of editing supervisor in one of the publishing departments.

There are many more candidates for these trainee positions than there are jobs. Each applicant must take a test designed to reveal his knowledge of English and his general aptitude for editorial work. Many fail the test, but there are always more than enough who pass it to fill the training program quota.

Following is a letter written to an applicant who failed the test.

Dear Miss Gambrell:

You failed our editing test, and I cannot accept you as an editorial trainee. We have enough people who passed the test to more than fill our quota.

Cordially,

Rewrite the letter for Mr. Weinberger's signature.

■■■■■■■■■■■■■■■■■■■■■■■■■■■■■■■■■■■■

CASE 6 RESPONDING TO AN UNREASONABLE REQUEST

PROBLEM: Mr. Weinberger has received this letter and has handed it to you to answer.

ROCKLEDGE COLLEGE OF EDUCATION
Curriculum Library and Materials Center
ROCKLEDGE, MISSOURI 64515

Dear Sir:

I'd like to have a file in our Curriculum Center that contains information about professional educators, authors, and illustrators.

Would it be possible to secure from you descriptive literature, pictures, brief autobiographies or biographies, and brief reviews concerning your company's leading people in these fields?

And if you don't have such materials on hand but could tell me where to get them, I'd appreciate that too.

Such a file would be so helpful to us in many ways.

Sincerely,

Peerless publishes several hundred new books each year, many written by new authors. In addition, Peerless has over 5,000 different books in stock at the moment (representing more than 3,500 authors and several hundred illustrators. Although the publisher obviously has some data about most of the people who write and illustrate his books, he does not keep a systematic biographical file on them. Compiling such a file would be very costly and require months of work. Besides, the information would quickly go out of date since the works of new authors are being published every week.

You will have to turn down this request. The only suggestion you can offer to the inquirer is that he might consult professional directories (*Who's Who, Who's Who in Education,* etc.) to obtain the information he needs.

BACKGROUND

Nearly every business receives requests with which it cannot comply. More often than not, the people making the requests are customers or potential customers. Perhaps because they think they are in a favored position, they believe they are entitled to receive almost anything they ask for. On the other hand, most of them probably don't realize that their requests are unreasonable.

SOLUTION A

Dear Mr. Kingston:

We find your request for biographical data on our authors, educators, and illustrators unreasonable. It would take us months to compile this information, and it would be out of date before we start because we are publishing books by new authors all the time.

Since you work in a library, you should be in a position to know about professional directories, such as Who's Who, and I would suggest that you do some research on your own.

Very truly yours,

Analysis of Solution A. Obviously, this is a very poor letter. In effect it calls the person asking for the information a fool and chides him for being so unrealistic. If the person is a customer, he will think twice before he buys anything else from the publisher. There is little doubt that the writer is annoyed—his annoyance shows through in every sentence, particularly the last one.

SOLUTION B

Dear Mr. Kingston:

Your letter to Mr. Weinberger has been given to me, and I am pleased to answer in his absence.

If it were possible, Mr. Kingston, to send you data on professional educators, authors, and illustrators, I would. Unfortunately, we do not have such information conveniently available, and it would be a formidable task to gather it. Every year Peerless publishes hundreds of new books; therefore, any biographical data we might assemble would go out of date quickly. For such information, we rely primarily on professional directories, such as Who's Who and Who's Who in Education.

Perhaps such directories will help you too. In any event, I hope you will be able to obtain the information you need without too much difficulty.

Sincerely yours,

Analysis of Solution B. In Solution B the writer reasons with the correspondent, proving tactfully that the task would not be worth the effort since time would render the information almost useless in a short period. The tone is positive; the language, persuasive. Note that rather than saying, ''Why don't you consult professional directories'' (which would imply that the reader hasn't done so), the writer turned the phrase into a positive one: ''we rely primarily on professional directories . . . .''

■ ■

PROJECTS

A   Roland Baxter, of Kansas City, wrote Mr. Weinberger asking for copies of Peerless Publishing Company's annual reports for the years 1925 to the present. As a doctoral thesis, he is writing a history of annual reports showing how styles have changed over the years in financial reporting.

Peerless has in its archives one copy of every annual report issued since the company was founded in 1921. These copies are very valuable, however, and the company does not allow anyone to take them out of the building. Write Mr. Baxter (for Mr. Weinberger's signature), suggesting that if he can visit Peerless, you will make arrangements for him to spend as much time examining the reports as he would like. In addition, indicate that you can make a photocopying machine available to him for reproducing certain pages from the reports.

B   Respond to the following letter for Mr. Weinberger's signature.

Dear Sir:

Our Personnel Department is sponsoring a course for executives in how to listen, and we would like to borrow your excellent "Listen—and Learn" cassette tapes so that we can reproduce them for use in this class.

Since we are a nonprofit organization, our funds are limited, and I would hope that you could give us the privilege of recording these tapes without charge. We would, of course, return your tapes in excellent condition.

The course starts in two weeks, so I would like to have the tapes shipped immediately.

Thank you for what I know will be a favorable reply.

Yours very truly,
Dwight F. Menzies

The request is an unreasonable one, and you must deny it. The price of the set of tapes is $120, and your agreement with the author is that he will receive 5 percent royalty on each set sold. If you permitted the tapes to be duplicated, you would not only establish a precedent whereby other organizations could ask for the same privilege but would also jeopardize your copyright and deny the author his royalty income.

■■■■■■■■■■■■■■■■■■■■■■■■■■■■■■■■■■■■

CASE 7 SAYING NO BECAUSE OF COMPANY POLICY

PROBLEM: The following letters, addressed to ''President, Peerless Publishing Company,'' are on your desk. Peerless does not sell directly to individual book buyers; the company distributes its books to retail trade and college bookstores who, in turn, sell to consumers. Therefore, in accordance with company policy, you must deny both requests.

> Dear Sir:
>
> It would be very much appreciated if you could make out a gift certificate to Doctor and Mrs. Keith Ansell which would apply on their purchase of one of your books. Enclosed please find a check for the amount of $14.
>
> > Yours,
> >
> > Sharon Salamanca

> Dear Sir:
>
> The Glenwood Bridge Club is interested in selling cookbooks as a project for raising money to help needy children in this area. Could you inform me of your policy in this matter? We are most interested in the Margaret Langdon Picture Cookbook.
>
> > Very truly yours,
> >
> > (Mrs.) Greta Wylie

BACKGROUND

Often requests must be refused because they conflict with company policy. The two examples above are typical. Many manufacturers do not sell direct to consumers because they would be competing with their own customers— retailers.

SOLUTION A: Letter to Miss Salamanca

Dear Miss Salamanca:

I regret to inform you that we cannot honor your request for a gift certificate for the purchase of our books. We do not sell our books directly to individuals but only to retail stores.

Your check is enclosed.

Yours truly,

SOLUTION A: Letter to Mrs. Wylie

Dear Mrs. Wylie:

While I can appreciate sincerely the worthwhile purpose behind your plan to sell the Margaret Langdon Picture Cookbook in order to raise funds for needy children, we are not in a position to participate.

You can appreciate that bookstores are in the retail business, having all the problems and overhead of any business organization, and it would be considered unfair practice for manufacturers to bypass these retail outlets (our main outlets for our books) and sell directly to others in competition with the stores.

Our present discount schedule would call for invoicing your club at the full list price of this cookbook. We do hope sincerely that you have a means of raising money for the needy-children fund, and we regret our inability to assist you.

Sincerely yours,

Analysis of Solution A. Although the letter to Miss Salamanca explains why her request is refused, it is a poor example of business communication.

1. It is blunt to the point of rudeness.
2. Its tone is unsympathetic and grudging. Miss Salamanca may simply be ignorant of business practice; she needs to be told how to obtain a gift book certificate.

Although the letter to Mrs. Wylie shows empathy, it is badly written:

1. "While *I* can appreciate . . . *we* are not in a position . . . ."
2. The word *participate* (last word in the first paragraph) is not appropriate. Participate in what?
3. The word *appreciate* (third word in the second paragraph) is not precisely the correct one. Indeed, the entire paragraph is awkwardly constructed, full of jargon, and somewhat condescending.
4. The last paragraph is not clear. The first sentence (differently worded) belongs in the second paragraph, and the last sentence leaves the reader puzzled.

SOLUTION B: Letter to Miss Salamanca

Dear Miss Salamanca:

Enclosed is the check for $14 that you sent us to purchase a gift certificate for Doctor and Mrs. Keith Ansell.

Our books are sold only through college and trade bookstores; therefore, you will have to purchase them at your local bookstore—Claridge's or the Stuart College Bookstore, in Leesburg. You may arrange for a gift certificate with either of the two stores; both stores carry an excellent stock of books from which the Ansells could choose.

Sincerely yours,

SOLUTION B: Letter to Mrs. Wylie

Dear Mrs. Wylie:

We are pleased to know that you are interested enough in the Margaret Langdon Picture Cookbook to want to sell it as a means of raising funds for needy children. Certainly your objective is an admirable one, and we wish we could assist you.

However, you see, Mrs. Wylie, we can offer a discount only to bookstores through which our books are distributed. To do otherwise would place us in competition with these stores. Perhaps your club can find another means of raising money. Not long ago, I ran across a small paperback book, Fund-Raising Ideas for Clubs and Organizations, published by Five-Star Press, which you may find helpful. Perhaps your local bookstore has a copy.

Sincerely yours,

Analysis of Solution B. Both the letter to Miss Salamanca and that to Mrs. Wylie are good examples of saying no tactfully. Note the three-step pattern that is typical of effective no letters:

1. An expression of appreciation for the invitation to help.
2. An explanation of why the request cannot be granted.
3. An expression of hope that a different solution can be found.

■ ■

PROJECTS

A Mrs. Millicent Arness, of the Hoopstown Public Library, wrote asking for twenty copies of the Peerless general catalog. She said she gets many calls for publishers' catalogs and thinks it would be a good idea to have several handy so that they can be given to those who ask for them.

The Peerless general catalog contains over 800 pages and costs $5.60 to produce. It is supplied in single copies free to large buyers of books—book dealers, librarians, school administrators, college professors, and others; but because of the cost of the catalog, copies are rarely given to individual consumers.

Write the response for Mr. Weinberger. Assume that you will send two copies of the catalog to Mrs. Arness—not the twenty she asked for.

B   Lloyd Demaret, office manager of a large printing house, wrote asking to be put on the mailing list for six copies of an employee publication, *Peerless Paragraphs*. This monthly monograph often contains confidential information and is restricted to employees. You don't know how Mr. Demaret got his hands on a copy. Write the response for Mr. Weinberger's signature.

■■■■■■■■■■■■■■■■■■■■■■■■■■■■■■■■■■■■■■■

CASE 8
RESPONDING TO AN IRATE CRITIC OF COMPANY PRACTICE

PROBLEM: In support of bookstores that sell Peerless books, the company advertises its new products in several magazines. One of these magazines is *Quench,* a highly controversial monthly magazine that speaks boldly on all issues—political, social, educational, and scientific—often attacking public figures and social institutions.

In Mr. Weinberger's absence, you are to respond to the following letter.

Dear Mr. Weinberger:

Why would a reputable company such as Peerless support, through advertising, a muckraking periodical like Quench? I cannot understand why you would assist in the desecration of our institutions and the character assassination of our leading statesmen, educators, and scientists. Your business and your profits depend on protecting and sustaining our American way of life—not on destroying it.

I expect to hear an explanation from you, Mr. Weinberger. It is not inconceivable that your products could be boycotted for such advertising practices, and if your explanation is not a satisfactory one, I shall take steps to see that Peerless books are not distributed—at least in this community.

Yours truly,

J. D. Douglas

BACKGROUND

All major companies receive letters from people who are highly critical of a company's advertising and selling practices. Some writers are well-meaning and state their positions reasonably. Others are irrational and threatening.

Of course, the company cannot afford to panic in such situations, but at the same time, it cannot afford to ignore these critics. In the interest of good public relations, most critical letters require a response.

SOLUTION

Dear Mr. Douglas:

Thank you sincerely for your letter concerning our policy of advertising Peerless books in <u>Quench</u>.

I am sure you will agree, Mr. Douglas, that by placing advertising in Quench or any other magazine we are not necessarily endorsing the editorial policy of the magazine. By and large, we and other businesses select printed advertising media on the basis of readership. As is true with most companies, we are constantly experimenting with various media; whether we continue such advertising usually depends on the results it obtains. This is a standard practice of American business firms.

Peerless advertises extensively in all types of media. It would be presumptuous of us to adopt the policy of advertising only in those publications whose editorial policy we agree with. Some advertising managers have a personal editorial preference for publications that others find offensive. Yet none can afford to base his business judgment on personal preference. As a business owner, you will understand, I am sure, the role that economics plays in such decisions.

Thank you for expressing your point of view so frankly, Mr. Douglas, and for giving us an opportunity to express ours.

Sincerely yours,

Analysis of the Solution. The writer has not revealed annoyance with Mr. Douglas, even though he may have seethed when the Douglas letter came. He explains tactfully and convincingly the company's position; and, although the response may not satisfy Mr. Douglas, a more rational person would accept it as a reasonable position. This is about all one can do in such situations. It would be foolish for the writer to tell Mr. Douglas that he, too, thinks it is bad practice to advertise in a magazine like *Quench* (and he very well might), for he would be criticizing his employer—and if he is writing *for* his employer, he must defend his employer's practices.

■ ■

PROJECTS

A   Reply to the following letter for Mr. Weinberger's signature.

Dear Mr. Weinberger:

I am writting in behalf of the Pearl City Environment Association in protest of your support of a printing firm that pollutes our river and air. This firm, which prints many of your books, is the R. S. Ogre Company. Every day of the week we see dirty, black smoke pouring out of the company's plant, and the Langorous River, on which the building is located, is fouled and filthy with the chemicals Ogre dumps into it.

Our group has protested to the mayor of Pearl City many times and has met with the Ogre bigwigs on numerous occasions about this matter. The only answer we get is, "We're working on it." Yet nothing happens—just more pollutants spill out to destroy the beauty of our city.

The only recourse left to us is to protest to those who support this company. As a large publisher, you have the obligation to take your business away from this irresponsible printer. I expect to hear from you.

Very truly yours,

Gardner V. Pristine

Although Peerless has no control over the pollution activities of its suppliers, Mr. Weinberger is sympathetic with and concerned about Mr. Pristine's claims. In your reply, take whatever stand you believe Peerless should take in matters of this nature.

Mr. Pristine did not indicate whether a copy of his letter to Mr. Weinberger was being sent to the R. S. Ogre Company. With that in mind, do you think Mr. Weinberger will want to send a copy of his reply (the letter you are preparing, of course), as well as a photocopy of Mr. Pristine's letter, to the president or some other official of Ogre? (It's true that Ogre prints many books for Peerless.) If your answer is yes, will you let Mr. Pristine know the correspondence is being shared with Ogre executives—or will you use the "blind carbon copy" approach discussed in Part 1?

B   Prepare a response to the following letter for Mr. Weinberger's signature.

Dear Mr. Weinberger:

As president of the Lamonica Valley Concerned Parents Association, I must express my shock and disgust at Revolt of a Radical Realist, by Chauncey Arcane, that you recently published. How can a company with your reputation champion the cause of this bloody revolutionist—one who would destroy our sacred ideals and institutions?

This is an offensive and irresponsible act, Mr. Weinberger, and I protest strongly in behalf of mothers and fathers everywhere. The language is filthy and the ideas expressed by this punk Arcane totally un-American. If you do not withdraw this book at once, I will see to it that the schools and libraries of Lamonica Valley stop buying from Peerless and that your books disappear from their shelves.

Very truly yours,

Mrs. Mona Standish

Take whatever position you wish in responding to Mrs. Standish. It is true that Chauncey Arcane is a highly controversial figure. His ideas on social reform are somewhat radical—indeed, Mr. Weinberger does not agree with Arcane's position. Mr. Arcane is, however, a gifted writer (the reviews of his book have been highly complimentary).

SAYING NO TO REQUESTS FOR DONATIONS

PROBLEM: Almost every week Mr. Weinberger receives requests that Peerless contribute to this charity or that worthy cause. A majority of these requests must be refused—no company, no matter how large or how profitable, can afford to support every campaign for funds. A typical letter received at Peerless is from Mrs. Frances Laytham, director of Clarkson Day Care Center, which opened recently in your community. Mrs. Latham asks Peerless for a contribution toward the Clarkson fund drive. Because you have received a number of such requests, you have decided to develop two or three "pattern" letters that can, with slight adaptations, fit most situations.

BACKGROUND

Every business organization receives many requests for contributions. Although most organizations do contribute to various local campaigns, setting aside a percentage of profits for that specific purpose, they can never honor all the requests they receive. Some firms support only one united fund organization (called by that name, or Community Chest, or a similar name). Others give most of their contribution fund budget to a united fund group and, in addition, set aside money for other charitable organizations that do not share in the united fund.

In any event, requests for contributions (including "complimentary" advertising space) must be screened very carefully. It is very hard to justify a no to one organization when you have just said yes to a similar one. More important, the charge of discrimination is always a possibility, especially among religious and ethnic groups. The subject of donations, then, is a very sensitive one in the public relations area.

Most large companies set up a special committee to study contribution requests, and the committee ponders over and discusses each request before reaching a decision. One purpose of such a committee is to share the responsibility for turning down a request. The negative decision of a group carries more weight than that of an individual; and certainly it is less painful to the person who has to convey the decision when he can say, "The Committee decided," rather than "I decided."

SOLUTION A

Dear Mrs. Laytham:

Thank you for your letter in which you ask us to support your drive for funds for Clarkson Day Care Center. Our Donations Committee, which has the responsibility for allocating our budget for contributions, handles all requests for funds. I am therefore referring your letter to that group. No doubt you will hear from the chairman soon after the committee reaches a decision.

Sincerely yours,

Analysis of Solution A. In companies where all requests for donations are turned over to a special committee, a letter such as this is appropriate. Note that the writer is noncommittal but tactful.

SOLUTION B

Dear Mrs. Laytham:

Thank you for writing us to request a contribution to Clarkson Day Care Center.

Each year we set aside a generous budget for contributions to local activities. In fact, last year we gave to various organizations the largest amount in our history. Even then, we were able to give to only a fraction of the groups that sought our help. I am sure you will understand that we cannot give financial support to all.

Reluctantly, then, we must refrain from participating this year. In your case the decision is particularly painful for us because we are well aware of the fine public service you are performing.

Best wishes in your drive, and I hope that at some later date we may be able to share in this effort.

Sincerely yours,

Analysis of Solution B. This pattern letter emphasizes the we-can't-give-to-everyone theme. It is sympathetic in tone, tactful, reasonable, and friendly.

SOLUTION C

Dear Mrs. Laytham:

Thank you for writing me about the need for funds to operate the Clarkson Day Care Center you have recently established.

Certainly we at Peerless are sympathetic with your objectives, Mrs. Laytham, and wish it were possible to participate in this endeavor. Because the requests for our financial support have become so numerous (last year we had over 120 requests), we have had to confine our company contributions to the three major community funds: Citizens All, Charity Council, and Givers Anonymous.

You will be interested to learn that we have a policy of matching contributions made by our employees to recognized charities and nonprofit institutions. Thus we undoubtedly will be contributing indirectly to Clarkson Center, which is, of course, on the approved list.

Sincerely yours,

Analysis of Solution C. In the kind of letter represented by Solution C, the writer makes two important points: (1) company policy is to support only community funds, and (2) the company has a matching contribution plan for employees.

SOLUTION D

Dear Mrs. Laytham:

Thank you for writing us asking for support of Clarkson Day Care Center.

Last year we had over 120 requests for financial aid. Fortunately, we were able to make contributions to nearly half of these organizations. One of the hardest decisions we have to make is determining which organizations do and which do not qualify for our support (we'd like to support every worthy cause). To help do this, we have established a point system to rate the various causes objectively. It's the only way we have found to bring objectivity into our decisions.

Although we cannot honor your request this year, I assure you that all of us at Peerless appreciate the valuable work you are doing. It is a great public service, and we wish you much success in your endeavors.

Cordially yours,

Analysis of Solution D. Some companies are sensitive about the subject of how they select the organizations to which they contribute. Solution D explains one company's procedures.

■■■■■■■■■■■■■■■■■■■■■■■■■■■■■■■■■■

PROJECTS

A   The Patterson Guild is a small, private art school near Lexington, Kentucky. Because of the high expense of operation, the administration has announced that the school must close its doors at the end of the current academic year. Although the students understand the problem and appreciate the administration's attempts to deal with it, they are not willing to accept the school's fate and have decided to solicit funds from various organizations to keep the Guild in operation. The "Committee to Save Patterson Guild" has written to Mr. Weinberger asking for financial help from Peerless (Peerless publishes art books that are used at Patterson Guild).

   Although Peerless is sympathetic, the Contributions Committee has voted not to make a contribution to the Patterson Guild students. The company cannot, according to the Committee, support "every cause, no matter how much we may sympathize with it." Write the letter for Mr. Weinberger's signature and address it to Rachel DeVille.

B   A local organization known as "Patriotic Americans for Puritan Principles" is soliciting funds to support its work. In his letter asking for money, the president (Roger T. Beckett) stated the objective of the organization: "To protect the American way our forefathers fought and died for."

After a thorough investigation, the Contributions Committee found nothing favorable about the organization. Several civic leaders and local government agencies said they believe it is an extremely radical group. Write the appropriate letter to Mr. Beckett.

C   The Oldtimers Club, of Racine, Wisconsin, wrote Mr. Weinberger asking for free copies of damaged and out-of-date books for its library. Peerless has made arrangements with a number of organizations throughout the country to supply such books to young people's libraries in especially needy areas and to philanthropic organizations concerned with the welfare of young people. The demand is, of course, greater than the supply. Write a response, addressing it to Mr. Phineas H. Coltran.

■ ■

CASE 10   REJECTING AN INVITATION TO PURCHASE ADVERTISING SPACE

PROBLEM: Mr. Weinberger received the following letter. He asked you to draft a reply for his signature, saying, "We can't do it."

Dear Mr. Weinberger:

The Suburban Art League is having its annual ball in October at the Lakewood Club. The proceeds from the ball will go toward establishing a scholarship fund for gifted young artists.

In connection with the ball, we are printing a special souvenir program. This program is designed by local young artists and printed in four colors.

Advertising space is available in these programs ($200 for a full page, $130 for a half page, and $75 for a quarter page), and we hope you will want to be represented in the advertising pages. Hundreds of people will see your ad and know that your company supports this very worthy activity.

Another reason that I believe you will want to help us is that many of your employees are members of the Suburban Art League, and they will be proud to see their company's name in the program.

May I hear from you?

Sincerely yours,

N. A. Jurasek

BACKGROUND

Business firms receive many requests to purchase advertising space in school yearbooks, directories, programs for sports and cultural events, and so on. Although there is some advertising value in such publications, it is mostly "institutional" (public relations). Most businesses look upon such advertising as a contribution, and the printed advertisement often consists of just the simple message "Compliments of the ABC Company."

Although many business firms support local community activities by purchasing advertising space, such requests are often so numerous that many must be turned down. Refusing such requests is a delicate matter—every organization needs money to support its activities, and local businessmen are obvious sources. The solicitor's appeal is to the businessman's conscience, his responsibility to the community he lives in. Often, though, the solicitor emphasizes the theme "We keep you in business and you owe us something."

SOLUTION A

Dear Mr. Jurasek:

I am sorry that we are not able to buy space in the souvenir program of the Suburban Art League Ball. Our advertising budget is exhausted.

Very truly yours,

Analysis of Solution A. Of course, Solution A won't be very convincing to Mr. Jurasek. He will accept the statement that the advertising budget is exhausted, but he won't believe that Peerless can't find the money elsewhere. More important, the letter does not achieve its real mission: to say no but to retain the friendly feeling of Suburban Art League members toward the company. Solution A is too cold, too curt—it will produce bad feeling.

SOLUTION B

Dear Mr. Jurasek:

A recent study made by our personnel department revealed that our employees hold memberships in 93 different organizations. Naturally, we are proud of the fact that our employees are active in their respective communities.

Because there are so many worthwhile organizations, we find it impossible to give financial support to all of them. This is why we must decline the invitation to advertise in the souvenir program of the Suburban Art League Ball. We think yours is an outstanding organization and are delighted that many of our employees are members; but if we were to favor the League while denying the solicitations of the many other equally worthy organizations, we would put ourselves in a most embarrassing—and indefensible—position.

Best wishes, Mr. Jurasek, to you and your colleagues in your efforts to raise funds for your scholarship program. It's a great idea!

Sincerely yours,

Analysis of Solution B. We do not claim that Solution B will make Mr. Jurasek happy (only a yes response would do that), but it is a tactful and reasonable no employing the fair-play theme.

Note the following:

1. The first paragraph—in a very positive manner—actually sets the stage for the refusal of Mr. Jurasek's request.
2. The second paragraph not only states the refusal but also gives a logical and defensible explanation of it.
3. The last paragraph attempts to retain Mr. Jurasek's goodwill.

■ ■

PROJECTS

A You must refuse this invitation in Mr. Weinberger's name. Assume, however, that Mr. Weinberger will send a personal check for $25 as a donation.

Dear Mr. Weinberger:

The Willard T. Peck Memorial Committee is sponsoring a dinner dance at the Morristown Heights Country Club on May 17. The purpose of the event is to raise funds to carry on the work of this renowned ornithologist who has done so much to establish and preserve bird sanctuaries all over the state.

A special program is being printed, and we have decided to accept advertising in it. A full-page ad will cost you only $100 (we do not accept smaller ones). Naturally, we hope that you recognize the benefits of our work and will give us your support. Please submit the copy for the ad you wish to place, along with your check for $100, to me by April 20.

Very truly yours,

Boyd M. Gallagher

B Peerless receives many invitations to advertise in high school yearbooks all over the country. Apparently students, aware that they are using books published by Peerless, feel that since they help to "support" Peerless, Peerless should contribute to their causes.

Although the company frequently takes advertising space in yearbooks of high schools located in the Des Moines area, it cannot afford to advertise in all the thousands of annuals published throughout the country. Actually, the students themselves are not the buyers of the textbooks they use—local school boards purchase the books that teachers and administrators choose. Therefore an advertisement would be more of a contribution than a promotion vehicle.

Write a form letter, as from Mr. Weinberger, to send those soliciting advertising for high school yearbooks. Use whatever rationale you think appropriate for refusing the invitation.

■ ■

PROBLEM: The editor of the employee magazine, *Intercom,* has written a memo to Mr. Weinberger asking for suggestions for improving the publication. There has been considerable criticism of the magazine by management, and the editor has asked top executives in the company for comments. Mr. Weinberger has given you his ideas but tells you to prepare your recommendations under your own name.

BACKGROUND

Executives often ask employees for suggestions to make the company a more efficient organization—suggestions about improving personnel practices, saving time and effort, cutting costs, and so on. Many firms have suggestion boxes into which employees are encouraged to deposit their ideas in writing. Cash bonuses are often awarded for suggestions that are accepted and put into use.

Memos of recommendation may be formal or informal, depending on the subject.

SOLUTION A

TO: J. R. Sanchez	FROM: S. Colfax
SUBJECT: Suggestions for <u>Intercom</u>	DATE: May 27, 19—

There are several ways in which I think <u>Intercom</u> can be improved. I would leave the title as it is, but there ought to be more photographs, a "Letters to the Editor" column, a new masthead, better typeface, more stories about the typical worker, and a gossip column. Also, I think you should have an "Employee of the Month" award.

I hope these suggestions will be helpful.

S.C.

Analysis of Solution A. Solution A has several shortcomings:

1. Although the recipient will probably understand that the writer is responding for Mr. Weinberger to a specific request, it would be better to mention that fact.
2. The memo starts off negatively. Although the request was for recommendations for improving *Intercom,* there would be no harm in starting off with some positive points.

3. The memo is too general, too sketchy. The recipient will be bewildered by some of the suggestions; they should be expanded.
4. The eight different suggestions would be more effective—and more readable—if they appeared as enumerations.

SOLUTION B

TO: J. R. Sanchez   FROM: S. Colfax
SUBJECT: Intercom   DATE: May 27, 19—

Mr. Weinberger has asked me to respond to your memo concerning Intercom, and I am glad to do so.

First, let me say that there are many good things about Intercom. I like the informal style, the editorial quality, the "Shop and Swap" column, the "What's New in Books" feature, and many other things. But I know you want suggestions rather than praise, and mine follow.

1. Although a new title for the magazine has been suggested, I believe it would be a mistake to change it. Everyone recognizes the publication by Intercom, and it still seems to me to be entirely appropriate.

2. More photographs would help—photographs of employees celebrating anniversaries, being "showered" at engagement parties, and receiving special recognition.

3. A "Letters to the Editor" column would be especially popular. It would have good readership and, at the same time, give employees a chance to "sound off" on their pet likes and dislikes.

4. A new masthead would help, and I would like to see us engage a professional designer to do one.

5. The general appearance of the magazine needs dressing up. I would also like to see a professional designer do this.

6. After studying the issues for the past year, I feel convinced that we have too many management stories and too few stories about the typical worker. It seems to me that this should be an employee magazine, not a management magazine.

7. I recommend that the magazine establish an "Employee of the Month" award. A committee of employees would select this person on the basis of recommendations of supervisors and department heads. We might run the employee's picture with a brief biographical sketch and story about his special recognition.

8. Finally, may I suggest that a monthly "gossip" column be added. I believe Ron Perkins, who did a column for his college paper, could do the job. Of course, this column would be mainly for and about the ordinary worker—nothing scandalous, of course, but on the order of a good-natured "snoop" column.

If you wish, I'd be glad to discuss these recommendations further with you. I am sure Intercom can be a more effective instrument for good employee relations.

S.C.

Analysis of Solution B. Solution B overcomes the flaws of Solution A. Note that the writer enumerated the points in a clear, readable style.

SOLUTION C

TO: J. R. Sanchez   FROM: S. Colfax
SUBJECT: Intercom   DATE: May 27, 19—

Mr. Weinberger has asked me to respond to your memo concerning Intercom, and I am glad to do so.

First, let me say that there are many good things about Intercom. I like the informal style, the editorial quality, the "Shop and Swap" column, the "What's New in Books" feature, and many other things. But I know you want suggestions rather than praise, and mine follow.

Title

Although a new title for the magazine has been suggested, I believe it would be a mistake to change it. Everyone recognizes the publication by Intercom, and it still seems to me to be entirely appropriate.

Design

A new masthead would help, and I would like to see us engage a professional designer to do one.

The general appearance of the magazine needs dressing up. I would also like to see a professional designer do this.

Photographs

More photographs would help—photographs of employees celebrating anniversaries, being "showered" at engagement parties, and receiving special recognition.

Features

1. A "Letters to the Editor" column would be especially popular. It would have good readership and, at the same time, give employees a chance to "sound off" on their pet likes and dislikes.

2. After studying the issues for the past year, I feel convinced that we have too many management stories and too few stories about the typical worker. It seems to me that this should be an employee magazine, not a management magazine.

3. I recommend that the magazine establish an "Employee of the Month" award. A committee of employees would select this person on the basis of recommendations of supervisors and department heads. We might run the employee's picture with a brief biographical sketch and story about his special recognition.

4. Finally, may I suggest that a monthly "gossip" column be added. I believe Ron Perkins, who did a column for his college paper, could do the job. Of course, this column would be mainly for and about the ordinary worker—nothing scandalous, of course, but on the order of a good-natured "snoop" column.

If you wish, I'd be glad to discuss these recommendations further with you. I am sure <u>Intercom</u> can be a more effective instrument for good employee relations.

S.C.

Analysis of Solution C. Solution C is exactly like B except that the suggestions have been grouped into four separate categories—Title, Design, Photographs, and Features. These identifications make the suggestions easier to follow.

■ ■

PROJECT

You have been asked to write a memorandum recommending certain changes in company policy, practices, or procedures. The following subjects are possibilities. Make your own assumptions as to the current status in the company.

> Improving Facilities and Services in the Company Library
> Improving the Handling of Mail for Executives
> Revising the Guide to Writing Company Letters
> Boosting Employee Morale
> Improving the Company's Public Relations
> Improving the Company's Accounting System (or Marketing, Advertising, Data Processing, etc.)

You may wish to choose a subject that relates to the college you are attending—the bookstore, cafeteria, parking facilities, enrollment procedures, athletic program, student government, campus regulations.

Make your memo at least two pages long and supply visual guidelines.

■ ■

CASE 12 REPORTING ON MEETINGS AND CONFERENCES

PROBLEM: Mr. Weinberger has asked you to represent him on the Forms Standardization Committee, a group recently formed to study ways of saving time and money through more intelligent design, use, and distribution of company forms. At the first meeting of the committee, you were appointed secretary, with the responsibility for making sure the meeting place is properly arranged, each meeting is announced, and minutes are distributed after the meeting is over.

BACKGROUND

Although meetings are often joked about as necessary evils—nearly every executive thinks he attends too many—it would be difficult, if not impossible, to run a business without them. Often meetings provide the only face-to-face opportunity for key people in an organization to communicate with each other.

A meeting can be any kind of get-together—from a conversation between two people to a convention attended by thousands. When an executive refers to "those meetings," however, he is probably talking about meetings of committees he belongs to, usually made up of from half a dozen to twenty or so people.

Nearly every organization has several committees that meet frequently. These committees are of two types: standing committees and ad hoc committees. Standing committees are permanent; the membership changes from time to time, but the committee stands. Ad hoc committees are formed to do a specific job and are dissolved when that job is over. Typical of an ad hoc committee is one appointed to direct a company drive for Community Chest funds. When the drive ends, the committee disbands.

Planning the Meeting. When meetings are unpopular with the people who attend them, the reason is probably poor planning in the first place. Everyone resents wasting time, and some meetings are notorious time wasters. A meeting worth being called is worth being planned. Planning includes (1) keeping each participant informed about time and place of the meeting, (2) preparing and distributing an agenda, (3) setting up the meeting room, and (4) seeing that the necessary materials and equipment are provided.

Keeping Participants Informed. Everyone who is to attend a meeting must be informed about the time, place, and program. Those who have an assigned part in the program are given special attention: the effective chairman will go over with each one in advance what he will present, how long it is likely to take, whether discussion will follow the presentation and who will moderate it, the types of visuals and other audience aids that may be used, and how the meeting will be run. If nothing else, such a premeeting conference will let each program participant know that the chairman is in command and expects everyone to do his part.

Alerting each participant is not a one-shot affair that takes place the day before the meeting. It should start right after the previous meeting—or as soon as the planning of the next program begins—and continue right up until the day of the meeting. A final check by telephone—"Are you all set for the meeting this afternoon?''—is quite in order. The chairman can't let himself forget that people get so wrapped up in their own jobs that a meeting seems an interruption in their regular routine, even when they are to have an important part in it.

The Agenda. Every meeting that is held on a regular schedule should have an agenda—that is, a list of topics to be discussed and the names of those who are to present them. An agenda gives purpose and direction to a meeting and gives a meeting more importance in everyone's eyes.

The agenda for a typical committee meeting can be an informal document, taking any form the chairman or committee secretary chooses. Here is one type.

FORMS STANDARDIZATION COMMITTEE

Agenda for October 29, 19—

Skyline Room, 10:30 a.m.

1. Data-processing installation study
    R. C. Cox

2. Personnel forms
    Sol Slater

3. Stock-control forms simplification study
    C. R. Wilkes

4. New letterhead design
    Nina Bracher

5. Reduction of composition costs
    Timothy Curtis

6. Filing problems created by new forms
    Millie Fein

7. Carbon packs vs. padded forms
    Arthur Hobbs

8. Visit to Pitney-Bowes
    R. C. Cox

R. C. Cox, Chairman

The Meeting Room. Meetings of standing committees are usually held in the same place each time, and it isn't necessary to remind people about it. However, when there is a change, it's up to the chairman or the committee secretary to see that everyone is notified in advance. One way to do this is to put the new meeting place on the agenda and call attention to it by some device such as an arrow or the words "Note new meeting place."

Obviously, the place for a meeting should be well-suited to the purpose. But if the room isn't suitable, there is not much anyone can do about it in a business office—one has to take whatever is available. (Hotel and other commercial meeting rooms are another matter; usually something *can* be done about it.) The chairman or committee secretary can see to it, however, that there are plenty of chairs, that all the lights are working, and that the room is well-ventilated. He inspects the room an hour or so before the meeting (or as soon as it is vacant) to assure himself about such things as clean ashtrays in ample quantity, a dust- and litter-free table, and a clean chalkboard with plenty of chalk and an eraser.

Materials and Equipment. When special equipment is needed for a meeting, it is usually up to the person who is going to use it to look after his own needs. Even so, the committee chairman should volunteer to be of whatever help he can. Film projectors, tape recorders, and other equipment requiring electric outlets will deserve special attention. The distance between the machine and the nearest outlet has often created havoc until someone dug up an extension cord. Many a meeting has been spoiled because the outlet was DC and the equipment for AC. Some visual aids require a darkened room, and the person who wants to show a film freezes in his tracks when he discovers too late that the windows have no blinds. Users of projection equipment often discover to their dismay that there is no screen or that the room is too small for the equipment. Even worse is the discovery that the operator engaged to run the film projector forgot to show up, whereupon several self-styled experts hover over the machine trying to thread the film and get "the thing going." And so on. Any crisis can happen when visual equipment is to be used, and the alert chairman (or committee secretary) plans ahead to see that it doesn't!

Most meeting rooms have a chalkboard, and chalk and erasers must be on hand. It is not easy to predict whether the chalkboard will be used during a meeting—it's a spur-of-the-moment visual aid—but it is amazing how many meetings are held up while someone goes in search of chalk or an eraser.

Each participant in a meeting should have writing paper and a pencil or two in front of him, and the committee secretary should supply these materials. He also distributes other materials that will be needed—reports, books, and other printed materials.

Taking the Minutes. The secretary usually records the minutes of meetings of important committees. Minutes furnish a record of decisions reached and action taken, remind participants of things to be done, provide a historical record for the company, keep top management and others informed, and pinpoint responsibility for recommendations and actions.

If you are to take the minutes, it is wise to study the agenda carefully beforehand and to learn the names of the committee members. If the people in the group are strangers to each other, try to get the names of the participants beforehand, and then prepare stand-up name cards and arrange them at various places.

If you are unable to get the names of the people beforehand and the group is fairly small, make a rough seating chart after you get to the meeting; then fill in the names as quickly as you hear them.

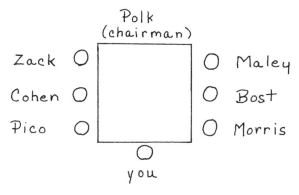

If the group is very large and it is important to know who said what, ask the chairman to have each person identify himself when he makes a statement.

Recording the Minutes. The recorder must be a discriminate notemaker. He must listen for key ideas and write just enough to get the main points the speaker is making. For example:

What the Speaker Said	What the Recorder Wrote
I see very little to recommend a change in policy that requires committee approval of all forms before they are printed. People have a natural tendency to develop a form for every purpose, and it isn't very long before we've got a stockroom full of forms that nobody uses. Just to let people know that any form they design for official use must be approved by a committee is a healthy thing and serves three basic purposes: it helps to cut down the number of forms designed in the first place, it simplifies the filing problem, and it saves time and money.	RCC: No need to change policy requiring committee approval of forms. Committee approval accomplishes three purposes: 1. Cuts down number of forms 2. Simplifies filing 3. Saves time and money

Writing Up the Minutes. Minutes of meetings can take several different forms.

The Heading. There are only two rigid rules about the heading of the minutes: it should contain the date of the meeting and the name of the committee or group. Here is one type of heading:

FORMS STANDARDIZATION COMMITTEE
Peerless Publishing Company
Minutes of Meeting, October 29, 19—

Here is another. Note the omission of the company name; it really is unnecessary since minutes are usually distributed only within the company.

MINUTES
Forms Standardization Committee
October 29, 19—

Minutes are often prepared on interoffice memorandum forms, in which case the heading might appear as follows:

PEERLESS PUBLISHING COMPANY
Interoffice Memorandum

TO: Forms Standardization Committee   FROM: R. C. Cox,
         cc: L. Nugent, P. Weinberger   Chairman
         S. Ellis, J. Katzenbach

SUBJECT: Minutes of Meeting, October 29, 19—   DATE: October 30, 19—

The Body. The style of the minutes themselves is also a matter of individual preference. In choosing the style, the recorder must consider the form that will be most useful for reference purposes.

Obviously, the topic discussed and/or the name of the person presenting it should be displayed in some way. By and large, the topic is more important than the person, but there may be exceptions. The safe way is to display both the topic and its discussion leader. It is also a good idea to number the topics so that they may be easily referred to by number in any subsequent communications (you may remember that the topics on an agenda are numbered). Some recorders like to identify the topic in the margin like this, because it stands out.

1. Data Processing   Ranier Consultants' report on data process-
   Installation Study   ing will be completed by December 12.
   (R. C. Cox)   The preliminary report indicates they will
                            recommend a computer installation for
                            customer billing and payroll. RCC will give
                            full report . . . .

But because this arrangement eats up space, others prefer a regular side heading like this.

1. Data Processing Installation Study (R. C. Cox)
Ranier Consultants' report on data processing will be completed by December 12. The preliminary report indicates they will recommend a computer installation for customer . . . .

Even in meetings where there is no set program and the discussion is free-for-all, it is wise to assign topic headings to major issues being discussed. Remember that minutes ought to be useful for reference purposes.

When discussion follows a presentation, its summary appears below the presentation like this.

1. Data Processing Installation Study (R. C. Cox)	Ranier Consultants' report on data processing will be completed by December 12. The preliminary report indicates they will recommend a computer installation for customer billing and payroll. RCC will give full report . . . .
Discussion	Mr. Hobbs asked how much time would be allowed for converting present procedures to computers. Mr. Cox estimated six months to a year.
	Miss Fein's question about provisions for training present personnel in the new procedures was answered in this way: Training sessions will be set up, by department, and these will continue for as long as they are needed. Special instructors from IBM will be engaged.

SOLUTION

The minutes of the meeting of the Forms Standardization Committee are shown on pages 212–213.

Analysis of the Solution. Note the following points concerning the minutes illustrated:

1. The items that were listed on the agenda (page 207) are given the same numbers on the minutes.
2. Names of people who made presentations or who contributed to the discussion are given.
3. Note that Item 3, although not discussed at the meeting because of department reorganization, is accounted for.
4. Observe that all assignments given out at the meeting are carefully documented.
   a. Item 1   (RCC will prepare a full report and present it at a meeting of all department heads.)
   b. Item 3   (CRW promised a report for the December meeting.)
   c. Item 6   (Mr. Cox will issue the invitation.)
   d. Item 7   (Mr. Hobbs is to gather data and report at the January meeting.)
   e. Item 8   (CRW, NB, RWZ, and RCC will drive their cars.)

MINUTES
Forms Standardization Committee
October 29, 19--

1. Data Processing   Ranier Consultants' report on data processing will be
   Installation   completed by December 12. The preliminary report in-
   Study   dicates they will recommend a computer installation
   (R. C. Cox)   for customer billing and payroll. RCC will give full
                          report to department heads when study is completed.

   Discussion   Mr. Hobbs asked how much time would be allowed for
                          converting present procedures to computers. Mr. Cox
                          estimated six months to a year.

                          Miss Fein's question about provisions for training
                          present personnel in the new procedures was answered
                          in this way: Training sessions will be set up, by
                          department, and these will continue for as long as
                          they are needed. Special instructors from IBM will
                          be engaged.

2. Personnel Forms   All personnel forms have been standardized. All
   (Sol Slater)   department managers solicited suggestions on the new
                          forms and composite forms submitted in Varitype
                          form. The most controversial form was the Personnel
                          Change Notice (5090) and especially the items under
                          "Separation." However, the revision seems to be
                          generally acceptable. Not everyone agrees on the
                          form and content of all the newly designed forms,
                          but all agreed to experiment with them and keep a
                          record of their suggestions.

3. Stock-Control   Department reorganization caused the delay of the
   Forms Simpli-   study. CRW promised a report for the December meeting.
   fication Study
   (C. R. Wilkes)

   Discussion   Mr. Cox asked whether a methods analyst is being con-
                          sidered as a staff addition, and CRW replied that
                          Miss Ethyl Aschner, formerly of Data Control, Inc.,
                          has been employed.

4. New Letter-   The new letterhead design was displayed and enthusi-
   head Design   astically endorsed by the Committee. NB indicated
   (Nina Bracher)   that a second color, in addition to black, is still
                          to be chosen and several are being considered. Gold
                          seems to have the edge at the moment.

5. Reduction of   We should consider "cold type" (Varitype) for all
   Composition   forms composition. It is about half the cost of
   Costs   machine composition and is quite attractive. We
   (Tom Curtis)   accepted the Varitype composition shown. The easily
                          adjusted type line for typewriter spacing is the
                          biggest advantage. Another way to cut composition
                          costs is to reduce the number of typefaces.

Discussion		Mr. Hobbs asked about flexibility in terms of composition schedules, and TC said that assurance has been given by Foley Letter Shop that schedules will definitely be met.
		Mr. Wilkes feels that the readability of Varitype is not so good as machine composition. (The Committee felt that this was not a problem since there is no "continuity reading.")
6.	Filing Problems Created by New Forms (Millie Fein)	Most people who design forms do not consider the problems created for Records Maintenance when forms are improperly designed. Size of the form and layout of the top portion of the form are particular problems. MF suggested that Mrs. Roach, in Records Maintenance, be invited to inspect and approve all forms when they are designed.
	Discussion	It was recommended by Mr. Cox, and approved by the members, that Mrs. Roach be invited to become a member of this Committee. Mr. Cox will issue the invitation.
7.	Carbon Packs vs. Padded Forms (Arthur Hobbs)	Recent studies in the company have shown that carbon packs are definite time-savers over padded forms. AH recommends that all frequently used forms be printed in carbon packs.
	Discussion	The Committee feels that we do not have sufficient cost information on which to base a decision. Mr. Hobbs is to gather data and report at the January meeting.
8.	Visit to Pitney-Bowes (R. C. Cox)	The visit to Pitney-Bowes is scheduled for December 8. CRW, NB, RWZ, and RCC will drive their cars; the group will be at the Ash Avenue entrance at 9:30 a.m.
9.	Other Business (R. C. Cox)	Mr. Cox announced that he will represent the Forms Standardization Committee at a special meeting of the Management Council on November 14 at which various company committees will report on their activities during the past year.
	NEXT MEETING:	The next meeting will be held November 30. We have invited C. A. Kiernan, of Moore Business Forms, to speak on trends in forms design.

R. C. Cox, Chairman

Distribution

Members of the Committee: Bracher, Cass, Curtis, Fein, Hobbs, Johnson, Moskowitz, Slater, Wilkes, Zelden (absent)

Others: Mr. Weinberger, Mr. Nugent, Mr. Katzenbach, Mr. S. Ellis

The committee secretary can underline or circle in red each member's assignments on his copy of the minutes when the copies are distributed. For example:

```
7.  Carbon Packs vs.    Recent studies in the company have shown that
    Padded Forms        carbon packs are definite time-savers over padded
    (Arthur Hobbs)      forms.  AH recommends that all frequently used
                        forms be printed in carbon packs.

    Discussion          The Committee feels that we do not have sufficient
                        cost information on which to base a decision.
                        (Mr. Hobbs) is to gather data and report at the
                        January meeting.
```

5. The minutes show the plans for the next meeting, a good way of giving advance notice.
6. The names of all committee members should appear somewhere. The minutes on pages 212–213 illustrate one way of listing them. Here may also be noted those who were absent from the meeting.

■ ■

PROJECT

You are secretary of the Employee Activities Committee of Peerless Publishing Company. This committee is made up of seven people, and the chairwoman is Mary Beth Rooney. The group was formed to deal with such matters as planning recreational activities, recognizing employee achievements and anniversaries, operating an employee suggestion system, and so on. The following notes were made during the meeting of April 3.

Catherine Vining recommended that the profits from vending machines in the building ($2,440.55 last year) be used to establish a scholarship fund for children of employees. The members of the committee participated in a full discussion of this suggestion. There was one dissenting voice. Bert Whelan raised the question as to how the recipient or recipients would be chosen for the scholarship, and he pointed out the difficulties of administering such a program. He wound up by saying that the program would create ill feelings among employees whose children were not selected—that it would not accomplish what it set out to do. On the other hand, Paul Zackowitz felt that the suggestion was a worthy one. He said that an independent committee (outside the company) should be appointed and that candidates for the scholarship award should be recommended by their high school principal, based on scholarship, leadership, and need. Helen Chu agreed with Mr. Zackowitz and further suggested that two scholarships of $1,000 each be awarded each year rather than one. The group agreed on the two-scholarship idea and also endorsed Mr. Zackowitz's suggestion about administering the program through an outside committee. Amy Rhodes felt that the scholarships should be limited to those who are interested in a career in publishing, citing the need for editors and expressing the feeling that such scholarships would fill not only a need insofar as the students themselves are concerned but a publishing need as well. This idea was rejected by other committee members. The general consensus was that the scholarship idea was good enough to be thoroughly explored. Paul Zackowitz and Amy Rhodes were asked by Chairwoman Rooney to find out how other companies, particularly in publishing, handle scholarship programs. She further recommended that committee members talk with local high school principals and perhaps some teachers to see what criteria might be set up for the scholarships and to get ideas for names of people who would make the final judgment on winners of the scholarships. A full report will be given by Zackowitz and Rhodes at the next meeting on April 27.

Concerning the formation of a Bowling League, Bert Whelan reported that 17 employees have signed up as interested in participating. He is having a meeting of these people Monday, April 7, to organize the teams. He has made arrangements to purchase bowling shirts with the Peerless emblem imprinted on the back (the employee is to pay half the cost of the shirt). The shirts will not be ordered until after the first organization meeting.

Chairwoman Rooney announced that suggestion boxes have now been installed on each floor of the building and forms for making suggestions distributed to each department manager. The policies and procedures concerning employee suggestions will appear in the next printing of the *Peerless Employee Handbook*. She also reported that the balance in the treasury of the Employee Activities Committee now stands at $3,426.17.

Amy Rhodes reported that 300 copies of the anniversary brochure of the 25-Year Club will be published in June. The printing cost per copy is $1.85, and Mr. Weinberger, the president, has said that the cost can be assumed by the company.

The meeting adjourned.

Prepare minutes of the meeting, condensing the discussions as appropriate and setting up the minutes in a form of your own choosing. These are unedited notes, so watch out for poor grammar, word choice, and so forth.

■ ■

part

8

EMPLOYMENT COMMUNICATIONS

YOUR JOB

You are approaching graduation, and the time has come for you to begin to make definite plans for employment. You know of course that in order to enter the world of business you must first land a job. What you need now is the know-how to get the job you want. In fact, your first and most important job is to sell yourself.

CASE 1 ASSESSING AND SELLING YOUR QUALIFICATIONS FOR EMPLOYMENT

PROBLEM: Before you start pounding the pavement in search of a job, you need to think through the answers to some hard questions: In what kind of job would I be happiest and most productive? In what location? What assets do I have—personal, professional, educational, and social—that I can "sell" to a prospective employer? How can I present these qualifications so as to gain his favorable response?

BACKGROUND

Most people, during their working lives, will write one or more of the following types of letters: an inquiry about a job opening in a business firm, a request for permission to use the name of someone as reference, a response to an invitation from a company to apply for a position, a letter accepting or declining a position, a resignation letter, a recommendation of someone for a position.

Jobs and the Job Market. The amount of effort you must exert to land the job you want will depend largely on the competition for that job. The employment market itself fluctuates. One year there may be a scarcity of engineers, and those who qualify can choose their own employer. The next year there may be an overabundance of engineers, and competition is tough.

Some jobs are always highly competitive—certain positions in advertising, for example. Even ordinary jobs that might be a dime a dozen in industry as a whole can become highly competitive in a certain company where the pay is high and the prestige great. For example, without too much effort you can usually get a pretty good job as a salesman. But a sales position in some blue-chip companies is always hard to come by.

218

It's a good idea, no matter what the job market is like when you read this, to learn the principles of employment letter writing. Even if you don't need this know-how to get your first job, chances are that you can use it later. Many people change jobs several times during their working lives. They want to live in a certain section of the country, or they are dissatisfied with working conditions and opportunities for advancement in their present jobs, or they want to change to another kind of work. Often these people ''prospect'' by letter; that is, they send written applications to various companies, hoping to get a good lead on the job they want.

What Do You Have to Sell? Your first step in getting the job you want is to determine what you have to sell. The business firm that lays out cash for your services is just as eager to get its money's worth as if it were buying, say, a computer installation. You can be sure that company executives think long and hard before buying a computer, looking at equipment from various manufacturers to compare cost, efficiency, and service. Most of them are equally cautious when hiring people, at least those with management potential. They make comparisons among the applicants available.

You can be sure, too, that the computer salesman knows precisely what his equipment will do for a firm and why it would be a smart investment. He plans his sales strategy carefully in terms of the organization that he hopes to sell. Doesn't it make good sense that you should plan just as carefully your sales strategy for the organization that is in the market for your services?

The first thing in planning your sales strategy—perhaps the only thing—is to answer the question, Why should a firm want to hire me? If you can show that you would be a good investment for an organization, you are well on your way to getting the job you really want.

You should know every bit as much about your sales features as the computer salesman knows about his equipment's sales features. While the computer offers such features as greater speed, better customer service, and greater economy, your assets are education, experience, and personality. In answering the question, Why should a firm want to hire me? you should write down the things you have to sell.

But, first, let's look at what the employer wants when he is buying talent; then we can do a more intelligent job of sizing up ourselves in terms of his needs. Every salesman relates the features of his product to the needs of the customer, and you must do the same. You try to find out what the customer (firm) wants in the way of knowledge, attitudes, and skills and then emphasize them in your employment application. This is simply good salesmanship. The personnel manager or other executive to whom you apply *expects* it.

What Do Employers Want? The things employers want when they hire people are no different today than they ever were, and chances are that they will never change. They include, among other things, the following.

A Return on Their Investment. It is no secret that an employer expects every worker to produce a profit for him. This profit may be in the form of increased company revenue, more effective selling or customer service, savings on costs, greater production, and the like. An accountant is expected to produce several times his salary by pointing out where money is being wasted, by establishing time- and people-saving systems, and by producing a financial records system that will guide management in long-range planning. A salesman is expected to produce net revenue for the company far in excess of his salary. A corporation president earning $100,000 a year may be responsible for decisions that result in revenue amounting to a thousand times his salary.

If every worker produced only enough to pay for his salary, then there would be no profit. Let's be realistic: No effective executive ever receives in salary all that he produces. Those who do take home more income than they produce for the company don't stay around very long.

A company expects to lose money on certain employees during the first year, especially management trainees. The cost of training the new employee and orienting him to the job amounts to far more than he will produce for several months—maybe a couple of years. Sooner or later, though, the company expects to realize a profit on that investment through his ability to make the right decisions, to improve operations and procedures, to increase production, to make more sales. That's the reason companies can afford to gamble on promising new employees—and it is the only reason.

Human Effectiveness. Business is essentially people: thus it is a team effort. Few college-trained people work all by themselves. They deal with many people who influence the firm's success—suppliers, customers, competitors, and the general public. If business is to succeed, its employees must work effectively with all these people. Internal employee relations are just as important; the outward impression a business makes depends largely on internal harmony or lack of it. It is equally necessary, then, that you get along well with fellow workers, managers, supervisors, and subordinates. Indeed it is not enough merely to "get along" with them; often you must cooperate, lead, influence, motivate, and follow.

Business, therefore, is interested in knowing what kind of person you are when it comes to working with people. You may be a genius and have straight A's on your college transcript, but if you can't cope with the give-and-take of daily human relationships, you aren't going to be much good in a position that requires you to supervise, cooperate, and perhaps compromise.

If you're going to be happy operating a calculator, doing library research, or performing experiments in some hidden-away laboratory, it probably isn't important that you think about your effectiveness in human relationships. But such jobs are rare, and most of them don't pay much. The jobs that pay the most are those that require leadership—the ability to motivate others to get a job done or to accept a point of view. That's why a manager or a top salesman gets more money than a machine operator.

The Right Job Attitude. The employer is interested in your attitude toward work. He expects you to have enthusiasm for your job, the company, and the people in the company. He wants you to be so interested and enthusiastic, in fact, that you will give him more time than he actually pays for.

The old slogan, "An honest day's work for an honest day's pay," does not apply to the ambitious person. It isn't strong enough! The employer would change it to read, "Give the job all you've got and don't worry about the pay." If this seems selfish and hard, then you must think about the problems that the typical business is faced with. Competition is keen and many businesses fall by the wayside because they are outsmarted or because their management simply isn't effective. Management wants people who are dedicated to the company's growth, who are keenly competitive, and who are success-conscious.

The greater your responsibility, the more hours you can expect to put in on your job. That's why men on the move take a briefcase full of work home on evenings and weekends. They don't think about how many hours they work or whether they are being paid enough; they think only of doing their job. It is a fact that those who work hard without worrying whether they're being paid enough usually get the plums in business. They earn them.

Imagination. Business thrives on the imagination of its workers. That is why top management looks for the inquisitive person, the innovator, the thinker. The employee who thinks imaginatively about how to save money, increase production, compete more effectively, or get a bigger share of the market is highly prized. Of course, business doesn't expect you to turn everything upside down in your first month on the job, but most progressive firms won't expect you to settle comfortably in your job and continue to do things the way they have always been done. They want improvement, and improvement means change.

Of course, some executives won't reach out for new ideas because they don't want to rock the boat. If you run into one of them, don't get the idea that his is a typical attitude. The most successful companies have executives at the top who encourage innovation and creativity.

Knowledge. No matter how skillful you are in human relationships, how imaginative in designing new systems or products, and how positive your attitude toward your work, there is no substitute for job knowledge. If you advertise yourself as an accountant, you are expected to know the fundamentals of accounting theory, cost methods, auditing procedures, modern data processing, and the like. A good secretary must, among other things, be able to take dictation no matter what the speed or the material and transcribe it into flawless letters and reports (perhaps doing a great deal of editing in the process). A salesman must know markets, buying motives, sales psychology, and so on. In your job campaign, then, it is important that you emphasize the education that equips you for the job you are after.

Communicating Ability. Because this is a book on communication, you may get the idea that communicating ability is listed as a "must" in self-defense. Not so. The truth is that one of the biggest complaints about those who aspire to management is that they are poor communicators. And we're talking not only about people whose primary work is writing communications but also about salesmen, accountants, secretaries, market researchers, financial analysts, and others. If you have better-than-average ability to express yourself orally and in writing, emphasize this on your list of qualifications, for it is a fundamental requirement for management success.

Ambition. Never was the demand for management talent so great as it is today. This demand is attested to by the fact that hundreds of large companies are forced to carry on expensive programs to train managers from the ranks. Obviously, in considering talent, management wants people who aspire to positions of responsibility, not people who either lack the interest or the talent to move up in the organization. Ambition is not a vice; it is a virtue. Don't be afraid to let people know that you don't want to sit still—that you want to grow in your job. Of course, you wouldn't be so foolhardy as to expect the vice president's job the first year, but at the same time you don't want to leave the impression you will always be satisfied with the job you begin with.

Assessing Your Qualifications. Now let's get back to the question, Why should an organization want to hire me? To answer that intelligently, you need to find out as much as you can about the employer's expectations.

If you know that, for a certain position, an employer prefers people with experience—and you have very little—you would be foolish to emphasize experience as one of your prime assets. Or if you learn that a position you want demands a good knowledge of Spanish and you've had only a couple of years of high school Spanish, you probably will want to emphasize your readiness to become fluent in the language rather than your proficiency in it. Try, then, to learn all you can about the prospective employer's preferences and requirements so that you can fit your presentation to his particular needs.

Suppose you are answering this advertisement that appeared in a metropolitan newspaper.

```
Management trainees in  marketing research.
Minimum two years of college, preferably in
marketing  and/or business  administration.
Heavy writing.   Apply Box 73, Times.
```

Not much here, you say? Actually, the employer has said a great deal.

1. He wants applicants with management aspirations ("management trainees").
2. He does not expect applicants to have work experience.

3. He wants people with at least two years of college (and you'll be favored if you have a marketing or business major).
4. He wants people with the ability to write well and handle a large volume of writing.

Given these clues, you are ready to match assets against requirements.

First, you will review your college work and highlight those courses and achievements that you think will impress the employer.

Second, you will emphasize your ability to express yourself in writing.

Then what? You will want to let the employer know what kind of person you are. Your activities in college, your work experience, your hobbies, your long-range goals—all help to reveal things about you that an employer will want to know.

Presenting Your Qualifications. After you have thought about the job, the employer's needs, and your fitness for the position—and only then—you are ready to summarize your qualifications in the form of a sales presentation.

The presentation of an applicant's qualifications may be called a data sheet, personal profile, qualifications summary, or résumé. By whatever name it is called, the qualifications presentation should enable the prospective employer to see at a glance the extent of the applicant's education and experience as well as something about him as a person. Suitable headings and an uncrowded appearance help the data sheet do this.

Preparing a data sheet will give you a head start on the application blank, which is usually required, and help you get ready for the job interview.

Since your data sheet is your sales presentation, personalize it. Use your imagination (and good taste) in adapting the conventional headings and their sequence. The way in which you describe your qualifications will, of course, depend on the job you are applying for.

Make sure that the physical appearance of your data sheet is top-notch: a good grade of bond paper; clear, clean typing; good spacing and arrangement; no misspellings or grammatical errors. If you are not an expert typist, hire one to do the job.

Your data sheet will make a better impression if it is an original. Using originals can be expensive if you send data sheets to a number of prospective employers. But when you consider how important landing that job is to you, you may decide to spend the extra money for originals. A really sharp mimeographed sheet, an offset-printed one, or a professionally printed one is acceptable, but a carbon or a fluid-duplicated copy is not. A copy of a data sheet, no matter how crisp, will imply that you are giving it wide distribution. That may be true, but each employer likes to think he is your first choice.

Keep your data sheet to two pages if you can. In some cases one page may be enough, but don't squeeze and condense your story just for the sake of brevity.

Above all, don't be modest in stating your qualifications. The data sheet is a sales presentation and you are expected to point out your good qualities.

The one-page data sheet shown below is what Martin T. Hammond's presentation might look like if he were answering the add (page 222) for a management trainee in marketing research. Mr. Hammond rightly emphasizes his education, specifically those courses most relevant to the position he is applying for.

SOLUTION A

```
                         MARTIN T. HAMMOND
                1977 DuBlanc Avenue, Monroe, Louisiana 71201
                       Telephone:  (318) 515-1234

           Position Wanted:  Marketing Research Management Trainee

     EDUCATION

     Degree:  B.B.A. (will be graduated in June, 19--), Centenary College,
              Shreveport, Louisiana.  Major:  Marketing

        Marketing Courses:
           Marketing Principles      Advertising         Retail Merchandising
           Marketing Research        Sales Management    Fundamentals of Buying

        Other Business Courses:
           Business Communication    Accounting          Money and Banking
           Business Statistics       Business Law        Government and Business

        Comments:  I maintained a B average in my business subjects and was
        on the Dean's List.  I especially enjoyed my marketing courses.  In
        Marketing Research, I made four A's and two B's on required research
        reports; two reports were exhibited as models of excellence.

     EXPERIENCE

     June-September, 19-5  Warehouse clerk, Tracy's Discount Store, Monroe,
                          Louisiana.  Filled customer orders, maintained
                          inventory, supervised two part-time helpers.

     July-August, 19-4    Deliveryman, Davey's Pharmacy, Monroe.  Drove truck,
                          assisted in stockkeeping, did some floor selling.

     June-September, 19-3 Route salesman, Cavell Home Products.  Sold aluminum
                          cooking ware from house to house.

     19-0 - 19-2 (various Laborer (repaired city streets and helped with re-
         dates)           planting city parks), filling station helper, paper
                          carrier, lawn tender.

     ORGANIZATIONS AND HOBBIES

     Organizations:  Debating Society, Marketing Club (treasurer), Tau Kappa
     Epsilon (social fraternity), Interfraternity Council, tennis team.

     Hobbies:  Building and flying model airplanes, tennis, writing short stories.

     PERSONAL DATA

     Birth Date:  October 29, 19--  Weight:  170  Height:  6'  Health:  Excellent

     REFERENCES

     Dr. Edward Hale, Professor of Marketing, Centenary College, Shreveport,
     Louisiana 71104.

     Mr. A. T. Mitchell, Manager, Tracy's Discount Store, Monroe, Louisiana 71201.

     Judge R. N. Toffenetti, 1416 DuBlanc Avenue, Monroe, Louisiana 71201.
```

Analysis of Solution A. Now let's look at each part of a well-prepared data sheet, such as that of Martin Hammond.

Heading. Whether you use in the heading "Résumé of," "Data Sheet," etc., or just your name is optional. If you feel something is needed to head the form, here are several variations.

Résumé of

MARTIN T. HAMMOND
1977 DuBlanc Avenue
Monroe, Louisiana 71201

(318) 515-1234

MARTIN T. HAMMOND

Job Qualifications Summary

1977 DuBlanc Avenue
Monroe, Louisiana 71201

(318) 515-1234

Personal Profile

MARTIN T. HAMMOND

Prepared for Western Oil Company

Position Wanted. Personnel managers strongly urge applicants to specify the job they are applying for. If you do not know the title of the job—or indeed whether there *is* a job for you—identify the general area in which you are interested. Unless you apply for a job in the personnel department, the personnel manager himself won't actually hire you. He will simply screen your papers and forward them to the executive in whose department the vacancy exists. Naming the job you are after will make the papers travel faster to the person in the organization who should see them. Besides, your case is strengthened considerably when you know what you want and ask for it. Such vague generalities as "marketing work" and "general management" tell the prospective employer almost nothing.

Education. Most college students have only a modest amount of job experience; the main thing they have to offer an employer is their education. That part of your education which equips you to handle the job you are applying for should be emphasized so that it gets immediate attention.

In addition to the format shown in Martin Hammond's data sheet on page 224, here are two other ways in which you could show your educational background.

EDUCATION

Three years at Centenary College, Shreveport, Louisiana (19— - 19—), studying marketing and business administration. Had to leave school before graduation for financial reasons.

Major courses included economics, marketing principles, salesmanship, business management, accounting (three semesters), business statistics, sales management, business psychology, and industrial relations.

A.A.	Norwalk Community College, Norwalk, Connecticut, 19—
	Major: General Business
B.B.A.	Centenary College, Shreveport, Louisiana, 19—
	Major: Marketing

Courses in Marketing and Related Fields:

Marketing Principles	Sales Administration
Advertising	Retail Management
Market Research	Merchandising Techniques
Salesmanship	International Marketing
Business Writing	Buying for Marketing

High School	Monroe, Louisiana. Graduated in 19—
	Business courses included typewriting, general business, and business machines.

Experience. Employers are interested in almost any kind of work experience—it doesn't have to be specifically related to the job for which you are applying. Working for others shows a certain amount of independence and maturity. If you bagged groceries in a supermarket, sold magazines, or supervised young people at a summer camp, list these activities. Experience should be described in reverse chronological order—that is, the most recent job first.

In relating your experience, give the date, title of the job, name of the person or firm, and a brief description of your duties. If you have had actual experience in the type of job for which you are making application, enlarge on this with a longer description.

Organizations and Hobbies. The purpose of listing the organizations you belong to in college and your hobbies is to give the prospective employer some clues about the kind of person you are. Your out-of-class activities say something about your mixing well with people, your leadership ability, and your general personality. Note that Mr. Hammond mentions writing as one of his hobbies. Again, this supports his earlier statement about his writing ability. In another data sheet for a different job, he might have, though not necessarily, omitted this activity.

Personal Data. There is no point in giving your life history under the heading "Personal Data." Sufficient vital statistics for the data sheet are your age, physical facts, and general health. Elaborating on them will not help to sell you—and the data sheet is a sales instrument. You will have ample opportunity on the application blank or in a personal interview to go into more detail. On their data sheet some people include place of birth, national origin (Irish, for example), and religious affiliation. Such information is not important and is best omitted.

References. It is generally recommended that you list three references on the data sheet, although it is acceptable to simply state, "References supplied upon request." Since education is your most marketable product, make sure one of your references is a dean, a professor, or other college person who knows you well. But don't force any references; the lady down the street for whom you mowed lawns when you were fourteen wouldn't make a very impressive reference.

Another person on your reference list should be someone who can vouch for your character. You can use the name of your priest, minister, or rabbi if you feel such a reference is appropriate. A prominent citizen or a local businessman who knows you and your family will also serve the purpose.

It is no secret that you list as references only those who you know will say the right thing in your behalf. Obviously, an employer doesn't expect you to list your enemies as references, and he knows that you have chosen your references because they think well of you.

It is a cardinal rule that you never use a person's name without first asking for permission. This can be done by a telephone call, a visit, or a letter. Such a letter might look like this.

> Dear Judge Toffenetti:
>
> Graduation is only a few weeks away, and if everything goes right, I will receive my B.B.A. degree from Centenary June 2. I don't know who will be happier—me or my dad!
>
> Now I'm getting ready to look for a job. My interest is in marketing research, and I hope to find a management trainee position in some large company, preferably in New Orleans or Atlanta.
>
> May I include your name as a reference on my application? If you will do this favor for me, just write your "OK" at the bottom of this letter and return it to me in the enclosed stamped envelope.
>
> Best wishes to you and Mrs. Toffenetti. I will be in Monroe about June 8, and I hope to see both of you then.
>
> Sincerely yours,

SOLUTION B

A variation in the presentation of qualifications is shown in the two-page data sheet on pages 228–229. This was prepared by Sara Jacobsen to support her application for a secretarial job she heard about from the placement director of the University of Fort Lauderdale. The director shared with Miss Jacobsen the notes she had made during a phone call from Loughborough Paper Company about an opening as secretary to the comptroller, R. H. Brewer.

> Secretary, experienced preferred (if experienced, could quickly become executive secretary). Considerable dictation. Some statistical typing. Must write some letters and simple reports. Should have good knowledge of accounting and math. Apply in writing. (Very good job.)

As Miss Jacobsen studied these job requirements, she mentally noted what she should emphasize in her data sheet: experience, secretarial skills, writing ability, and knowledge of accounting and math. She recognized that as comptroller, Mr. Brewer was no doubt the chief accounting officer of his company, and she planned to use this clue to guide her in preparing her data sheet. If the position had required outstanding shorthand and typing skill, she would have given more emphasis to these skills. If the ability to supervise

```
                        Qualifications of
                          SARA JACOBSEN
                          17 Cayuga Lane
                   Fort Lauderdale, Florida 33308
                     Telephone:  (305) 936-4421


    Position applied for:   Secretary to Mr. R. H. Brewer
                            Vice President and Comptroller
                            Loughborough Paper Company

    EXPERIENCE

        At present          Administrative assistant to the Dean of Faculties,
                            University of Fort Lauderdale.  In this position,
                            which I have held all this academic year while a
                            student, I have the following responsibilities:

                            1.  Take all the Dean's dictation (often heavy);
                                type her memorandums and reports, many of
                                which are statistical; receive visitors;
                                answer the telephone; keep the Dean's appoint-
                                ment calendar; and do the filing.

                            2.  Write many letters and reports for the Dean's
                                signature to job applicants, other deans and
                                administrators, faculty members, parents,
                                students, and others.  Assist the Dean in
                                research for reports and articles she writes
                                for publication.

                            3.  Supervise two part-time clerks.

                            4.  Assist in the preparation of budgets, personnel
                                reports, and financial proposals.

        19-4                Clerk-stenographer, Florida Credit Corporation.
                            In this summer job, I took some dictation and typed
                            contracts, letters, bank documents, and financial
                            statements.

        19-3 - 19-4         Salesclerk (part-time after school and on Saturdays),
                            Craig's Variety Store.  In this job, I waited on
                            customers and assisted in the office and the stock-
                            room.  Did some light typing and filing of invoices.

    EDUCATION

        College

        Attended University of Fort Lauderdale, 19-- to 19--, majoring in
        Secretarial Science.  Will be graduated in June with A.A. degree.
```

people had been stressed, she would have provided more details about her experience as a supervisor.

Analysis of Solution B. Unlike Martin Hammond, Sara Jacobsen presents her work experience first. In this way she emphasizes what she has actually done that helps her qualify for the specific secretarial job she is applying for. She also details college secretarial and business courses she has completed.

Qualifications of Sara Jacobsen   Page 2

    Secretarial and Business Courses Completed:

      Shorthand (120 words a minute; hold Gregg certificate)
      Typewriting (78 words a minute; hold Gregg certificate)
      English (composition, vocabulary, letter writing, report writing)
      Secretarial Procedures
      Accounting (principles, cost, and intermediate)
      Data Processing (including computer programming)
      Mathematics of Accounting and Finance (two semesters)
      Economics
      Business Machines

    <u>High School</u>

      Graduated from Fort Lauderdale High School, 19-5. Took the business curriculum, which included shorthand, typewriting, secretarial practice, personal development, business English, and office machines.

    <u>Scholastic Honors and Activities</u>

      National Honor Society
      Psi Beta Chi (social sorority), University of Fort Lauderdale
      Executive Secretaries Club
      Fort Lauderdale Choral Society (Vice President)

OTHER INTERESTS

    Sing with the Fort Lauderdale Choral Society and the First Baptist Church choir and play the piano and the guitar.

    Swimming, water skiing, deep-sea diving.

PERSONAL DATA

    Birth Date: January 1, 19-2
    Physical: Weight, 120; height, 5'5"
    Health: Excellent

REFERENCES (by permission)

    Dr. J. Frank Halderman, Chairman, Department of Secretarial Administration, University of Fort Lauderdale. Telephone 462-1527 (Ext. 27).

    Dr. Phyllis Tangerman, Dean of Faculties, University of Fort Lauderdale. Telephone 462-1527 (Ext. 31).

    Rev. Frank C. Carter, First Baptist Church, Fort Lauderdale. Telephone 847-4756.

■■

PROJECT

Prepare data sheets for any two of the following twenty positions, emphasizing in each one the skills or abilities you possess that match the employer's requirements.

1 PERSONNEL ASSISTANT (Job Evaluation). Excellent opportunity for college-trained man or woman in Personnel Department of large advertising agency. Must have at least two years of college, preferably in personnel or business administration. We'll train you, and you earn as you learn. Write to Box No. M 1465, Post. An equal opportunity employer.

2 PERSONNEL INTERVIEWER. We want people who are interested in a career in personnel administration, and interviewing prospective employees is an ideal place to start. Business training (some college) required. Must be able to speak well, present good appearance, write reports. In this job you will learn to interview, screen, and test applicants for jobs. Send résumé to Box 14, Times.

3 MANAGER TRAINEE. Publicly owned multimillion-dollar building company needs young man to train for manager of new subdivision. Must have feeling for organization, marketing, sales/display, advertising, and public relations. Security, salary, and fringe benefits of major corporation. Excellent starting salary for the right person. Write Mrs. L. Jones, Suite 309, Bradley Building.

4 MANAGEMENT TRAINEE. Interested in finance? Our company has 3 openings for young college persons who have good training in finance and are interested in managing a finance or budget department. Excellent starting salary and fringe benefits. Nationally known corporation, excellent chances for advancement. Address Box 98-C, Star-Ledger. E.O.E.

5 HOSPITAL ADMINISTRATION. Want young man or woman to train as hospital administrator. Degree preferred but not essential. Applicant should have general knowledge of accounting. This job requires an individual who can work well with people and who is strong in communication skills. Modest beginning salary but outstanding opportunities for frequent financial and career advancement. Send résumé to J. I. Trumble, 2401 Blueridge Avenue, Morristown.

6 MANAGEMENT TRAINEES—AVIATION ACTIVITIES. Firm dealing in aviation activities (we have several government contracts) desires to interview men and women who have management aspirations. Good benefits, fine starting salary. Address Box 123, Inquirer.

7 SALES CAREER. Century-old international financial institution has opening for 2 counselors in investment and insurance. Complete 2-year training program. Will consider those with no experience. For interview, send brief personal history to Box No. M 1434, Chronicle.

8 SALES. Top opportunity for ambitious go-getter. Any good experience in auto or route selling will help. Salary plus commission. Write Cynthia Olwell, 217 Mayfair Building.

9 SALES. We are a nationally recognized sales and marketing personnel agency, and we are seeking an intelligent, motivated, people- and sales-oriented individual capable of justifying and maintaining a 5-figure income with consistency. Previous history of success in sales or personnel would be advantageous but will consider good college business administration background. Must be able to communicate effectively on all levels from recent college grad to executive. Ability to work successfully with a minimum of supervision a must. Candidate selected will take over currently productive desk. Call John Mulholland, Ajax Agency. Have résumé ready.

10 SALES OPENINGS. We have several excellent openings for people interested in selling. Our clients include food manufacturers, retail furniture dealers, magazine publishers (space selling), time-sharing firms, and many others. Name your interest—we have the job if you're qualified. Tell us about yourself. Box 0072, Times-Herald.

11 MARKETING/PUBLIC RELATIONS. Rare opportunity in education field. We are interviewing for several openings in our marketing management training program. If you like people, are ambitious, a hard worker, and college-trained, then you will be thoroughly trained in our successful marketing methods. Earn an excellent salary. Opportunity for advancement into management as fast as ability and performance warrant. Send résumé to Box 27, World Globe.

12 ACCOUNTANT—AUTOMOTIVE. Fast-growing auto dealership requires accountant to work closely with general manager in overall operations. Applicant must have strong background in accounting principles and be looking for a permanent position with a bright future. Some experience in automotive accounting preferred. Reply Box 2 (Mrs. Agnes Lawson), Examiner.

13 ACCOUNTING MANAGER. Growing firm has immediate need for fully qualified, aggressive accountant who can quickly develop to take full charge of general accounting and auditing functions. Knowledge of cost accounting and budgeting techniques desired. Excellent opportunity for the right person. Full package of employee benefits and salary commensurate with education and experience. Submit résumé to Daily Blade, Box 47113.

14 ACCOUNTING—SYSTEMS AND PROCEDURES. Headquarters of national association has opening for a person with good background in accounting and economics. This is a non-data-processing-oriented position. If you have initiative and imagination, a thorough knowledge of business procedures, and a better-than-average ability to express ideas in writing, please send us your résumé. Box C-40, Tribune. An Equal Opportunity Employer.

15 JR. INTERNAL AUDITOR. Office of controller in large expanding firm is seeking an individual in a full-time junior auditor's position. If you are a 2- or 4-year graduate or a student attending night school in accounting and want to earn while you learn, here is an excellent opportunity. No experience necessary. Salary commensurate with education. Write to Oscar Jesurun, Star Foods, Inc., 6900 Landover Road. Equal Opportunity Employer.

16 ADMINISTRATIVE SECRETARY. No shorthand. For this spot you must be a thoroughly trained individual with emphasis in business administration, office procedures, and supervision. Lots of public contact, so you must enjoy working with all sorts of people. Can advance to department manager. Good typing ability, letter writing, routine reports. Pleasant private office. Assist president in public relations work. Résumé to Box 16, Clarion.

17 EXECUTIVE SECRETARY. Great opportunity for person with high level of stenographic skills. Work for VP of Marketing, assisting him in planning, research, contacts with sales representatives, advertising and promotion, and so on. General knowledge of accounting helpful but not necessary. Prefer some college. Good salary, with all benefits, sophisticated offices. Send qualifications summary to J. T. Evans, Albert Gamble Building.

18 ADMINISTRATIVE ASSISTANT—INTERNATIONAL AND CRIMINAL LAW. Well-known lawyer seeks versatile person to be his right arm. You'll handle various administrative matters and may even attend court cases. Fast-paced and challenging opportunity, with typing and shorthand skills. No law experience. More of a management job than secretarial—managing the boss, supervising small clerical staff, etc. "Takeover" type desired! Write to Lawrence Applebaum, Box 4747, Centertown.

19 ADMINISTRATIVE AIDE—URBAN RENEWAL. As executive secretary to senior partner of firm dealing with urban renewal, you will be in a key administrative position where you can utilize your executive talents along with your shorthand and typing. Excellent future and benefits. Want to be "involved"? This is the place. Write to Betty Grayson, 1102 Riddell Building. An E.O.E.

20 MEDICAL SECRETARY. Medical secretary (work for Chief Medical Officer) with good skills and knowledge of medical terminology. Exciting opportunity. Write to Personnel Manager, Providence Hospital.

■■■■■■■■■■■■■■■■■■■■■■■■■■■■■■■■■■■■

CASE 2

WRITING THE APPLICATION LETTER

PROBLEM: Let's repeat the advertisement for which Martin T. Hammond prepared his data sheet.

```
Management trainees in  marketing research.
Minimum two years of college, preferably in
marketing  and/or business  administration.
Heavy writing.   Apply Box 73, Times.
```

What kind of letter would you write in answer to this ad?

BACKGROUND

The data sheet is essentially a personal history which concentrates on dates and events. But even though it is an individualized presentation of one's qualifications, it is not intended to be a highly *personal* one. That is, there is little opportunity in the data sheet to reveal one's sincerity, ambition, and enthusiasm.

The really personal document in employment communications is the letter of application. It may be written in answer to an ad, it may be written because the writer has been referred to a job opening by a friend, or it may be entirely unsolicited. In each case, however, the purpose of the application letter is to obtain an interview; it is therefore a sales letter. Its job is to attract favorable attention and to persuade a prospective employer that the data sheet—as well as the applicant himself—is worth looking at.

The application letter is generally accompanied by a data sheet; therefore, it does not merely repeat the dates, events, and achievements in the data sheet. It *supports* that presentation by giving the employer a more personal statement of an applicant's interest in and fitness for a particular job.

You won't need a long letter to do the job—certainly not more than one page. If your data sheet is complete, there isn't much to be said in the application letter. The letter should be built around one or all of these points:

1. Why I want the job and feel qualified for it.
2. What my interests, ambitions, and aspirations are.
3. What I expect to do for you, the employer.
4. When I'm available and how I can be reached.

We mentioned that the application letter is a sales letter. And so it is. But remember that you are not selling a bag of flour. For example:

> Wouldn't you like to have an eager, dynamic, resourceful college graduate working for you—a man with ideas, imagination, and ambition? I'm your man.

Such a beginning sounds bombastic—even laughable—to the typical executive who reads it. He is likely to put the applicant down as a know-it-all. While you don't want to hide your light under a bushel, neither do you want to give the impression that you have all the answers. Managers are well aware that the big talkers are rarely the big doers. Even old hands don't know all the answers. As they struggle with the brain-wracking problems of their jobs, imagine how they feel toward the fellow who makes the work sound like a cinch.

Unless you are applying for a very competitive position that you know will require you to display your ingenuity, don't. Occasionally, tricky letters will work—in advertising agencies, for example, where shock effects are part of the game. For example, one applicant for an agency job affixed his picture to a cover of *Time* magazine, calling himself "Man of the Year." Inside was a biographical sketch, such as *Time* might publish, emphasizing the applicant's talents, ingenuity, education, and so on. For the purpose, it must have been effective, because he got the job.

For the typical job in business, however, you will want to strike a chord somewhere between the boastful and the modest. Certainly you won't approach an employer on your knees with "You probably wouldn't want to hire an accounting graduate with no experience, would you?" There is no harm in saying frankly what you believe you can do for a firm.

Above all, don't copy a letter someone else has written, no matter how good the author says it is. Your letter should be you—honestly you—and nobody else.

For your letter use a good grade of white bond paper ($8\frac{1}{2}$ by 11 inches) that matches the paper used for the data sheet. Never use a company letterhead (believe it or not, some people have written application letters on hotel stationery) or tinted paper. Leave generous margins all around. You want your letter to invite reading.

Another point is worth repeating: Exhaust every source to find the name and title of the person to whom your letter should be addressed. Then be sure that the name is written the way the recipient likes it and that the title is accurate. If Mr. J. Walter Meade is Director of Marketing, don't address him as Mr. J. W. Mead, Marketing Department.

The first thing to keep in mind as you answer the ad in the case problem is that you are probably going to have plenty of competition. This is no reason to make your letter shout, but it *is* a good reason to make your letter good looking, accurate, and somewhat persuasive. By the way, if you consider yourself a little weak in grammar and punctuation, have an English major (or your instructor in business communication) check it for you.

SOLUTION A

Gentlemen:

I want to apply for the job in marketing research you advertised. My data sheet is enclosed.

I very much want to work in Atlanta because I have relatives there. I need the job because I am helping to support my parents (my father is disabled).

I am sorry I don't have any experience, but I hope you will not hold that against me. College students don't have much of an opportunity to get experience, and we have to start some place.

Sincerely yours,

Analysis of Solution A. You don't have to be told that this is a very poor letter, assuming that the organization to which it is sent is not charity-minded (most aren't!). All you have to do is think how you would feel if you were doing the hiring and received such a letter.

1. The opening is trite and ordinary; probably a hundred others will say the same thing. Also it is not clear where the applicant learned about the job (the *Times*).

2. The writer concentrates on why *he* wants the job—not why the firm might want to hire him. Beware of personal reasons for applying for a job, such as the fact that relatives are nearby. And never say you *need* work; this puts you in the position of a beggar, and you are expected to have some pride. Lots of people have financial problems—and young college graduates are no exception—but keep the problems to yourself.

3. Don't apologize for lack of experience. The person getting started in business isn't expected to have worked at anything except part-time or temporary jobs, most of which are unrelated to his main interest.

4. The last sentence in paragraph 3 is sarcastic. If the reader gets this far, it will surely sink the applicant.

5. The writer offers no details about when he will be available, how he might be reached, whether he could come for an interview, and so on. The last paragraph should suggest action, leaving no doubt in the employer's mind that an interview is desired and giving details on how it might be arranged.

SOLUTION B

1977 DuBlanc Avenue
Monroe, Louisiana 71201
May 16, 19—

Box 73
Atlanta Times
916 Peachtree Street, N.W.
Atlanta, Georgia 30309

Gentlemen:

The position you advertised in the May 14 Times for management trainees in marketing research is exactly the opportunity I had hoped to find. As I read the ad, I felt that you were talking to me.

As you will see by the enclosed résumé, I will be graduated from Centenary College in June with a major in marketing. I feel that I have an excellent marketing education (21 semester hours in my major), supported by a broad program in business administration and liberal arts. Of special interest to me was my course in marketing research. Not only did we study modern techniques, but we were required to read and report on significant current books in the field—including two by E. B. Weiss and the highly controversial Markets and Media, by Marshall McGoogan. Writing those reports and others requiring the use of sampling techniques and interviews was the most interesting part of my work (and my grades in this course prove it).

In college I held several part-time jobs and was still able to maintain a good grade-point average while carrying a full academic load.

On June 7 I will complete my work here and can come to Atlanta any day after that. Will you allow me the privilege of talking with you in person and telling you why I believe I can be useful to your firm in the exciting field of marketing research? If you prefer to telephone me, you may reach me at (318) 515-1234.

Sincerely yours,

Martin T. Hammond

Analysis of Solution B. This effective letter has features that you could give a similar letter of your own.

Heading. Type your address and date as shown. The address to which you expect a reply to be sent is a must, even though it is included in your data sheet.

Inside Address. Some ads indicate the company's name and ask that the applications be addressed to "The Personnel Director." In this case, you will use the salutation "Dear Sir." If the person's name is given, you will, of course, use it in the salutation. Remember, make every effort to learn the name and use it.

Opening Paragraph. You can open your application letter in various ways. The one illustrated is effective for three reasons:

1. It comes right to the point; the writer doesn't beat around the bush in applying for the job.
2. It reveals that the writer is genuinely interested in the job.
3. It identifies the source of information about the job.

Here are other possible openings:

The enclosed résumé, I believe, will provide evidence that I am a logical candidate for the position of management trainee in marketing research that you advertised in the May 14 Times.

Will you please consider me an applicant for the position of management trainee in marketing research that you advertised in the May 14 Times?

My interest and specialized training in marketing make me an exceptionally well-qualified candidate for the position of marketing research trainee as described in the May 14 Times. Will you please consider me an enthusiastic applicant?

If the name of the company or the type of business is mentioned in the advertisement, the following would be effective openings.

Marcal is a name that I know very well, not only because you distribute your products nationally but also because you have an excellent reputation among marketing people for innovations in food packaging and distribution. I would consider it a privilege to work in your marketing research department (Times of May 14) and would like to be considered a trainee applicant.

A genuine interest in food distribution, a desire to make a career in marketing research, energy and ambition, and a specialized college training in marketing—these are the things I can offer in response to your advertisement in the May 14 Times.

Some writers prefer the opening immediately above because it puts the applicant's primary sales features right up front.

Second Paragraph. You will have to think long and hard about what goes into your second paragraph. The opening introduces you and gets the employer interested. The job of the second paragraph is to convince him that you have the qualifications he is looking for.

Ask yourself the question, "What human-interest features about my experience or education might the executive want to know that I didn't include in my data sheet?" In Solution B Martin Hammond has assumed that the progressive marketing man knows who E. B. Weiss is and has at least heard about Marshall McGoogan. Even if he hasn't, it is probably worth taking a chance to show that Mr. Hammond is familiar with the current literature in the field. Note the emphasis on writing ability in this paragraph.

The second paragraph obviously is a good example of why you can't copy somebody else's letter. You need to single out your own special attributes for emphasis, and no two people have the same ones.

Third Paragraph. It is a good idea to let the employer know that work doesn't scare you and that you like challenge. He will interpret this as willingness to apply yourself and to learn. Mr. Hammond got both points across.

Closing Paragraph. The closing paragraph should be an action paragraph, telling the employer that you want an interview and suggesting ways in which it might be arranged. Of course, not everybody can travel several hundred miles for an interview, as suggested in Mr. Hammond's letter. If it is out of the question for you, then you can simply leave the matter open, hoping the company will be sufficiently interested in you to pay your travel expenses or perhaps suggest an interview with one of their nearby representatives. Or you might say something like this:

> Will you allow me the privilege of an interview? Do you have a representative in this area with whom I might discuss my qualifications?

This statement implies that you won't be able to travel to the employer's headquarters at your own expense but are willing to go a reasonable distance.

Signature. Type your name exactly the way you sign it. And don't forget to sign the letter! It is surprising how many people, after struggling for hours or days over the contents of an application letter, spoil the entire effect by failing to sign it.

The Salary Question. Some advertisements ask applicants to state the salary expected. Most advertisements don't. Never bring up the subject of money unless you are asked to or unless you have a burning financial problem and a few dollars makes a big difference. If you must have a certain amount in order to live and pay off your debts, then be frank and say how much.

> As to salary, I feel that the minimum I could accept is $8,500.

If money is not the crucial issue (salaries for college trainees are surprisingly close in similar industries), don't even bring up the subject.

Referral Application Letter. The best entrée you can have to a job is when you are recommended by a person whom the employer knows and whose opinion he respects. For example, your major professor receives word from a personnel director that a certain type of person is wanted to fill a vacancy and your qualifications happen to match the requirements. Such a recommendation gives you one leg up the ladder; the employer doesn't have to puzzle about who you are and why you are applying.

Such an application letter may be similar to the one addressed to Mr. Brewer, below. The main difference is that you will mention, in the opening paragraph, the name of the person who suggested that you apply. For example:

Dear Mr. Carlson:

Professor George T. Courtright, chairman of the Accounting Department at Monmouth College, has suggested that I apply for the position of cost accountant that you spoke to him about earlier this week. The job sounds very interesting to me, and I should like to be considered for it.

or

Dear Mr. Carlson:

Will you please consider me for the position of cost accountant about which you recently spoke to Professor Courtright? He recommended that I write to you and apply for the job.

The second and succeeding paragraphs will be similar to those you would write in answer to an advertisement. You would be wise, however, to capitalize on the name of the person who recommended you. For example:

I feel that I had excellent training in accounting at Monmouth (24 semester hours in my major), supported by a broad program in business administration and liberal arts. Of special interest to me was Professor Courtright's course in data processing techniques as they affect modern cost accounting procedures. Here we studied . . . .

Following is the letter Sara Jacobsen might write to apply for the position of secretary to Mr. Brewer (pages 227–229).

Mr. R. H. Brewer
Vice President and Comptroller
Loughborough Paper Company
320 Broadway
Miami, Florida 33142

Dear Mr. Brewer:

Mrs. Farnsworth, placement director at the University of Fort Lauderdale, described the secretarial position available in your accounting department. It is at her suggestion that I am making application for it.

Ever since I took a business curriculum in high school, I have had trouble deciding between secretarial work and accounting as a career. I did extremely well in these subjects in high school and college and have had experience in both areas during the past year. I made up my mind at the beginning of my second year at the University of Fort Lauderdale that I would make secretarial studies my major and accounting my minor. Since the position as your secretary offers an opportunity to work in both fields, it seems ideal for me.

A statement of my qualifications is enclosed. I shall be pleased to provide further details at a personal interview, and I can come to your office when it is convenient for you.

You may reach me at 462-1527 (Ext. 31) until 3 p.m. each day and at 936-4421 after 4 p.m.

Sincerely yours,

Sara Jacobsen

Unsolicited Application Letter. Sometimes you may have your heart set on a job in a particular section of the country but do not have any leads on jobs or firms. One way to get leads is to obtain newspapers from cities where you want to work and see if there are advertisements that appeal to you. Another way is to contact local firms that are likely to have a branch or main office in that city. In some cases, you will simply have to choose the type of firm you want to work for, obtain the addresses of several leading firms in the city of your choice, and write to the personnel directors. (In many cities you can obtain telephone directories of any city in the United States.)

Suppose you live in Charlotte, North Carolina, and want to work in San Francisco. If you're like most people, you can't afford to make the long trip from Charlotte to San Francisco, at least without some definite hope that you will have a job when you get there. Your interest is petroleum accounting, and you have selected five major oil companies to which you will direct your inquiries about job opportunities.

Following is a letter you might write. Of course, the letter will be accompanied by a data sheet.

Comptroller
Western Oil Company
1518 El Camino Real
San Francisco, California 94136

Dear Sir:

Do you have a place in your department at Western Oil Company for a young man who

1. Hopes to make a career of accounting—particularly in the petroleum industry?
2. Has a broad background in accounting but knows that he must prove himself by on-the-job training?
3. Is eager to learn and not afraid to dig in?

In June I will be graduated from King's College, Charlotte, North Carolina, and I am eager to find a challenging job in the San Francisco area.

My data sheet is enclosed. Would you let me know, please, whether you are interested in my qualifications?

Cordially yours,

■■■■■■■■■■■■■■■■■■■■■■■■■■■■■■■■■■■■■■■

PROJECTS

A Write application letters to accompany the data sheets you prepared in Case 1, page 230.

B Carlton J. Sibley, assistant personnel manager of the Jason Products Corporation, has informed your major professor of an opening in a certain department (choose the type of position in which you have an interest and the necessary qualifications). Your professor has suggested that you apply. Write an application to Mr. Sibley, assuming that you will accompany it with a data sheet.

C Select an area of the United States in which you would like to work (or a company with overseas operations). Write an unsolicited letter of application that you could send to several firms.

■■■■■■■■■■■■■■■■■■■■■■■■■■■■■■■■■■■■■■■

CASE 3 FOLLOWING UP APPLICATION LETTERS

PROBLEM: You have received no response to your application for the position of marketing research trainee (case problems 1 and 2), and you decide to write a follow-up letter.

BACKGROUND

If you receive no answer to an application within a reasonable time—say, two or three weeks, depending on the distance the letter has to travel—it is wise to follow up. The objective of the follow-up letter is to remind the firm of your interest—not to show impatience or anger. Responses to applications may be delayed because the papers are being circulated among several people; if one of these people is away on a business trip or vacation, the decision is held up until his return. You should be notified, of course, that your application has been received and that there might be a short wait before you will hear anything definite, but don't count on it.

Your follow-up letter can serve to provide additional information that will help your cause. In fact, some authorities recommend that the applicant deliberately withhold a nugget or two from the original letter. But since you may not have a chance to write a follow-up letter, you naturally will not want to withhold your most important ''sales features'' from your application letter itself.

SOLUTION A

Gentlemen:

When can I expect to hear from you about the position I applied for as marketing trainee? I can only conclude that you are not interested in my qualifications; but if you are, I will need to know very soon, for I am considering other opportunities that have recently come up.

Sincerely yours,

Analysis of Solution A. If the applicant who wrote Solution A had been on the list of possible candidates, the letter would surely have taken him off. It reveals impatience and annoyance. Equally important, the applicant's suggestion that he is no longer in the running is too easy for the recipient to agree to. Negative suggestions rarely make sales!

SOLUTION B

Gentlemen:

When I wrote you on May 16, applying for the job of marketing research trainee (your advertisement in the May 14 Times), I neglected to mention that one of my senior projects in marketing research was a report on recent marketing trends in the food industry. I think you might be interested in a brief summary of that report and am enclosing a copy.

When may I expect to hear from you concerning my application? I am eager to know whether I am being considered so that I may complete my plans.

Cordially yours,

Analysis of Solution B. Solution B is likely to get a favorable response if the position has not been filled. The writer uses good salesmanship by supporting his previous application papers with a sample of his work—a technique many people have found very effective.

Note that the writer asks about the status of his application, but he does not put the question in the form of a demand. Observe the phrase ''so that I may complete my plans.'' This is more subtle and tactful than ''because I am considering several other offers,'' which is a veiled threat.

■■■■■■■■■■■■■■■■■■■■■■■■■■■■■■■■■■

PROJECT

About two weeks ago you applied for one of the positions listed on pages 230–232, but you have not had a response to your application. In the meantime, you have been offered another position that you must accept or decline within two weeks. You would prefer the first position you applied for (the salary is better and the opportunities are more attractive). Write the appropriate follow-up letter.

■■■■■■■■■■■■■■■■■■■■■■■■■■■■■■■■■■

CASE 4

THANKING THE INTERVIEWER

PROBLEM: You have been interviewed for the marketing research position that you applied for. You spent most of your time with the manager of marketing research, Theodore Patton, but you also met his boss, Mr. Conrad, the marketing director, and Mr. Conrad's assistant, Mrs. Archdale. You believe it would be a good idea to write Mr. Patton to thank him for seeing you and to restate your interest in the job.

BACKGROUND

A thank-you letter following a job interview will give you an advantage over applicants who don't think of writing (most people don't). Even though the firm to which you are applying is local, it is better to write than to telephone and to do so no later than a day after the interview.

SOLUTION A

Dear Mr. Patton:

Thank you for allowing me to meet you this week to discuss the position of marketing research trainee.

The job is most attractive to me and offers the kind of opportunity that I am looking for. I know I would find the work challenging and rewarding.

Please express my appreciation also to Mr. Conrad and Mrs. Archdale.

Sincerely yours,

Analysis of Solution A. The type of follow-up letter you write will depend on how things went at the interview. If you feel that you were favorably received and that you have a good chance of getting the job, the solution above is fine. If your letter is friendly, positive, and sincere, you will reaffirm the employer's interest, saying in effect, "Now that I've met you, I know I want the job." And it doesn't hurt to mention the names of others with whom you talked besides the principal interviewer. You never know where the center of influence is.

Suppose you got the impression at the interview that you were lacking in certain desired qualifications. Your letter might then be somewhat different, as the following solution illustrates.

SOLUTION B

Dear Mr. Patton:

Thank you for allowing me to meet with you this week and discuss the position of marketing research trainee.

The job is most attractive to me and offers the kind of opportunity that I am looking for. I know I would find the work challenging and rewarding.

After learning more about the job, I realize that my knowledge of advanced statistical methods may be somewhat light. The subject interests me, however (I did well in the elementary course in college), and I would expect to become more expert in it. Cole University offers advanced courses in statistics, and I would plan to enroll in its evening division.

Would you please express my appreciation also to Mr. Conrad and Mrs. Archdale for giving me so much of their time.

Sincerely yours,

Analysis of Solution B. In this letter you are telling your interviewer that you recognize you are lacking knowledge of advanced statistical methods and you are honest enough to admit it to yourself and to the interviewer. A prospective employer would be impressed with your awareness as well as with your desire to gain expertise.

■■■■■■■■■■■■■■■■■■■■■■■■■■■■■■■■■■■■

PROJECTS

A   Assume that your follow-up letter in the project on page 242 resulted in an invitation to come for an interview. After the interview, you are more certain than ever that you want the position. Write a letter expressing your appreciation for the interview and reaffirming your interest in the job.

B   One of the letters you wrote for Project C (page 240) resulted in an invitation to come for an interview, expenses paid. The interview completed, you return home convinced that you would enjoy working for that particular firm. Write a thank-you letter.

■■■■■■■■■■■■■■■■■■■■■■■■■■■■■■■■■■■■

CASE 5 ACCEPTING A JOB OFFER

PROBLEM: You have been offered the position as marketing research trainee. Mr. Patton wrote you, telling you what your salary will be, when you are to report for work, and that you must undergo a physical examination. He also sent you a copy of the booklet *Welcome to New Employees*, describing company policies concerning hours of work, vacations, cafeteria hours, recreational activities, and so on.

BACKGROUND

The person offering you a job will expect you to respond immediately to the offer. Although you could telephone your acceptance, you should respond in writing, particularly if the invitation you receive is in writing.

SOLUTION

Dear Mr. Patton:

You don't know how delighted I am to accept the position of marketing research trainee with Marcal. As you suggested, I shall report to the medical department at 8:30 a.m. on June 16 for my physical examination and will come to your office immediately afterward.

The prospect of joining your team is exciting and I look forward to the experience. You may be sure that I will read Welcome to New Employees from cover to cover!

Cordially yours,

Analysis of Solution. This promptly written response accepts the job, confirms all the requests made by your new employer, and tells him that you are enthusiastic about getting started.

■■■■■■■■■■■■■■■■■■■■■■■■■■■■■■■■■■■■■

PROJECT

You have received word that the position for which you were interviewed (Project B, page 243) is yours. You are to report for work at nine on Monday, June 27, going first to the Personnel Department for a medical examination, indoctrination, and so on. Respond to the job offer, indicating that you have decided to accept it.

■■■■■■■■■■■■■■■■■■■■■■■■■■■■■■■■■■■■■

CASE 6 REJECTING A JOB OFFER

PROBLEM: The other company to which you submitted your application (see the project in Case 1, page 230) has just made you a job offer. However, you must turn down this offer because you already have accepted another firm's offer.

BACKGROUND

When you accept a job offer, the courteous thing to do is notify the other companies to which you have submitted your application that you are no longer in the market for a position with them. Do this whether or not you actually receive a job offer that you must decline.

SOLUTION

Dear Mr. Lyles:

Thank you for considering me for a position in your marketing research training program. However, I have accepted a similar job with Marcal Distributors, and I wish to withdraw my application with your firm.

While I know I would have enjoyed working at Midfair, I feel that the job I am taking offers a better opportunity to concentrate on packaging, which is of special interest to me.

It was a pleasure talking with you. I appreciate all your kindnesses.

Sincerely yours,

Analysis of Solution. The letter to Mr. Lyles is thoughtful and courteous. It doesn't say, "I got a better job." In effect, it says, "I got a job better tailored to my interests and needs."

■■■■■■■■■■■■■■■■■■■■■■■■■■■■■■■■■■■■

PROJECTS

A You have accepted the position of assistant personnel manager of the Badger Products Company. Therefore you feel that you should write to Ms. Ruth Edwards, personnel manager of the Dilworth Corporation, who interviewed you for a similar job with her company but has not made you a job offer. Write Ms. Edwards the letter you feel is appropriate.

B The day after you accepted Badger's job offer (Project A), you received an offer from Dr. Harold Jackson, personnel manager of Billings Associates, Inc. Write him a letter in which you turn down his offer.

■■■■■■■■■■■■■■■■■■■■■■■■■■■■■■■■■■■■

CASE 7 THANKING YOUR REFERENCES

PROBLEM: Judge R. N. Toffenetti, a family friend, and Professor Edward Hale, your marketing professor, were two of the references you listed on your data sheet. During a telephone conversation with Professor Hale this morning, you mentioned that you had accepted a very good job offer. You haven't been in touch with Judge Toffenetti since you accepted the position as management trainee in marketing with Marcal Distributors, Atlanta, Georgia.

BACKGROUND

Once you have obtained a position, it is important that you write those whom you listed as references on your data sheet to thank them for their help. You have no way of knowing whether your prospective employer actually sought the opinions of your references, but it is safe to assume that he did. Writing to thank those who helped you is the courteous and thoughtful thing to do, and it is also good insurance in case you want to use their names as references again.

SOLUTION A

Dear Judge Toffenetti:

Well, Judge Toffenetti, I have accepted a position as management trainee in marketing with Marcal Distributors in Atlanta. It looks like a great opportunity, and I couldn't be more pleased.

Next week I will leave for Atlanta and start searching for a place to live (I'm to report to work a week from this coming Monday). My folks think Atlanta is a long way off, but I think they're getting used to the idea of my living there.

Thank you for letting me use your name as reference in my application. You must have said the right thing!

Respectfully yours,

Analysis of Solution A. This letter courteously thanks the judge. It also says, ''I am thoughtful enough to appreciate the privilege of using your name as a reference.''

SOLUTION B

Dear Professor Hale:

As I told you on the telephone, I landed the job with Marcal and I start work August 15. I will leave here next Tuesday to try to locate a place to live—hopefully in the suburbs.

You must know how much I appreciate your help in getting this position. Your letter of recommendation obviously carried a great deal of weight. Thank you for the confidence you have in me. I hope I can prove that I deserve it.

I'll write you a note when I get settled so that you may reach me if you ever get to Atlanta. You must drop in to see me—I'd like that.

Respectfully yours,

Analysis of Solution B. This letter is an appropriate and effective follow-up to a telephoned thanks to a reference.

■ ■

PROJECT

You have accepted a job offer from the Nettleton Industrial Corporation (select the position that interests you) and plan to begin work the first of next month. Write a letter to one of the references listed on your data sheet.

■ ■

CASE 8 — RESIGNING FROM A POSITION

PROBLEM: You have decided to resign from your position as assistant credit manager of Franklin Steel Company.

BACKGROUND

Although some people spend all of their working years with the firm that gave them their first position, most of us do not. We change employers for a variety of reasons: financial needs, distance from work, family problems, health, dissatisfaction with the job, lack of opportunity, and so on. And although we feel we should not stick with a job merely for the sake of "security," we also feel that spending a year here, six months there, a year and a half elsewhere—becoming a job-skipper—can be very damaging.

Before you change jobs, therefore, you ought to make sure that the cause of your dissatisfaction can't be eliminated. Sometimes a serious talk with your boss (or with his permission, someone higher up) can result in a solution. If you feel that your situation is hopeless and that there is nothing left to do but resign, you should discuss your intentions with your immediate superior and then put your resignation in writing. In doing so, remember that it is customary to give the company at least two weeks' notice of your intention to resign.

Naturally, it makes good sense to scout around to see what is available in other companies before you make that final decision to resign from your present position. Most people make a thorough study of the job market—even contact several prospective employers—before they take the leap. *Caution:* In making application for another job, it is best not to knock your present company or the people in it, no matter how you feel. When your prospective employer asks why you want to leave your present job, you are always safe in saying that it does not give you the opportunity you want.

A letter of resignation is a simple one to write if you are changing jobs for "non-people" reasons. If you are offered a job that pays better, if you must move to a more healthful climate, if commuting from your home to your present job location is inconvenient and expensive, or if the hours of work or the work itself are unsuitable, you simply "tell it like it is."

On the other hand, when your reasons for leaving a company involve other people—your boss, your fellow employees, or others in the firm—your approach may be somewhat different. Although you may still wish to "tell it like it is," doing so will create animosity (toward you more than toward anyone else) and might hurt (you more than anyone else). Proceed with caution, then, when writing a letter under such circumstances. Lambasting your adversaries will gain you nothing but the short-lived satisfaction of blowing off steam. Here's a resignation letter that's the result of a personality conflict.

SOLUTION A

Dear Mr. Korngold:

Please consider this my resignation from my position in Franklin Steel Company, effective August 1.

As I told you, I have decided to take a position in another company, although I have not made a firm commitment to any particular one. I do think I would be happier and more productive in publishing or advertising, and I expect to concentrate on firms that can offer me this opportunity.

Thank you for the help you have given me. I have learned a great deal from my job that should prove useful in my new work.

Sincerely yours,

Analysis of Solution A. Solution A is written on the assumption that the writer has not located another position but has several definite opportunities that he is considering. Let's analyze it from that viewpoint.

1. The opening paragraph states the writer's decision to resign and gives the effective date of his resignation.
2. There is no evidence of bitterness anywhere in the letter. The writer skillfully avoids mention of dissatisfaction, even though he may have been unhappy

with the person to whom he is writing. You may feel that the writer did nothing but "cop out," but remember that when this particular job and employer are only dim memories, he probably will be glad that he did not spill out what was really on his mind.

3. In the last paragraph, the writer is noncommittal. He simply expresses thanks for the help he has been given (and he surely received *some* help), but he doesn't dwell on it. Nor does he say that he enjoyed working with Franklin Steel Company—simply that he learned a great deal that will be helpful later.

SOLUTION B

Dear Mr. Korngold:

Please consider this my resignation from my position in Franklin Steel Company, effective August 1.

As I mentioned to you, I have never really adjusted to life in a big city, and I have long wanted to get back to Vermont, where I was reared and where my family still lives. The position I have obtained in Bennington—managing a small travel agency—is the kind I have been hoping to find. So the new job and the location made the opportunity too hard to turn down.

At the same time, I have really enjoyed my work at Franklin Steel, and I hate to leave my many friends. I am especially indebted to you for training me. You are a great teacher, and I shall always be grateful to you for your patience and your inspiration.

Sincerely yours,

Analysis of Solution B. The writer of Solution B obviously had a "non-people" reason for resigning and a much easier task than the writer of Solution A. In this letter, too, the writer:

1. Stated his decision to resign and gave the effective date of his resignation.
2. Referred to his previous discussion of the situation with Mr. Korngold.
3. Gave his reason for resigning and, in this instance, told the reader some details of his new position.
4. Expressed appreciation for the help given him.

■■■■■■■■■■■■■■■■■■■■■■■■■■■■■■■■■

PROJECTS

A You have held your first job for two years. You have enjoyed the work very much and learned a great deal from your boss and others with whom you associated. However, you have received an offer of a much better position—one that offers greater responsibility, a more convenient location for commuting, and a higher salary. It is an opportunity you feel you can't afford to turn down. After discussing the matter with your superior, Lydia Morehouse, you have decided to resign and take the other job. Write the letter of resignation.

B   Margaret Kincaid has decided to resign from her position as assistant training director. Her reason is that she has no freedom—her supervisor, Howard Frankenthaler, refuses to give her any real responsibility, hovers over her constantly, complains about the quality of her work without offering constructive suggestions, and goes out of his way to belittle her efforts. Although Margaret tried to be a conscientious worker, she couldn't seem to overcome the personality clash with Mr. Frankenthaler. When she tried to discuss the matter with him, he brushed her off with, "If you'll learn to do your work right, your chance for responsibility will come. You're nowhere near ready to take on anything bigger."

Margaret has looked around for other opportunities and has been offered a job as supervisor of central typing for the McGregor Company. Although it isn't exactly what she wanted, the salary is comparable and the opportunity for management seems much better. Write a letter of resignation that you would prepare if you were Margaret Kincaid.

■ ■

CASE 9   RECOMMENDING SOMEONE FOR A POSITION

PROBLEM: Frank McGrath is a copywriter in the Marketing Research Department and has been under your supervision for some time. Frank is a competent copywriter, but you have had much difficulty with his attendance. He is away from his desk a great deal, often calls in "sick," and is out of the office for several days each time. Because Frank couldn't keep up with his work, you have had to let him go.

Frank has applied to another company for a copywriting position, and you receive a letter from the personnel director of that firm inquiring about Frank's employment record. You will have to decide what you want to say in behalf of Frank McGrath.

BACKGROUND

At some time in your life you will probably be asked to give a recommendation for someone who has applied for a job. Many large companies write to references listed by job applicants—usually it is a form letter, obviously designed to look "routine." As in the following example, the letter often is set up in such a way that the person sending it only types in the inside address, the name of the applicant, and the title of the position applied for. Not shown but usually included, of course, is the date.

Mr. Edward B. Costello
910 Hewlett Street
Franklin Square, New York 11010

Dear Sir:

Your name has been given as a reference in the application of

Susan Wasserman

for the position of

Computer Programmer

Would you please give us your assessment of this applicant—work habits, ability, character, potential, personality, and any other traits and characteristics that would help us to evaluate her as a potential employee in our company? Your statement will, of course, be kept in strictest confidence. An addressed, stamped envelope is enclosed for your reply.

Very truly yours,

Responding to such a request can be very simple if you have a high opinion of the applicant and sincerely believe she would be an asset to the prospective employer.

Dear Mr. Seaton:

It is a pleasure for me to write in behalf of Susan Wasserman, who has applied for the position of computer programmer in your company.

I have known Miss Wasserman for over three years, first as a fellow programmer and later as her supervisor. I consider her an extremely competent person, completely dependable and extremely intelligent. She works well with people—she was always cooperative and pleasant. Her record here was outstanding.

When Miss Wasserman told me that she was leaving us (she had to return to Duluth to care for her invalid father), I was sad indeed. She will be missed here. Any organization that hires Miss Wasserman will be most fortunate.

Sincerely yours,

Writing a letter concerning someone about whom you are not so enthusiastic is more difficult. Here you must wrestle with your conscience. You could take the attitude that even though you consider the person incompetent or otherwise undesirable, it's of no concern to you—let the company to which he applied take the risk. True, it is somewhat painful to assume the responsibility for denying a person a job. Yet you do well to remember that if you were a manager seeking information about a prospective employee, you would expect honesty from those who write a recommendation.

SOLUTION A

Some people, rather than say something negative about an applicant whom they can't praise, resort to a noncommittal letter.

Dear Mr. Phineas:

It would be unfair of me to comment on the qualifications of Frank McGrath for a position with your firm. He was under my supervision for a very short time, and I did not have an opportunity to evaluate his competency.

Sincerely yours,

Analysis of Solution A. Of course, one could argue that the letter above is actually a denunciation of the applicant. That is, if the writer knew anything at all favorable about the applicant, he would have said it; therefore, what is left unsaid speaks as loudly as an outright denunciation. We do not say that such a letter should not be written. If the writer is honest—that he doesn't have an opinion—the letter is satisfactory. If he is hedging, however, we would take issue.

SOLUTION B

Dear Mr. Phineas:

In the best interests of both you and Frank McGrath, about whom you inquired, I cannot give him an unqualified recommendation.

Mr. McGrath was a copywriter under my supervision for six months. While he is competent as a copywriter, his attendance was sporadic. He was frequently late to work, often called in sick, and stayed away from work two or three days at a time. In spite of my having several discussions with him, the problem was never resolved, and finally I had to let him go.

Perhaps, Mr. Phineas, the position Frank had here didn't challenge him enough—or perhaps he had personal problems he couldn't resolve. Certainly he is a likeable fellow and seemed to get along well with his co-workers here. Unfortunately, however, I just couldn't get him going. Perhaps he will do better in a different working environment.

Sincerely yours,

Analysis of Solution B. It could be argued that the writer of Solution B has shot down Frank McGrath's chances at another job and, for that reason, is heartless. No one can say that such a letter is bad or that it is good. The writer apparently feels that he is placing his integrity on the line, and he must deal with his own conscience. He has, however, said some positive things:

1. Frank McGrath is a competent copywriter.
2. Mr. McGrath is likable and got along well with his co-workers.
3. The writer suggests the possibility that he himself may have been at fault because of his inability to motivate Mr. McGrath.

SOLUTION C

Dear Mr. Phineas:

It is a pleasure for me to recommend Frank McGrath as a copywriter. He worked under my supervision for six months, and I found him competent in his job. He was well-liked by his fellow workers.

Frank left our employ because the hours of work did not fit in with his personal schedule.

Sincerely yours,

Analysis of Solution C. What do you think of Solution C? Certainly the letter is not damaging to Frank McGrath even though there is a hint in the second paragraph that all was not well.

Many people would choose this alternative, feeling that Frank may have had some bad breaks and that he could be a very good worker in another company. But we would not accept this line of reasoning; the intent of the writer is to deceive.

■ ■

PROJECTS

A   As administrative assistant to the vice president for public relations in Basel Corporation, you supervise two clerk-typists. One of these positions was until a month ago filled by Millicent Crater. Miss Crater left of her own accord (her father was transferred to another city, and she wanted to go with her family), but you were about ready to release her. Her typing skills were very weak, and she never did catch on to the filing system. Also, her attitude was sullen, uncooperative—there was always a scene when she was asked to do a job over because of errors.

   You receive a form letter from Mudville National Bank, asking you to assess Millicent's work record while in your employ. Write the letter.

B   Another clerk-typist who once worked under your supervision, Barbara Cherner, was first-rate—a rapid typist, accurate, devoted to her job, and pleasant to be around. You were about to recommend her for a promotion to senior clerk when she left the company to be married. Four months after she left, you receive an inquiry from Jonesburg Realtors about Miss Cherner (now Mrs. Francis Donovan); she has applied for a position as clerk-typist. Write the letter.

■ ■

part

9

BUSINESS REPORTS

You are assistant personnel manager of the Warner-Dennison Company, a manufacturer of desks, chairs, and other furniture for business firms, government organizations, schools, colleges, and other institutions. Your job is to determine company personnel needs, supervise recruitment and placement activities, establish and maintain job specifications and descriptions, operate indoctrination and special training programs for employees, and so on. Your boss is Daniel L. Haskell, the personnel manager.

WRITING AN INFORMATIONAL REPORT

PROBLEM: Warner-Dennison publishes the booklet *This Is Warner-Dennison* and, as part of its indoctrination program, gives a copy to each new employee of the company. The booklet contains a brief history of the company, a description of its principal products, and information about such matters as work hours, vacation policy, insurance plans, and recreational programs. The booklet has 24 pages and is printed in two colors and illustrated throughout.

The manuscript for a new edition of the booklet is about ready to release for composition, printing, and binding. Mr. Haskell has asked you to get comparative cost estimates from three local printers and to give him the information in the form of a written report.

BACKGROUND

In every organization those responsible for managing the company's operations must have factual information about various subjects that they can use as the basis for making intelligent decisions. For example, the marketing director must have at his fingertips information about sales, personnel, competition, advertising media, budgets, customers, prices, transportation, and so on, if he is to answer such questions as these:

How are sales going?
Should we add another field representative in the Twin Cities area?
Why did we lose the Tucker account to Consolidated?
How is Dave Faulkner working out in the Spokane territory?
How well did the full-page ad in the six metropolitan dailies pull?

Are we under or over budgeted expenses?
What changes should we plan in our rate schedule for next year?
Why are there so many back orders in the El Paso office?
How can we speed up shipping?
What can we do to decrease postal costs?

The marketing director obviously could get the answers to some of these questions simply by picking up the telephone and asking various people for the information. In some instances, though, he cannot get the information he needs in the form he needs it through a phone call or even a personal visit. Thus he often must ask a responsible subordinate to "give me that information, please—in writing."

Although the typical marketing director or other business executive may give you some guidance in preparing a particular report, he seldom will "label" the kind of report he expects or tell you how to set it up. Even at the outset of your business career, the person asking you for a report will expect you to have an understanding of the mechanics of report writing and, more important, a fairly high level of skill in writing reports. Such an expectation may seem unreasonable, but it stems from a simple fact of business life: reports play a far more vital role in business management and involve more employees than do letters or other business communications. Many business workers, including high-level executives, who have limited responsibility for letter writing must write a great many reports of various types.

Classification of Reports. Businessmen ordinarily refer to all reports simply as memos or reports. The traditional classification of reports, however, is according to such criteria as the following:

Frequency of Preparation. A report prepared on a daily, weekly, monthly, quarterly, or annual basis is classified as a *periodic report.* Any other report is referred to as a *special report,* since it is not prepared according to a set schedule.

Subject. The subject of the report determines whether it is classified as a *financial report,* an *insurance report,* a *legal report,* or whatever.

Origin. The classification depends upon the department in which the report originates. For example, a report originating in the sales department is classified as a *sales report;* one in the personnel department, a *personnel report;* and so forth.

Format. A report that includes a cover, a title page, and other special parts and that has a body section organized according to a more or less standard pattern (introduction, summary, text, conclusions, recommendations, and so on) is classified as a *formal report.* Any report that does not fit that general description is usually referred to as an *informal report,* although those prepared as memorandums are sometimes called *memo reports* to distinguish them from other informal reports.

Tone or Language. Interestingly, and often confusingly, the terms *informal* and *formal* are used to classify reports by tone or language as well as by format. A report written in a personal, almost conversational style is called an *informal report.* Conversely, one written in an impersonal style is classified as a *formal report.*

Function. If a report does nothing but present factual information about a particular subject, it is usually classified as an *informational report* or *straight information report.* If it includes the writer's interpretation of that data and his conclusions or recommendations (or both), it is generally called an *analytical report.*

Purpose of Reports. From the report writer's viewpoint, the basic purpose of every business report is to provide complete, accurate information about a particular subject and to do so in a manner that will make it totally understandable and useful to the person requesting it. From the reader's viewpoint, the purpose may be anything from establishing a sound basis for a management decision to gaining current information with no immediate or specific application to his work.

At this point, we are concerned with reports that have the single purpose of providing factual information—those that are usually classified as informational reports. Most of the reports you will write, particularly at the outset of your career, will be of this type.

Typical Report-Writing Situations. As a responsible employee, you will be called upon to prepare a variety of straight information reports for your boss and other executives. In many instances, as in this case problem, you will be writing in response to specific requests by your boss. In others, you will be writing reports that are simply a part of almost every organization's operating routine. And sometimes you will be writing reports in response to requests directed to your boss by other executives but delegated to you by him.

The following situations are examples of occasions that require the writing of an informational report. The reports illustrate typical formats.

Situation 1. Periodically—often every month—salesmen, executives, and other employees who incur reimbursable business expenses in the performance of their jobs must prepare and submit to their supervisors an itemized statement of their travel, hotel, food, and other expenses. In most organizations, printed forms similar to the one shown here are used for this purpose. Thus, all the employee has to do is fill in the appropriate figures, give brief explanations of expenses when such descriptions are required by company policy or government regulations, attach whatever receipts may be required, sign the report, and send it to his supervisor for approval and subsequent routing to the accounting department.

Expense Report Summary

DETAIL OF EXPENSES

DATE	TRAVEL FROM	TRAVEL TO	AUTO MILEAGE (c)	TOLLS & PARKING	LOCAL TRANS. CAR RENTAL	PLANE	TRAIN	HOTEL	MEALS	ENTER- TAINMENT (a)	PHONE TELEGR. POSTAGE	MISC. (c)	DAILY TOTALS: LESS MEALS CONDUCTING EXHIBIT (b)	DAILY TOTALS: ALL OTHER
26	New York	Chicago			4 25	59 00		28 00	8 65		1 65			101 55
27					9 20			28 00	9 20		3 15			49 55
28	Chicago	New York			4 70	59 00			8 30					72 00
29														
30														
31														
1	New York	New York			5 20				5 80					11 00
2														
3														
4														
5														
6	New York	Knoxville			4 75	54 00		18 50			2 85			80 10
7	Knoxville	New York			5 60	54 00		18 50			4 20			82 30
8														
9														
10	New York	Buffalo			6 15			22 00	7 40		1 50			37 05
11	Buffalo	New York			6 35				6 70		2 00			15 05
12														
13														
14														
15														
16	New York – Washington	New York			3 70		33 50		8 15					45 35
17														
18														
19														
20														
21	New York	Pittsburgh			7 20	35 00		26 00	11 40		5 15			84 75
22	Pittsburgh				9 15			26 00	8 60		3 60			47 35
23		New York			6 80	35 00			5 50					47 30
24														
25														
TOTALS FOR PERIOD					73 05	296 00	33 50	167 00	79 70		24 10			673 35

GRAND TOTAL: 673 35

TOTAL MILEAGE
Mileage × ¢ per mile
Mileage × ¢ per mile

BOOK COMPANY EMPLOYEE NUMBER → 235 –

(a) Details to be shown on reverse side.
(b) Publications & Book Co. Only. See specific Division instructions.
(c) For leased car arrangements, supporting documentation must be attached.

MILEAGE EXPENSES / TRAVEL DAYS

Budget | Previous Months Total | Current Months Total | Year to Date

NOT TO BE COMPLETED BY SALESMEN

Note: For this purpose, travel means away from the city of permanent assignment.

ACCOUNTING USE ONLY

Expense Report Summary

Name: John W. Haines
Division: Marketing
Pub or Dept.: Customer Relations
Floor or Branch: New York
Travelletter No.: _____ T&E Account No. 294
Period Ending: March 25 ____ 19 —

	Due Co.	Due Me
LAST MONTH'S CLOSING BALANCE		12 80
ERROR CORRECTIONS – USE THIS LINE ONLY WHEN NOTIFIED		
CASH ADVANCES OR TRAVEL ORDERS DATE		
" February 26	200 00	
" March 6	100 00	
" March 21	250 00	
TRAVEL ADVANCES DATE		
"		
"		
TRAVEL REFUNDS DATE		
MONTH'S EXPENSES		673 35
AMOUNT OF REMITTANCE ENCLOSED OR SURRENDERED TO CASHIER		
TOTAL EACH COLUMN	550 00	686 15
INSERT DIFFERENCE BETWEEN TOTALS ABOVE INTO PROPER BOX	Due Co.	Due Me
CLOSING BALANCE		136 15

AUDIT CORRECTION (ACCOUNTING USE ONLY)
☐ CHECK THIS BOX IF REMITTANCE IS ENCLOSED

ACCOUNT NUMBER(S)
Not to be completed by Book Co. Personnel

Gen.Led. | Sub.Led. | Dept. | % or Amount

I Certify This Report To Be Correct: _John W. Haines_
Dept. Head Approval: _____
Additional Approval: _____

FORM 51-50000 (Rev. 11/71)

Situation 2. In an organization that pays its sales representatives on a commission basis or on a salary plus commission basis, the general sales manager may ask the assistant sales manager to give him a monthly report that shows the year-to-date commissions earned by the salesmen. To provide this information, the assistant might prepare the report on a plain sheet of paper in the format illustrated below.

E. H. MORRISON CORPORATION

Summary of Commissions Earned Through
Month of ___April___ , 19--

Salesman	This Year	Last Year	Increase	Decrease
Blank, C.	$4,657	$5,046		$ 389
Cord, L.	6,617	5,958	$ 659	
Dreyfus, J.	3,986	4,456		470
Espinoza, R.	5,566	6,437		871
Feingold, R.	7,094	6,493	601	
Tomaselli, F.	4,238	5,916		1,678
Young, R.	5,925	4,206	1,719	

Prepared by: *J. T. Williamson*
Distribution: C. T. Sousa, M. Blankenship, O. Flood, M. DeHarak,
R. P. Griffith, C. Lomax

Interoffice Memorandum

TO	T. J. Courtney		**FROM**	Carmen Soriano
DEPT.	Executive		**DEPT.**	Executive
SUBJECT	Employment Anniversaries		**DATE**	March 20, 19--

The following employees will celebrate their employment anniversaries during the month of April:

Name and Department	Anniversary
Collins, Andrew T. Payroll	April 4 (Fifth)
Holmes, Estelle (Mrs.) Executive	April 8 (Tenth)
Vincent, Carl Accounting	April 9 (Fifth)
Vincent, Pauline (Ms.) Marketing	April 16 (Fifth)

Situation 3. The president of the company likes to write a personal note to employees celebrating their fifth, tenth, fifteenth, and so on, anniversaries with the company. At the end of each month, his administrative assistant gives him a report like the one above.

Situation 4. The manager of each department in the company receives the following memorandum and turns it over to his assistant with the request, ''Please take care of this.''

Interoffice Memorandum

TO	Department Heads		**FROM**	Alton T. Pratt
DEPT.			**DEPT.**	Purchasing
SUBJECT	Magazine Subscriptions		**DATE**	August 14, 19--

Will you please help us make a roundup of the various magazines subscribed to by individuals in Far Western--that is, periodicals that are paid for by the company but received by individuals for their own use.

Please give me the name of each periodical, the name of the subscriber, and the disposition of the magazine (retained by the employee, thrown away, sent to the library, or whatever). Do <u>not</u> include magazines that employees pay for themselves.

Could I have the list for your department by September 1?

                                        A.T.P.

As in every situation, the assistant obviously must obtain the necessary information before he can begin to think about writing the report. In this instance, he might write a memo to each supervisor, adapting the memo from Mr. Pratt. More than likely, though, he would simply photocopy that memo and write a brief covering memo such as this one.

Interoffice Memorandum

TO   Mr. Prince   Mr. Cordoza   FROM James P. Fordham
        Miss Welch   Mrs. Yates
DEPT.   Ms. Latham   Mr. Zeldin   DEPT. Office Services

SUBJECT Magazine Subscriptions   DATE August 15, 19--

Please read the attached memorandum from Alton T. Pratt, in which he asks for a report on paid magazine subscriptions for individual use. Mr. Prince has asked me to gather this information.

I suggest that you use the following form when you respond.

Magazine	Subscriber	Disposition of Magazine			
		Keep	Discard	Library	Other

Could I please have your report by August 25?

As soon as he received the replies, the assistant would consolidate the information provided by the supervisors into a report like that shown on the opposite page. Note that even though the assistant actually prepared the report, he used his boss's name in the *From* line—a common procedure in a situation like this.

Most organizations develop a variety of standardized fill-in forms to fit as many recurring situations as possible. As in Situation 4 and as in this case problem, though, many reports cannot be prepared in such a simple, convenient manner. The letter below shows how the writer obtained the printing cost estimates requested by Mr. Haskell, and the solutions that follow illustrate two ways in which the writer could have written the report.

Gentlemen:

Would you please give me an estimate showing the composition, paper, printing, and binding costs for each copy of a new edition of This Is Warner-Dennison. Except as otherwise indicated by the following specifications, this new edition is to match the present booklet, a copy of which is enclosed.

1. 24 pages, 6 by 9 inches
2. Line and halftone illustrations on each page (see present booklet for number and distribution)

Interoffice Memorandum

TO   Alton T. Pratt   **FROM** H. R. Prince

DEPT Purchasing   **DEPT** Office Services

SUBJECT Magazine Subscriptions   **DATE** August 27, 19--

Here is a report of the magazine subscriptions in the Office Services Department, which is in response to your memo of August 14.

Magazine	Subscriber	Keep	Discard	Library	Other
			Disposition of Magazine		
Administrative Aide	Barbara Latham			X	
Better Offices	Gabriel Cordoza			X	
Communication Digest	Barbara Latham				Cut up and filed
Computer News	Richard Yates H. R. Prince	X			Central files
Data Management	H. R. Prince		X		
Forecast	J. L. Fordham	X			
Management Science	J. L. Fordham Irene Welch	X	X		
Methods Analyst	J. L. Fordham Gabriel Cordoza		X X		
Modern Accounting	A. K. Zeldin H. R. Prince	X X			
Supervision	A. K. Zeldin				Ames Coll. Library
Systems Digest	J. L. Fordham	X			
Today's Secretary	Irene Welch			X	

You will see that there is some duplication of subscriptions. However, in those cases, the employee feels that it is important to have his own copy for clipping and for future reference. I agree.

H.R.P.

3. Printed on 50-pound offset paper in two colors of ink throughout
4. Saddle-wire binding, 65-pound Monarch antique cover
5. Printing quantity of 1,000 copies

If you have any questions about this request, please call me.

Sincerely yours,

SOLUTION A

Interoffice Memorandum

TO   Daniel L. Haskell   **FROM** Susan T. Frey

SUBJECT Comparative Costs for Printing   **DATE** June 4, 19--
        This Is Warner-Dennison

In answer to your memo of May 19, here are estimates of unit costs for
composition, paper, printing, and binding of the booklet This Is
Warner-Dennison submitted by suppliers Carleton, Froelich, and Rhodes.

	Carleton	Froelich	Rhodes
Composition	$.492	$.515	$.541
Paper	.015	.020	.025
Printing	.112	.121	.130
Binding	.072	.081	.090
TOTALS	$.691	$.737	$.786

The specifications given to each printer were as follows:

1. 24 pages, 6 by 9 inches
2. Line and halftone illustrations on each page
3. 50-pound offset stock, printed in two colors throughout
4. Saddle-wire binding, 65-pound Monarch antique cover
5. Quantity of 1,000 copies

Please let me know if you wish to have additional information or if
you want me to get costs from other suppliers.

Analysis of Solution A. Solution A is an effective informational report because it:

1. Gives the reader the information he requested. Note the clear statement of the subject of the report in the heading and in the first paragraph and the reference to the reader's request for the information.
2. Includes no information that is not relevant to the subject of the report and to the reader's purpose in requesting it. In this connection, notice that the writer included a statement of the specifications given to each printer (next to last paragraph of the memo) and by doing so indicated that the cost estimates are truly comparative. Remember Mr. Haskell's request for *comparative* cost estimates?
3. Presents the information in a logical, easy-to-understand, and easy-to-use manner. Notice particularly the display of the three cost estimates, which makes it easy for the reader to analyze each estimate and compare the three estimates item by item as well as total by total.
4. Shows that the writer considered the reader's preferences with respect to such matters as writing style, tone, and report format. In this instance, we must assume that Mr. Haskell prefers a direct but personalized writing style (note such pronouns as *you* and *me* and, in the last paragraph, the writer's offer to be of further assistance) and a memo-type format.

SOLUTION B

COMPARATIVE COSTS FOR PRINTING
"THIS IS WARNER-DENNISON"

Purpose

To compare unit costs for composition, paper, printing, and

binding of the This Is Warner-Dennison booklet as submitted

by suppliers Carleton, Froelich, Rhodes.

Specifications

Estimates were based on the following specifications:

1. 24·pages, 6 by 9 inches
2. Line and halftone illustrations on each page
3. 50-pound offset stock, printed in two colors throughout
4. Saddle-wire binding, 65-pound Monarch antique cover
5. Quantity of 1,000 copies

Costs

	Carleton	Froelich	Rhodes
Composition	$.492	$.515	$.541
Paper	.015	.020	.025
Printing	.112	.121	.130
Binding	.072	.081	.090
TOTALS	$.691	$.737	$.786

Analysis of Solution B. If we make assumptions concerning the reader's preferences in such matters as writing style, tone, and report format that are completely opposite to those we made in the analysis of Solution A, this report is just as effective as Solution A. It gives the reader a clear, complete, concise, relevant statement of the information he requested, but it does so in a different order and in a more formal, impersonal manner. The most important thing here, as in every report-writing situation, is that the writer has taken into account the reader, the subject, and the purpose of the report.

The heading of this report indicates that the writer will prepare a transmittal memo to accompany it (see Case 1 of Part 3). Otherwise, the report would have a heading similar to this:

COMPARATIVE COSTS FOR PRINTING
"THIS IS WARNER-DENNISON"
A Report for Mr. Daniel L. Haskell
Prepared by Susan T. Frey
June 4, 19—

■ ■

PROJECTS

A   Your boss, Mr. Haskell, has asked for a report on the number of physically handicapped people employed by Warner-Dennison and how their performance is rated by their superiors in terms of safety, attendance, and job performance. This information has been requested by the executive vice president, Eugene L. Herbert, for a talk he is planning to give to a local civic organization. You are to supply whatever data you think will be helpful.

To get the information you need, you sent a questionnaire to all executives and department managers in the company asking them to give you the total number of handicapped workers employed in five categories—professional and technical, supervisory and management, clerical, craftsmen, and laborers—and to rate those in each category as above average, average, or below average. Following is the information you obtained.

Professional and technical: Total employed: 82. In terms of safety, 40 of these were rated above average, 41 average, and 1 below average. In terms of attendance, 33 were rated above average, 40 as average, and 9 below average. As to job performance, 32 were rated above average, 45 average, and 5 below average.

Supervisory and management: Total employed: 38. In terms of safety, 22 were rated as above average, 16 average, and 0 as below average. In terms of attendance, 16 were rated above average, 20 as average, and 2 below average. In job performance, 15 were rated above average, 21 average, and 2 below average.

Clerical: Total employed: 65. As to safety, 34 were rated as above average, 30 as average, and 1 below average. In terms of attendance, 35 were above average, 25 average, and 5 below average. In job performance, 27 were rated above average, 32 average, and 6 below average.

Craftsmen: Total employed: 110. In safety, 39 were rated above average, 67 as average, and 4 below average. In attendance, 40 were rated above average, 52 as average, and 18 as below average. As to job performance, 30 were considered above average, 60 as average, and 20 as below average.

Laborers: Total employed: 14. As to safety, 3 were rated above average, 10 as average, and 1 as below average. In terms of attendance, 4 were rated above average, 9 average, and 1 below average. Concerning job performance, 2 were rated above average, 8 average, and 4 below average.

Many of those reporting made enthusiastic comments about their handicapped workers. The most consistent reason given for the outstanding performance of these people is that they have a higher degree of motivation, presumably because they appreciate the opportunity to work.

Included in the handicapped category are people who are blind, partially sighted, and deaf, as well as amputees, paraplegics, and others crippled from various causes—polio, accidents, birth defects, etc.

Prepare the report as a memorandum.

B Following is an accountant's statement concerning financial operations of the Caldwell and Bonelli Company. Put the statement in the form of a report to the Executive Committee (a group of top executives).

Operations of the company for the month of March produced total revenues of $1,890,000, over budget by $147,000. Net operating income was $289,000, over budget by $114,000. Almost all categories of expenses are performing more favorably than budgeted, resulting in favorable comparisons for gross margin and operating income. Comparison with the same period last year reflects a sales increase of $314,000 and an NOP increase of $93,000, a rate which is 5.3 percent higher as a percentage of sales than the previous year.

Accumulative performance for the first quarter shows a slight under-budget condition of $58,000 in revenue. However, a revenue increase of $382,000 is shown when compared with the previous year. Net operating profit is $120,000 over budget and is $32,000 ahead of the previous year.

At March 31, Caldwell and Bonelli assumed complete responsibility for servicing both the Pump and Water Softening divisions in all matters relative to purchasing, production, warehousing and shipping, and common accounting services activities. Common personnel administration also became effective during March. It is anticipated that significant dollar savings and higher levels of efficiency will be realized.

In the Pump Division, March revenues amounted to $940,000, which is $85,000 over budget. General Sales contributed $66,000 of the increase, with the balance of $19,000 coming from Service Contracts. Net operating profit of $109,000 is $84,000 over budget. All categories of expense performed as expected in relation to total revenue levels. Provision for uncollectible contracts reflects the monthly adjustment necessary to amortize the deferred expense created at the end of last year. Manufacturing costs appear high in relation to budget; however, we anticipate that a reasonable adjustment will be made as a result of a physical inventory taken at April 3. The physical inventory provides the basis for transfer to a perpetual system.

In the Water Softening Division, revenue exceeded budget and previous year by $34,300 and $162,565, respectively. The superior revenue performance can be attributed to a continuation of the interest of customers in the ecological and environmental factors that distinguish our line.

Expenses for March were well in line with budget except for advertising, factory wages, and dealer service. Although these expenses were well ahead of budget, comparable reductions in expenses of maintenance, overtime, and breakage brought the total to a favorable figure.

CASE 2 WRITING AN INFORMAL ANALYTICAL REPORT

PROBLEM: As assistant personnel manager of the Warner-Dennison Company, you are having difficulty finding qualified people to fill the many requests for field sales representatives from the three western regional offices. Mr. Haskell and you have been discussing the high turnover, especially in the San Francisco office. He has asked you to find out what the problem seems to be by visiting all three regional offices and then to report your findings and recommendations to him.

BACKGROUND

Executives with the ultimate responsibility for making basic management decisions sometimes want more than complete, factual information about a subject. They often want to know what a competent subordinate thinks about a problem and what that person believes the appropriate solution or solutions might be. If you are a competent employee, then, you will receive requests for analytical reports. Each such request will be an excellent opportunity for you to demonstrate not only your thinking and writing ability but also your potential for advancement to a higher-level position.

What is an analytical report? Essentially, it is an informational report expanded to include the writer's interpretations of the factual information he has presented and the conclusions and recommendations that he has arrived at as the result of his analysis of it. An analytical report is obviously a valuable management tool in such situations as those outlined below. In each of these instances, the person receiving the analytical report would have not only the information necessary to reach a decision completely on his own but also the thoughts and recommendations of the writer. (The old adage "Two heads are better than one" is no more nor no less true in business than it is elsewhere!)

1. You want to buy a piece of equipment, install a new system or change an existing policy, and you write a report to justify your intentions.
2. The supervisor of Central Filing wants to set up a company archives section for storing valuable historical records and makes a proposal to the treasurer.
3. The marketing vice president thinks too many salesmen are spending money on car rentals and asks the general sales manager to justify the expenditures.
4. The personnel director compiles for the president a year-end report that includes information about staff growth, sources from which new employees were obtained, salary levels as compared with those in similar businesses, training programs conducted during the year, retirement policies, projected personnel needs, and the state of employee morale.

5. The sales service manager discovers a crisis in the Omaha office concerning customer services, goes to Omaha to get the facts, and writes a report to the marketing vice president recommending a course of action.
6. Customer billings are suddenly bogging down, and the company president asks for a report on the cost and effectiveness of a computerized system.
7. XYZ Company is considering establishing a new branch office in the Northwest, and the executive vice president wants a recommendation of the best location for it.
8. The personnel manager and other executives of the company feel that the constant shortage of qualified engineering technicians, secretaries, foremen, accountants, and computer personnel could be relieved by training employees in lower-level jobs for those positions. The executives also feel that there is a problem in providing advancement opportunities for professional people in the company—that is, upgrading and getting them ready to take on greater responsibilities. Consequently, the personnel manager asks his assistant to study the training programs now being offered, interview various people in the company to find out what they think the needs are for training, and to write a report stating his findings and recommendations.

   If you were the person asked to write the report in the last situation above, how would you go about it?

Preliminary Planning. Before you can even begin to plan your report, you need to know the answers to these basic questions:

1. What is the purpose of the report? Is it to provide information, to solve a problem, to make a recommendation, etc.?
2. Who is to read the report?
3. What is the most suitable form for the report?
4. How long is the report likely to be?

Purpose. It may seem obvious to you that every writer should know why he is writing a report, but in a surprising number of instances he doesn't. To be sure you know, write the purpose in your own words before you make your plan for gathering information and developing your report. For example:

1. To convince the shipping manager that the delays in getting out customer orders is costing us business.
2. To propose a new employment application form and recommend its adoption.
3. To study the various methods of computing depreciation on factory machinery and show the effect of each on profits.
4. To report the results of an attitude survey among customers and implications for long-range planning in the Customer Service Department.

   Note the terms *convince, propose, recommend, show the effect,* and *implications.* These are key words that will determine largely how the report is to be written. Only by knowing your purpose will you have an idea of what the report will contain and what facts and opinions to present in order to achieve your purpose.

Try to confine your report to a single project. For example, don't try to cover in one report to your boss a recommendation for a new approach to institutional advertising with a discussion of personnel and equipment needs in the promotion department, even though the topics may be somewhat related in your mind. Get the first idea accepted before attempting to sell the second one.

In informal memorandum reports, the purpose may be either stated or implied. In more formal reports, the purpose is usually specifically stated under the heading *Introduction* or similar wording. Regardless of the style of report you are using, make sure your reader understands your reason for writing it.

The Reader. We have already discussed the need to design your reports expressly for the reader. In this connection, you must try to find out in advance how much the reader already knows about the subject (if you don't, you are in danger of supplying too much or too little detail), what information you must supply in order to achieve your purpose, whether the reader prefers a great deal of detail or capsule summaries, what disposition is to be made of the report, and so on.

Form and Length. Select the form that is most appropriate in terms of (1) the purpose of the report and (2) the reader. If a one-page memo will do, don't "pad" the report with verbiage just to make it look impressive.

Gathering the Information You Need. Once you have settled on the purpose of the report and what it is to accomplish, the audience, and the probable form and length, you are ready to begin to gather your data. Suppose Mr. Haskell asked you to study the training programs now being offered, to interview various people in Warner-Dennison to find out what they think the needs are for training, and to write a report stating your findings and recommendations. Where would you start?

Reading. It would probably be a good idea to approach the subject of training by reading up on it. Even though you may consider yourself an expert on the subject, there is usually someone who has ideas that haven't occurred to you and who has put them in writing. In the first place, are you sure you know what training is? Of course you do—it's teaching people something they don't know. But is that enough? There are many kinds of employee training—indoctrination, orientation, apprenticeship, skill, refresher, upgrading, executive, and so on.

Admit to yourself at the outset that you don't know as much as you would like to know about your subject. Then search the files for other reports and proposals. If there is a company library, ask the librarian to help you locate articles in personnel and management journals, textbooks, handbooks, and so on. Watch for footnotes in these publications that may refer to studies or experiments that are available free in pamphlet form and look at the bibliographies for additional sources of information.

As you read, make notes on cards (4-by-6-inch cards are good for this purpose). By using cards you can easily add new material and throw out useless material, and you can reorganize in different ways the material you have collected. Be sure to identify the source of the material—you may want to quote from it, in which case you will want to give credit.

Interviewing. Once you have soaked up some learning on the subject of training and have an idea of what you want to talk to the managers and supervisors in Warner-Dennison about, you are ready to start your interviews. It's best to give advance notice to the people you plan to talk to, and you can do this by telephone or memo.

TO: Miss Edith Whelan   FROM: Susan T. Frey

SUBJECT: Survey of Training Needs   DATE: April 8, 19—
            in Warner-Dennison

Mr. Haskell has asked me to study the various employee training programs in Warner-Dennison and to report my findings and recommendations. In making my study, I want to talk to all the supervisors and managers in the company who are responsible for employee training. Certainly I want to learn more about your methods of training key-punch operators and what you think the company should do to extend its training opportunities.

May I see you a week from tomorrow—Tuesday, April 16, at 10? Perhaps you can spare me at least an hour. If you don't say no, I'll assume we have a date.

S.T.F.

In preparing for the interviews, you may want to design a brief questionnaire—either to leave with the interviewee or to use as your guide to asking questions.

Outlining Your Report. Assume now that you have collected the information you need for your report. You have a small stack of cards on which you made notes from reading, a larger stack on which you have jotted down notes from the interviews, and perhaps a batch of questionnaires that were completed by the interviewees. You are now ready to prepare a tentative outline of your report. Although you might have made an earlier outline to guide you in your reading and interviewing, you'll now have a better idea of what's going to go into your report and can prepare a good working outline.

Your very broad outline will look something like this:

1. Purpose—why the study was made.
2. Procedure—how you went about making the study.

3. Information—what you found out.
4. Conclusions—what the information that you gathered means.
5. Recommendations—what action the results of your study suggest.

Of course, you can't write to the outline above—it's too general. You must now proceed to put "meat on the bones." We pause here to say that some writers do not make a detailed outline before they start to write, saying that only when they have made a rough draft of the report will they know what they want to say. If you work best that way, there is nothing wrong with the procedure. However, we would recommend that you prepare an outline even if it's done *after* the rough draft. Doing so will tell you whether your report is logically organized. Many a report writer has discovered, after completing his writing and attempting to prepare a table of contents, that some topics don't fit the headings he selected! As you prepare your working outline, review your notes to make sure you have the entire project in proper perspective.

Purpose. The purpose of your report is no problem, although it may have two or three subheadings:

    Purpose
        Why the report was written
        For whom the report is intended
        Who authorized the writing of the report

Procedure. Your procedure—how you went about making the study—will require more thought. Here you may include such items as definition of terms, scope of the study, and methods you used in gathering the data.

    Procedure
        Definition of terms
            Education
            Training
            Indoctrination
            Orientation
        Scope of study
        Methods of gathering data
            Library research
            Interviews
            Earlier reports
        Training programs in other companies
            Westinghouse
            American Safety Razor
            Bendix
        Need for additional training programs
            Office and clerical
            Factory
            Sales and sales promotion
            Data processing
                Key punch
                Computer programming
                System analysis

At this point, you may decide that *Procedure* isn't a good heading and will choose instead *Introduction* or *Scope and Methods* or something else.

Information. Outlining the basic information—what you found out—will be a little more challenging. Here you will draw upon all the notes you made on your cards, arranging and rearranging the cards in various topical sequences until you have a sequence that suits you. (This is a major advantage of using cards—you can sort and re-sort them.)

The outline for the information section might appear as follows:

Types of training at Warner-Dennison
    Indoctrination
    Orientation
    Apprenticeship
    Skill
    Refresher
    Upgrading
    Executive
Company-sponsored training
    On-the-premises courses
    Outside residence courses
    Correspondence training
    Seminars
Unsponsored training
    Schools and colleges
    Correspondence
    Meetings and conventions

Or you may prefer to set up the outline in more traditional form, with roman and arabic numerals, letters, etc.

I. Need for additional training programs
  A. Office and clerical
  B. Factory
  C. Sales and sales promotion
  D. Data processing
    1. Key punch
    2. Computer programming
    3. Systems analysis
      a. Basic educational requirements
      b. Probable future needs
        (1) Office
        (2) Factory

In the report itself, most business writers prefer to omit numerals and letters and to distinguish between headings by means of type and indention.

SURVEY OF TRAINING NEEDS AT WARNER-DENNISON

PURPOSE

The number one text heading is flush with the left margin and in caps.

Why the Report Was Written

    The number two heading is flush with the left margin, free-standing, upper and lower case, underlined.

<u>Background</u>. The number three heading is indented five spaces, is in upper and lower case, and underlined. The copy "runs in" (follows on the same line).

Historical considerations. The number four heading is indented five spaces, only the first letter is capitalized, and the copy runs in.

or

SURVEY OF TRAINING NEEDS AT WARNER-DENNISON

PURPOSE

<u>Why the Report Was Written</u>

<u>Background</u>

Historical considerations. The history of training . . .

The number of headings you use in your report should be restricted; thus, if you need more than the four or five illustrated, you'd better restudy your organization. Although you should certainly have sufficient headings to guide your reader easily through your copy, you merely confuse him when you carry them to the extreme.

Conclusions and Recommendations. Depending on how you treat the information section of your report, you may decide to make your next heading *Conclusions.*

Conclusions
Strengths of present training programs
Weaknesses of present training programs

The conclusions may stand alone or be combined with the final heading of your outline, *Recommendations.* The outline for the *Recommendations* section might appear as follows:

Recommendations
Programs to be added
Programs to be eliminated
Expansion of classroom facilities
Equipment requirements
Teaching personnel
Administration of training

Plans of Organization. There are two basic patterns of organization in a report. The one you have just seen is inductive: you state the problem, tell how you are going to approach it, discuss the problem in detail, and suggest ways in which it should be solved. In other words, you proceed from the particulars to the general statement or conclusion.

The other pattern is deductive: the writer first states the results (summary, conclusions, recommendations) and then proceeds to the back-up material that supports the results.

Inductive	Deductive
Introduction	Summary (conclusions and recommendations)
Body of the report	Introduction
Summary (conclusions and recommendations)	Body of the report

The deductive pattern is preferred by many executives, particularly those who must read many long reports and who want to get the main point quickly without having to wade through all the details first. Those who prefer the inductive pattern say that the conclusions reached by the writer may be so startling to the reader that he develops a negative bias before he learns why those particular conclusions were reached. The following solution to the case problem follows the inductive pattern.

SOLUTION

TO: Mr. Daniel L. Haskell   FROM: Susan T. Frey

SUBJECT: Sales Personnel Study in   DATE: January 27, 19—
         Western Regional Offices

As you know, I recently spent a week in each of the three Western regional offices talking with the managers and their field supervisors about the personnel turnover problems we're having. Here is a brief report.

LOS ANGELES

Los Angeles is short two salesmen (and has been since October), and the Bakersfield and Riverside territories have been left virtually uncovered since that time. One other salesman, Arnold Hooper (San Diego), is on the verge of resigning.

The reasons given for the resignation of Alger (Bakersfield) and Hughes (Riverside) were just about identical: dissatisfaction with basic salary, inequitable incentive arrangement, and low mileage allowance. I understand that both received a substantial increase in salary from Jeffers and Bates, our major West Coast competitor.

While Hooper does not emphasize money as the basis of his unrest, it is certainly a major factor. Hooper's problem seems to be his inability to accept supervision, at least from the present field manager.

The Los Angeles office has found no effective sources of recruitment of new salesmen, relying almost entirely on newspaper ads in the Sunday Times and word-of-mouth recommendations of other salesmen. There do not appear to be any likely candidates on the horizon.

PHOENIX

Phoenix is fully staffed at the moment, although a couple of people are unsettled about their jobs (Millard in Phoenix and Carpenter in Flagstaff). The district manager told me that neither is performing up to his capacity and that their loss would not be a serious blow.

Phoenix seems to have no difficulty obtaining highly qualified candidates for sales positions. As a matter of fact, several applicants there look quite promising. This office has established exceptionally good relations with several colleges and universities in the area and obtains many candidates from these institutions.

SAN FRANCISCO

The San Francisco office is short one salesman; however, they have had several promising interviews and believe they will fill the vacancy before the end of the month. The situation here, however, is not so rosy as might be imagined.

While San Francisco seems to have little trouble in filling its vacancies, the turnover rate is extremely high. Of the fifteen salesmen in this office, seven have been with the company less than a year, four less than two years, and only one more than five years. According to the exit interviews, most of those who leave the company do so because of dissatisfaction with salary and incentives. However, a number seem to have some difficulty getting along with their field managers.

RECOMMENDATIONS

I have the definite impression that we are in serious trouble in the matter of hiring and retaining an effective sales staff. Even among those people who choose to remain with the company, morale is low. To overcome the situation, I recommend the following:

1. Salary Study. That a study of salaries of our salesmen as compared with those in the industry as a whole and with several similar firms within each geographical district be undertaken.
2. Supervisory Training. That a how-to-supervise training program be established for district managers, field managers, and sales supervisors.
3. Personnel Recruitment. That a conference be held in each district under the supervision of our personnel department to instruct managers and field managers on the techniques of recruiting, testing, interviewing, and hiring salesmen.
4. Management Contacts. That more frequent contacts with management be provided all salesmen by scheduling more district and national conferences.
5. Field Memo. That a "field memo" or some such news-inspiration piece be distributed every month to field salesmen.

After you have read this report, I would like to talk with you further about some of the problems I found and enlarge on the recommendations I have made.

Analysis of the Solution. The writer informally and briefly discussed the situation pertaining to each branch office, analyzed the strengths and weaknesses of each office, and recommended several ways of solving their common problems.

■ ■

PROJECT

Educademy offers educational programs by means of correspondence (home study). Last year the school launched a new Computer Programming course (COBOL Language), placing advertisements for the course in eight men's and women's special interest and general consumer magazines. By the end of May, 19—, over a thousand inquiries (coupons) had been received from readers who wanted additional information about the course. After mailing a catalog and other promotion literature, Educademy turned over the coupons to its sales representatives who were to contact in person the people who responded to the advertisements. However, there were 682 respondents who did not enroll, and Educademy was curious as to whether they had received satisfactory information about the course from the school; whether they were actually called on by an Educademy representative, and if so, whether he was courteous, informative, and helpful; why the respondents failed to enroll for the course; and what the respondents were like—occupation, age, income, education, etc. This information, it was felt, would be helpful to Educademy in learning something about the people who responded to the ads, in determining whether it had chosen the appropriate media for advertising the course, and in evaluating the efficiency of its follow-up mail and direct selling efforts.

The decision was made to send a questionnaire on April 15 to each of the 682 people who responded to the advertisements but failed to enroll, in an attempt to get answers to those four questions. The mailing consisted of a covering letter, a two-page questionnaire, and a stamped return envelope. The cutoff date of June 30 was established for the return of the questionnaires, and by that date 114 questionnaires had been completed and returned to Educademy (nearly 17 percent!).

The eight magazines used for advertising were *Redbook, Popular Mechanics, Modern Romances, Cosmopolitan, Cavalier, Popular Science, Esquire,* and *True Story.* The rate of return varied considerably for each magazine. The returns for three of the magazines—*Modern Romances, Cavalier,* and *Esquire*—were too few to allow Educademy to draw any conclusions.

Following are the details of the study. Each figure in the Percent Returned column has been rounded off to the nearest whole number.

Magazine	Total Questionnaires Mailed	Total Questionnaires Returned	Percent Returned
Redbook	153	34	22
Popular Mechanics	123	15	12
Modern Romances	19	2	11
Cosmopolitan	99	17	17
Cavalier	20	5	25
Popular Science	108	18	17
Esquire	74	9	12
True Story	86	14	16

Of the *Redbook* readers who responded to the questionnaire, 88% received literature from Educademy about the Computer Programming course. An Educademy representative had contacted 56%; he was generally rated as courteous, informative, and helpful. The primary reasons for not enrolling in the course were: (1) "Can't afford the course right now," and (2) "Not enough spare time." Of the total respondents, 61% were between 19 and 34 years of age, 28% between 35 and 44 years of age, and 11% over 44. As to education, 77% were high school graduates, 15% were college graduates, and 8% did not complete high school. Of the respondents, 54% were married and many had 1, 2, or 3 children at home; 70% were female. The most common responses to the question, "What is your occupation?" were "student," "secretary," and "housewife." As to income, 38% had an income under $6,000, 39% between $6,000 and $10,000, and 23% over $10,000.

Of the *Popular Science* respondents, all received literature from Educademy about the Computer Programming course; half of them had been called on by an Educademy representative, who was rated as courteous, informative, and helpful. Primary reasons for not enrolling were: (1) "Not enough spare time," (2) "Want resident course rather than correspondence," and (3) "Want FORTRAN language instead of COBOL." Of the respondents, 45% were between 19 and 34 years old, 27% between 35 and 44, and 28% over 44. All were male. Of those who answered the questionnaire, 76% had a high school education, 12% were college graduates, and 12% did not finish high school; 51% were single. Occupations listed included student, bookkeeper, laborer, computer programmer, mechanic, and military serviceman. As to income, 38% received an income under $6,000, 31% between $6,000 and $10,000, and 31% over $10,000.

Of the *Cosmopolitan* readers who responded to the questionnaire, 94% had received literature from Educademy about the Computer Programming course, and 65% were contacted by an Educademy representative. The representative was generally rated as being courteous, informative, and helpful. Reasons given for not enrolling in the course were: (1) "Can't afford the course right now," (2) "Want a resident course," and (3) "Don't have the time." Of the respondents, 59% were 19 to 34 years of age, 26% were between 35 and 44 years old, and 15% over 44; 67% were female, 59% had a high school education, 23% did not finish high school, and 18% were college graduates; 62% were single. The most frequent occupations listed were housewife, secretary, teacher, and student. As to income, 23% had an income of less than $6,000, 37% of between $6,000 and $10,000, and 40% of over $10,000.

All *Popular Mechanics* readers who responded said they had received literature from Educademy about the Computer Programming course. Of those who responded, 67% had been called upon by an Educademy representative, and he was rated as courteous, informative, and helpful. Primary reasons given for not enrolling in the course were: (1) "Can't afford the course right now," (2) "Want a degree program," and (3) "No help to future ambitions." Of the respondents, 67% were between 19 and 34 years of age, 23% were between 35 and 44, and 10% were over 44. As for education, 87% had a high school education, 7% were college graduates, and 6% did not complete high school;

40% were single. Occupations mentioned were clerk, store manager, secretary, technician. As to income, 33% earned less than $6,000 a year, and the same percentage had an income between $6,000 and $10,000. The rest (34%) earned over $10,000.

Of the *True Story* respondents, 85% had received literature from Educademy about the Computer Programming course. Only 21% of the respondents were called on by an Educademy representative, who was generally rated as courteous, informative, and helpful. Reasons given for not enrolling were: (1) "Can't afford the course right now," (2) "Course not fully explained," and (3) "Didn't receive enough information about the course." Of the respondents, 90% were between 19 and 34 years of age, 10% were between 35 and 44; 94% were female. Of those who answered, 85% had a high school education and none was a college graduate; 63% were married; several had children at home. Occupations mentioned were housewife, clerk, and stenographer; several were unemployed. As to income, 64% had an income of less than $6,000, 25% had an income between $6,000 and $10,000, and 11% over $10,000.

From these data, the advertising manager of Educademy concluded that although the returns were not heavy, from them he got a better "feel" for the prospect. He also believed that the five magazines represented in the final tabulations were good media to use for the Computer Programming course. His analysis of the demographic factors (age, education, income level, etc.) led him to believe that the group was appropriate for the course advertised.

He was encouraged that the representatives were rated by everyone as courteous, informative, and helpful. He gathered from this that they had the necessary knowledge and enthusiasm to sell the course.

The advertising manager was surprised at the percentage of women who responded to the advertising. He and others had felt that the primary market was male.

He was most distressed by the fact that so many prospects were not being called on (in one case, only 21%).

Based on his analysis, the advertising manager felt that several proposals could be made. In the first place, he wants to continue to advertise in the five magazines from which he made tabulations but to give up the others. Even those five, however, he wants to evaluate constantly for results. He thinks that follow-up studies such as this should be conducted periodically to guide the school in the future, for changes not only in the product but also in promotion methods.

He wants to slant future advertising and promotion to women.

Finally, he feels strongly that the school should reemphasize to its representatives the importance of calling on prospects and wonders if a monthly bulletin on the subject should be issued to the representatives.

Prepare a report from the data given. Assume that it will be given to the Director of Marketing, Kenneth L. Bradshaw.

What format will you use? Either of those discussed and illustrated in Case 1 would be appropriate—the decision is yours.

■ ■

CASE 3   WRITING A FORMAL ANALYTICAL REPORT

PROBLEM: The president of Warner-Dennison, H. J. Holtzclaw, has asked the personnel manager, Mr. Haskell, to study the feasibility of establishing a suggestion system whereby employees would be paid for ideas that result in greater efficiency or reduction of costs. Mr. Holtzclaw wants to know how such a system might operate in Warner-Dennison and requests Mr. Haskell's recommendations.

Mr. Haskell has delegated the assignment to you, and you are to study various suggestion systems in use in other companies and present what you think would be an effective set of standard operating procedures. You will submit your report to Mr. Haskell; he may possibly forward it to Mr. Holtzclaw without comment.

BACKGROUND

Tone. When you write an analytical report such as the one requested in this case problem, what should the tone be? Should it be personal and informal?

> I think our present orientation program for new employees is weak in several respects:
> 1. It isn't long enough—a half day won't do the job that needs to be done.
> 2. It overemphasizes company procedures at the expense of the "people" side of our business.
> 3. The presentations are dull. I think the programs would be a lot more interesting if the new employees had a part in it.

Or impersonal and objective-sounding like this?

> The following suggestions are offered for the improvement of Dailey's present orientation program for new employees:
> 1. Lengthen the program. It is believed that sufficient time is not now provided.
> 2. Place more emphasis on personnel. The program seems too procedurally slanted.
> 3. Provide opportunities whereby the new employees will participate. This would help to make the programs more interesting.

When you come right down to it, the writers of the two foregoing examples have said the same thing. The first one has used personal pronouns, contractions, colloquialisms, and active voice. The second writer has avoided personal pronouns, is more guarded (''The program *seems* too . . . ,'' ''*It* is believed that . . . ''), and has used passive voice.

What is the "right" tone? There's no pat answer to that question. You must know who is going to read the report and what will impress him (them) most favorably before you can decide on the appropriate tone and language. The subject of the report also has a bearing on tone. A memo to your boss suggesting a new procedure for covering the telephones when the secretaries are out to lunch will probably be somewhat casual and personal. But if your report covers a weighty subject like "Demographic Factors in Future Marketing Strategy," the tone is likely to be a good deal more formal.

The trend in report writing is away from the stiff, formal style and toward a style that is more personal—easy to read and understand. The faith the reader has in the writer's honesty, his integrity in separating fact from opinion, his motives in general—these determine whether a report is accepted as objective or as biased.

If it becomes a matter of personal preference, we recommend that you lean toward an informal style in your reports. They'll be more interesting and more persuasive.

We can give you three generalizations about the tone of your reports—and they are only generalizations.

1. Reports that travel upward, especially to top management, generally call for a more formal tone than those that travel laterally or downward.
2. Reports that are to be circulated outside the company are usually more formal in tone than those kept within the "family."
3. Reports on matters of great weight or that are based on considerable research and investigation are more formal in tone than those concerning routine matters.

There are exceptions, of course, to all generalizations; and you can choose the appropriate tone only when you know what your readers expect or would be likely to prefer.

Objectivity in Reports. Some company guides on report writing, as well as numerous books, suggest that all business reports should be objective. What is meant by the word *objective?* No doubt most people use the term as a synonym for *factual.* Yet few reports written in business are strictly factual; indeed, many of the reports you will write—unless you're engaged in scientific research—will be valuable mainly because they present your *opinions,* with or without facts to back them up.

If you're asked by your boss to recommend a procedure for processing promotion letters more quickly, you will have to dig up all the facts about the present procedure and the reasons why it isn't satisfactory. Maybe you discover that the equipment breaks down frequently and time is wasted while repairs are being made. This is a fact, and the solution to the problem is simply to replace the machines. But might the machines give many more years of good service if they were rebuilt? Or if you have to replace them, what kind of equipment will do the best job? These are matters of opinion, even though you may have some facts to support them.

Often, people who say they prefer objective reports mean they want them written in third person, passive voice. Compare:

1. It is believed that a successful outcome resulted because the samples were chosen scientifically.
2. I think we got good results because we chose our samples so carefully.

1. It is strongly recommended that the procurement section be abolished and that its functions be assigned to the Treasurer's office.
2. I recommend that we eliminate the procurement section and turn over its function to Mr. Hoyer's office.

Although the ''1'' examples are more formally expressed than the ''2'' examples, they are not necessarily more objective. A formal tone can convey opinions, too; the opinions are simply less obvious when expressed as *It is recommended* rather than *I recommend.*

Tone, then, does not in itself convey objectivity or lack of it. A truly objective report is factual, without emotion or personal prejudice. You should not get the impression that if you avoid such personal pronouns as *I, we, you,* and *they* and write in passive voice, you will automatically achieve objectivity.

Fact Versus Opinion. No matter what tone you decide on for your reports, it is important that you let your reader know when you're stating a fact and when you're giving an opinion. Assume that, during the week of the World Series, department managers reported 212 employee absences—three times the rate in a typical week. You are pretty certain that the reason for so many absences is that the World Series "interfered" with attendance, but you don't really know. You would *not* write:

During the week of October 3, there were 212 employee absences. This is three times the rate in a typical week, and it is because the World Series was being played and the employees stayed home to watch it on television.

In the absence of hard data, you would probably write:

During the week of October 3, there were 212 employee absences—three times the rate in a typical week. The fact that the World Series was being played that week probably accounts for a number of these absences.

Although in the second example you have offered an opinion, it is stated as an opinion by use of the word *probably.* Yet the above example is not satisfactory either, because we don't know whose opinion it is. If it is solely the writer's, he should have said in the last sentence:

It's interesting to note that the World Series was being played that week, and I suspect this would account for a number of these absences.

If the writer was expressing opinions offered by the department managers reporting the absences, he would have said in the last sentence:

> It's interesting to note that the World Series was being played that week, and most department managers think this accounts for a number of these absences.

Specificity in Reports. Writers often confuse their readers when they are not specific in the facts or opinions offered. Let's take the example of the 212 employee absences during World Series week. Suppose you had reported the following:

> During the week of October 3, there were 212 employees absent from work . . .

If this is true, there is nothing wrong with the statement, of course. But the phrase "212 employees absent" does not mean the same as "212 employee absences." The first phrase means that 212 different employees failed to show up for work some time during the week; the second allows for the possibility that some people were absent for more than one day and that only 50 or so different *people* were absent.

In the matter of specificity, make sure you avoid generalizations when you have specific details that you can use. If you are writing a report to your boss about the status of job descriptions in the Personnel file, don't say:

> Most of the positions in Warner-Dennison are covered by job descriptions. Of these, some are satisfactory and some are not. But where descriptions are either inadequate or nonexistent, we are attempting to correct the situation.

when you can say:

> There are 133 different positions in Warner-Dennison. Of these, 100 are covered by what I would call accurate job descriptions. Of the remainder, 20 positions have descriptions in various "states of inadequacy" (some don't show the changes in jobs since they were prepared; others were written poorly in the first place). Within the past 22 months, 13 new positions were created but lack specific descriptions. All in the last two categories mentioned are being worked on now, and I expect they will be finished by February 17.

Readability of Reports. In writing your report, make it as easy as possible for the reader to grasp, with conviction, what you have to say. Following are suggestions for making your report readable.

Organization and Headings. We have already looked at the essentials of choosing an organization plan (deductive versus inductive) and outlining the content of your report (pages 271–275). Remember, then, to organize your report in such a way that the reader is constantly with you. Visualize yourself as taking him firmly by the hand, guiding him from point to point, never letting go. Don't lure him into uncharted byways.

To make sure your reader stays with you, be generous with headings in the report. And make sure the headings show proper subordination. Minor points are correctly shown *under* major headings in the following:

POPULATION
    Total Population
    Regional Distribution
    Urban, Rural, Suburban, and Interurban Distribution
CONSUMER INCOME
    Nature and Scope of Income
        National Income
        Personal Income
        Discretionary Income
    Income Distribution

When you have several minor headings under a major heading, it's a good idea to introduce them—in other words, tell your reader what you're going to tell him and then tell him. Thus:

METHODS OF APPRAISING MORALE

The generally recognized methods of appraising morale include:

1. The supervisor's or executive's impressions
2. The guided interview
3. The unguided interview
4. Analysis of production
5. The "listening-in" process
6. The questionnaire

The Supervisor's or Executive's Impressions

Relatively few supervisors or executives are trained observers of morale. They usually know how to get things done . . .

Pay particular attention to parallelism in headings. For example:

RIGHT	WRONG
MAJOR CAUSES OF TURNOVER	MAJOR CAUSES OF TURNOVER
REDUCTION OF TURNOVER	HOW TO REDUCE TURNOVER
RESULTS OF REDUCED TURNOVER	REDUCED TURNOVER SAVES MONEY

Word Choice. Keep it simple. Don't try to exhibit the breadth of your vocabulary in your report. Choose the plain words and straightforward expressions that nearly everyone understands.

Sentences and Paragraphs. Keep your sentences relatively short and uncomplicated. Avoid the extremes of too many short, choppy sentences on the one hand and, on the other, long, involved sentences that demand the reader's utmost concentration.

Don't be afraid to paragraph. Practice varying the length of paragraphs, remembering that a fairly brief opening and a short closing paragraph are more likely to gain the reader's attention.

Coherence. Your report will hang together for the reader if you provide transitional words and phrases between sentences and paragraphs. Your reader is more likely to stay with you if you use such bridges as *in addition, too, on the other hand, moreover, in the second place, therefore, however, yet,* and so on.

Margins and Spacing. Be generous with your margins. Allow at least 1 inch for the top, bottom, and side margins. Start chapter or section headings $1\frac{1}{2}$ to 2 inches from the top of the page. And make sure to use the same margins consistently throughout a report.

   Because double spacing is easier to read, we recommend that you use it for most of your reports—even longer ones. Indent paragraphs at least five spaces.

Pagination. Number all pages except those that precede your introduction (such as a title page). You may center the number at the top of the page or place it in the upper right or bottom right corner; we prefer the upper right corner.

Illustrations. Provide illustrations (maps, charts, tables, graphs, drawings, diagrams, etc.) when they will help your reader understand what you are talking about. When your report contains a great many figures, try to find ways to put them in tables and charts. Your report will be hard to read (and dull to most people) if your narrative contains a great many figures. Compare the narrative presentation below with the tabular arrangement that follows.

> As to advertising expenditures by media, in 19— we spent $15,000 on newspapers and magazines; $8,500 on radio and television; $18,000 on direct mail; $7,700 on transit advertising; $17,000 on premiums; and $6,400 on billboards. In 19— we spent $18,000 on newspapers and magazines; $10,500 on radio and television; $21,000 on direct mail; $3,500 on transit advertising; $12,000 on premiums; and $9,800 on billboards.

Advertising Expenditures	19—	19—
Newspapers and Magazines	$15,000	$18,000
Radio and Television	8,500	10,500
Direct Mail	18,000	21,000
Transit Advertising	7,700	3,500
Premiums	17,000	12,000
Billboards	6,400	9,800
Totals	$72,600	$74,800

   Wouldn't you agree that not only is the information easier to read in the table form than in narrative form but it is also easier to make comparisons of amounts spent by year?

Parts of a Formal Report. While a formal report does not always contain all of the parts discussed here, you should know about them. In a few instances, you will want to include at least some of them in formal analytical reports that you write.

Title Page. The title page typically contains four items of information: the title of the report, the name and title of the person or organization for whom the report was written, the name of the person who wrote the report, and the date on which the report was submitted. The placement of this information—indeed, the type of information given—varies. The title page for a report on school and college enrollment might be similar to the one shown here.

SCHOOL AND COLLEGE ENROLLMENT: 1975–1985

An Examination of Projected Enrollment in
Elementary School, High School, and
College and University

Prepared by

Thornton S. Louderbush
Assistant Personnel Manager
Warner-Dennison Company

For

The Long-Range Planning Committee
Warner-Dennison Company

May 5, 19--

Letter of Transmittal. A letter of transmittal is not always needed for reports that are not to go outside the company. However, if there is any doubt in the reader's mind about why he is getting the report, a transmittal letter or a memo is a good idea. Intracompany reports can be transmitted by means of a simple memo that does little more than identify the report, the sender, the receiver, and the date.

Interoffice Memorandum

TO	Arthur Knudsen, Chairman	FROM	Thornton S. Louderbush
DEPT.	Long-Range Planning Committee	DEPT	Personnel
SUBJECT	Report on School and College Enrollment: 1975-1985	DATE	May 5, 19--

Here is my report, "School and College Enrollment: 1975-1985," that you asked me to prepare. I look forward to discussing it with you at an early meeting.

T.S.L.

If, however, the report is prepared for people outside the company, the letter of transmittal is set up in business letter form and usually includes such information as why the report was written, acknowledgments of assistance, how the report was distributed, and so on.

Table of Contents. The table of contents orients the reader to the subject of the report and also facilitates future reference.

CONTENTS

Summary. The purpose of the summary is to give the reader a quick capsule of the writer's findings. Following is the summary of the report for the Long-Range Planning Committee. As you will see, it tells what the report is about, gives the source of the enrollment data, and includes a brief summary of the enrollments at various educational levels.

SUMMARY

This report is the end product of a study of school and college enrollments just completed, focusing on the 10-year period from 1975 through 1985.

Enrollment data contained in the report have been derived from an analysis of population forecasts for the age groups that feed into schools and colleges--i.e., the 5-13, 14-17, and 18-24 age groups. The basic enrollment figures produced in this study are as follows (in millions):

Level	1975	1980	1985
Elementary	33.7	32.1	35.2
High school	15.9	15.3	13.5
College	9.4	11.1	11.5
TOTALS	59.0	58.5	60.2

This study finds that educational enrollments will rise to 60.2 million for an increase of about 3 percent by 1985. The coming 10-year period will produce significant changes in the mix of enrollment numbers from one level to another and from one 5-year period to another. These changes are discussed in the sections that follow.

Introduction. The introduction in a report sets the stage for the reader so that he will have the necessary background to understand the report itself. The introduction contains information about how the writer approached his subject, limitations of the study (what he did not do), and so forth. Following is the introduction to the "School and College Enrollment: 1975–1985" report.

2

INTRODUCTION

    The shape and size of school and college enrollments during the next 10 years should not come upon us as a complete surprise. Many of us have known the general facts for some time, but it is doubtful that we are thoroughly aware of the precise nature of the changes to come and their timetable. For this reason, our report examines in detail the educational enrollments that can be expected during the next 10 years.

Scope of the Report

    This report focuses on educational enrollments (and their supporting population) for three traditional levels of formal education: elementary school (nursery school through grade 8), high school (grades 9-12), and college and university (2-year, 4-year, and graduate). We include enrollment in both public and nonpublic institutions at all three levels.

    We make no attempt in this study to relate our analysis to other areas of education, such as proprietary vocational schools, home study schools, adult education programs, or training in business, industry, and government. Nor do we attempt to deal with such important correlative questions as trends in curriculum and methodology, changes in organizational patterns, problems in school finance, or the crisis in Catholic schools. These require separate study in order to give them the focus and emphasis they deserve. We hope to explore some of them in later studies.

Body of the Report. The meat of the report is, of course, the body. Under appropriate headings, the text fleshes out the summary and supports the conclusions and recommendations. Essential details should be given, but temptations to digression should be resisted. The reader will grasp numerical data more easily if they are presented in tabular or graph form, as shown in this portion of the body of a report.

8

ELEMENTARY SCHOOL

　　We will experience two wide swings in elementary school (N-8) enroll-ments during the next 10 years. The first of these will occur between 1975 and 1978 in the form of a sharp dip, reducing enrollments by more than four million students. The later swing will reverse that loss, bringing enroll-ments back to within one million of the current level by 1985. Both swings are entirely the reflection of predictable shifts in the size of the population age group that supplies the elementary school with its students.

Population

　　When we study elementary school-age population (5-13), we must do some educated guessing. At least one-half the children who will enroll in elementary school between now and 1985 are not yet born. The rate at which they will be born is dealt with later in this report.

　　The elementary school draws its enrollments almost exclusively from the age 5-13 population. This population will reach a low point in 1979, then turn upward again (see Figure 2).

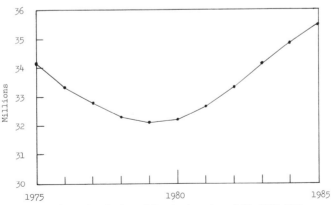

Figure 2.   Projected Population, Ages 5-13, 1975-1985

Conclusions and Recommendations. Not all formal reports call for the writer's conclusions and recommendations. In deciding whether to include this section, check the purpose of the report to see if such words as *recommendations, suggestions, conclusions,* or *opinions* were included in the original request or plans.

Some people think that conclusions should be separated from recommendations—conclusions being objective statements based on evidence

---

15

CONCLUSIONS AND RECOMMENDATIONS

The foregoing study of the employee-relations policies in 40 major

businesses in the United States leads to the following conclusions:

1. A profit-sharing plan, based upon percentage sharing wherein the

"partner in interest" consciousness is established, is the most effective

of all formulas for creating the capitalistic conception, with its

approval and allegiance to the profit system.

2. The formula of "percentage sharing" definitely creates the

partnership relation, which in turn promotes a closer, friendlier, and more

cooperative attitude on the part of the employee toward his employer.

3. Profit sharing on a percentage basis develops the same selfish

desire in the employee for the enjoyment of profits as motivates the

employer; hence there is established the "common interest" reflecting

itself in increased personal interest for company success and in doing all

those things that have an influence upon the making of profits.

4. The "conflict of interest" that centers in the wage question is

tempered and modified by the introduction of profit sharing--that is, the

employee looks in two directions for financial betterment.

It would seem, therefore, that Klaxton could profit from the installa-

tion of a profit-sharing plan; and it is recommended by the Task Force

that a committee be appointed immediately to propose an operating plan.

It is further recommended that a consulting firm, such as Byron

Breckenridge, Incorporated, be engaged to assist in drafting such a plan.

supplied in the body of the report and recommendations being the writer's own opinions of the action called for by the conclusions. Others feel that both conclusions and recommendations are the writer's ideas. We think they can usually be combined. Shown on the opposite page is the *Conclusions and Recommendations* section of a formal report.

The Appendix. The appendix of a formal report contains supplementary information that some readers may wish to see but which, if included in the report itself, would merely clutter and confuse. Some or all of the following might be included in an appendix:

1. Questionnaries used in making the survey
2. Additional tables
3. Copies of contracts and other legal forms
4. Publications and other literature appropriate to the subject
5. Other reports or quotations and excerpts from them

The items in the appendix should be labeled.

> Exhibit A. U.S. Estimated Population (by Age) Through 1980
>
> Exhibit B. Excerpt from The Business Environment of the 70s
>
> Exhibit C. Reprint, "Is Higher Education Too 'High'?" from Saturday Review, February, 1972

Labeling appendix items makes possible reference to them in the body of the report by exhibit number or letter designation.

> Professor Blumenthal, of Cornell, cites the increasing cost of a college education (Exhibit C) as a serious. . . .

If the appendix contains many tables, graphs, questionnaires, etc., you may want to list the items on a separate Appendix page and insert it in front of the exhibits.

Bibliography. The bibliography is a list of books, newspapers, magazines, reports, monographs, etc., consulted by the author when he gathered the information for his report. It has two purposes:

1. To provide the reader with additional references in case he would like to read further.
2. To acknowledge the work of the authors whose writings were consulted.

A typical bibliography from a report is shown on the next page.

Binding the Report. Formal reports are usually bound. The elegance of the binding depends on the importance of the report and the impression one wants to make. Some short reports are not bound at all but merely stapled at the left side (at least three staples, affixed vertically, are recommended). Others are housed in an elaborate cover and bound with comb plastic; and still others are hole-punched and placed inside a folder-type report binding. Stationery stores stock a wide variety of bindings, and companies that prepare a great many reports for clients develop their own special bindings.

16

BIBLIOGRAPHY

Archibald, Oscar, "A New Meaning for Incentives," Personnel Journal,
    January, 1971, p. 46.

"Everyone Profits," The Wall Street Journal, Sept. 16, 1972, p. 6, col. 2.

Kepner, Bertram J., and Olive S. Silverthorn, "Profit Sharing at
    Columbia Industries," Forward, March, 1972, p. 7.

Occupational Trends, U.S. Department of Labor Publication No. 18,
    Washington, July, 1972.

Scott, Walter Dill, et al., Personnel Management, 7th ed., McGraw-Hill
    Book Company, New York, 1970.

"Soledad Comes Back" (editorial), Washington Post, May 2, 1971, p. 20.

Thalmier, S. K., Rewarding Employees, LaSalle Press, Boston, 1972.

SOLUTION

A PROPOSED EMPLOYEE SUGGESTION PLAN
FOR WARNER-DENNISON

PURPOSE

To establish operating rules and procedures for an employee suggestion system for Warner-Dennison.

PROCEDURE

The suggestion plans of five different companies were studied, and the best features of all these were selected for a Warner-Dennison system.

THE PROPOSED PLAN

Suggestion Forms: A form similar to the attached should be printed in quantity and distributed to employees, together with an announcement of the general plan.

Suggestion Boxes: Suggestion boxes should be placed on each floor of the building and employees encouraged to drop their suggestions in the boxes.

Suggestion Plan Committee: A committee of six people, each representing a different department, should be named to administer the awards.

Awards (Class A): Where savings can be computed, an award equal to 25% of the first year's savings would be paid. If the award is $100 or more, half of the amount (based on estimated savings) would be paid as soon as possible after the suggestion is adopted. The remainder (based on actual savings) would be paid within a year after the suggestion is adopted.

If the award is less than $100, the entire amount would be paid as soon as possible after the suggestion is adopted.

Awards (Class B): Where savings cannot be precisely computed (for example, safety suggestions), awards from $10 to $50 would be made. When exceptional circumstances warrant, the Suggestion Plan Committee should be authorized to offer an award up to $100 for such suggestions.

Operating Rules

1. Ownership: All suggestions, upon submission, would become the property of Warner-Dennison.
2. Collection: Suggestions would be collected daily and date-stamped. This date would become the official date of the suggestion.
3. *Etc. (The full report will contain many more items—perhaps as many as 25.)*

CONCLUSIONS AND RECOMMENDATIONS

It is recommended that a suggestion system of the nature described be installed at the earliest possible time—by September 1, 19—, if possible. Companies that have an effective suggestion system report that it:

1. Encourages subordinates in making improvements and eliminating waste.
2. Provides an effective means whereby the worker can communicate with management.
3. Improves morale—gives employees a sense of contributing.

It is believed that Warner-Dennison would enjoy similar advantages from the installation of such a system.

Analysis of Solution. This report is formal in tone because it is likely to be forwarded to the president of the company without change by the person between the writer and the president. For much the same reason, the writer kept the report impersonal and objective.

■ ■

PROJECTS

A Write the following in a more formal, impersonal tone.

1 I think we should first find out why dealers are returning so many lawn mowers this spring.

2 Of course, we will look only at people who have the experience these jobs call for.

3 It's clear to me, based on the interviews I've had with top people here, that we've got to find a better way to compensate our executives.

4 I think the first step we should take is to make a careful audit of our supervisors to find out what they think the needs are for a training program.

5 I will continue my daily check on the efficiency of this new installation and report to you at the end of October—earlier if something important develops.

6 Would you like a further breakdown on the inventory situation in Dayton and Chattanooga? I have the information and can get it to you quickly.

7   When the figures arrive from Harrison, I'll be in a better position to make an accurate long-range forecast for you.

8   This is about as far as I can go until our committee meets again in December, after which I will report in more detail.

B   Write the following in a more informal, personal tone.

1   It will be observed that sales expenses during the period increased three times the rate of sales. Should this trend continue, it appears likely that the budgeted 16% NOP cannot be achieved.

2   On the basis of this experiment it would seem likely that Naugahyde is the superior binding material, at least in terms of wearing quality and washability.

3   Based on the results of the survey, the conclusion appears to be warranted that the market for Widgets is better in rural communities than in metropolitan areas.

4   Interviewers are hired and trained, in person, to conduct the survey, and their work is checked regularly for accuracy and validity. This procedure has proved very effective in statistical sampling.

5   The ability to commmunicate effectively is not an innate characteristic of mankind; instead, it is the result of observation, study, experimentation, and practice.

6   The principal consideration, when planning an efficient and practical layout of the offices of Reliant, is the direction and flow of work.

7   The opinions of trained and experienced librarians should be sought when undertaking to evaluate the reliability of statistical data.

8   It is the opinion of many executives that budget estimates should be made by the individuals who are to be held accountable for achieving the estimates.

C   Which of the following do you consider the more objective statement in each case?

1a   It is highly questionable that the savings forecast could, under the circumstances, be achieved.

1b   I'm not convinced that we could save as much as we have hopes of saving by putting in this new plan.

2a   It is improbable that the additional cost of having the salesmen's wives attend the marketing conference as guests of the company will be worth it in so-called "morale" value. Besides the heavy cost (which, incidentally, was not included in the budget for this meeting), there is a distinct possibility that the presence of wives will waste a large amount of time.

2b   Although I am intrigued by the idea that having the wives attend the marketing conference as guests of the company will be good for morale, I'm not sure that the benefits will equal the expense. We must consider, too, the "expense" of time: How much will the wives' presence eat into conference time?

3a   The facts are indisputable, and further consideration of the Mayberry Company as a prime contractor is out of the question.

3b The facts would seem to indicate that the Mayberry Company is not the best choice for a contractor.

D The following report was prepared at the request of Charles S. Fauxhall, president of Romeo Spice Company. Mr. Fauxhall said to the sales manager, C. T. Sayre, "How is that new car-leasing arrangement working out? Could you give me a rundown on your experience to date (including costs) and tell me what the future looks like? I want several people to have this information."

C. T. Sayre assigned the job to W. S. Hotz, assistant sales manager, who prepared the report. Make whatever changes you think will result in a better report. Use whatever form you think is appropriate.

INTEROFFICE MEMORANDUM

TO: Mr. Charles S. Fauxhall   FROM: W. S. Hotz
DEPT: Executive   DEPT: Sales
SUBJECT: Car-Leasing Plan—a View of   DATE: May 16, 19—
              the First Eight Months

At the conclusion of our first eight months in operation, we have 305 cars on lease from Lacy Corporation (302 are in operation and 3 are surplus—1 in St. Louis, 1 in Los Angeles, and 1 in Memphis). As far as we can determine, only three were lemons—an Indomitable, a Fearless, and a Mariah. Our relations with Lacy are excellent. They handle our requests rapidly and we have had a barely noticeable number of complaints from the field. In the case of the three lemons, information was forwarded immediately to district warranty people or to the service dealer who quickly corrected whatever was wrong.

During the first eight months, the average mileage per man per month was 1,625 on business and 368 personal for a total of 1,993. Annualized, that would be an equivalent of 19,500 business miles and 4,400 personal miles per car.

The running expense per car-month, including gas, oil, maintenance and repairs, tires, and tire repairs, was $68.50, or 3.43¢ per mile. The standing expense, including rental less depreciation, provision for depreciation, depreciation adjustment on cars sold, licenses, and taxes, insurance, accident and theft loss, and some miscellaneous items, is $115 per car-month, or 5.80¢ per mile. For instance, the cost of parking, storage, washing, and tolls was $15 per car-month, or .75¢ per mile. The total cost of the operation, as credited to us after payment made by drivers on their personal use of the cars, was $177 per car-month, or 8.87¢ per mile. The cost per mile for business usage was 10.9¢. An added item of interest—these 300 cars averaged 13.3 miles per gallon of gas; 1,250 miles per quart of oil; or a cost per gallon of gas of 36.6¢ and a cost for a quart of oil of 81.5¢.

Looking ahead to the coming year, our rental will decline by $6\frac{1}{4}$% or so per month due to aging and our fixed charges will be less. The maintenance will probably go up as the cars become older. We are told that the new models will be approximately $150 more per car and that the manufacturers have discontinued their fleet allowance of $50–$150. This additional cost would be offset by lower cost of money—thus, we will be saving on interest and a higher trade-in value on more expensive cars.

We propose to change the reimbursement plan to take care of the increased operating cost for those people driving their own cars. This plan, you will recall, was effective for those driving 5,000 miles per year whose jobs required them to do so. The present plan provided 4¢ per mile for the first 14,000 miles, 5¢ per mile for the next 4,000 miles, 6½¢ per mile for everything over 18,001, plus $720 a year for depreciation and actual insurance costs.

We plan to introduce a change which would eliminate the 4¢-per-mile bracket and would pay 5¢ per mile for 18,000 miles. Such a plan would cost the company, based on current travel in this class, approximately $17,000.

That expense may be offset by a proposal that the members of the Lacy car-lease plan who are now paying the company 4¢ per mile for private use of the car have that charge increased to 5¢ per mile, which is a more realistic figure. Based on personal travel in the range of one million miles, it will reduce the cost of the paragraph above in the amount of $10,000 and result in an overall cost to the company of $7,000.

We are planning to establish a new account on the monthly statement of expense for car expenses. This will carry the actual expenses during 19—, moving them from the Travel and Entertainment account. It isn't possible to budget this in 19—, and , therefore, it will show expenses only. With that experience behind us, we will be able to budget for 19— at the appropriate time.

E   The senior personnel clerk has been complaining to you, her boss, about the need for all new typewriters in the department (there are seven). According to your records, four are three years old, two are two years old, and one was purchased eight months ago. You ask the clerk to give you a report on the condition of the typewriters so that you can make a decision about replacing them. Her report is as follows:

You asked for a report on the condition of the seven typewriters in my department. They are all old and inefficient. We are wasting time with this old equipment; there are new models available now that would pay for themselves in the increased speed and quality of work. I recommend that we buy all new typewriters.

What is wrong with the report?

■ ■

part
10

COMMUNICATIONS
PROJECT

YOUR JOB As sales manager of the College Department in the Dallas regional office of the Merit Publishing Company, you supervise ten field representatives who call on professors and others at colleges and universities in Texas, Oklahoma, Arkansas, New Mexico, and Arizona. In addition, of course, you have such responsibilities as corresponding with professors, authors, bookstore managers, and others; seeing that your customers' orders are shipped promptly; attending educational conferences; and keeping in touch with your boss, Lyle P. Warren, and others in the New York office.

PART 10 COMMUNICATIONS PROJECT

PROBLEM: During the week of October 4, you receive the correspondence reproduced on the following pages. You are to study each piece of correspondence in each of the 33 situations and the notes about each situation. Solely on the basis of these, you are to decide the action to be taken and then prepare the necessary communications.

BACKGROUND

The Merit Publishing Company has its headquarters in New York City and six regional offices in various parts of the country. The company publishes dictionaries, encyclopedias, technical handbooks, and other reference materials; children's books, novels, biographies, and other trade books. The company derives the largest share of its income, however, from the sale of textbooks, filmstrips, and other educational publications.

The Dallas office, which is the headquarters for the Southwest Region, receives and fills orders from customers in Texas, Oklahoma, Arkansas, New Mexico, and Arizona. However, the New York office handles the collection of customer accounts and other financial records, the advertising of the company's products and services, the editing and manufacturing of books and other items, and similar matters.

As regional sales manager, you obviously receive a large volume of mail and therefore must devote much of your time to reading and answering it—with an absolute minimum of delay. And, as you might expect, the letters, memos, and other items that you receive run the gamut as far as writing style is concerned. Consequently, you will not be surprised to find that in this project you must work with letters and other communications that are not necessarily model examples of "good" business writing.

Another Merit "First"

... in Marketing

Illustration — Cover
of text

FOREST PRODUCTS MARKETING

By STEVEN T. McCAUGHEY

Professor of Marketing

University of the Northwest

Seattle, Washington

A new college textbook designed for forestry and business school students who
aspire to marketing or general management positions in the forest industries.

"As forest products companies become increasingly concerned
with finding and serving markets for the finished output of the
mills, more and more forestry school graduates will have to be
knowledgeable in the field of marketing." (David J. Keane)

Send for your examination copy today!

Merit Publishing Company
1640 Stemmons Freeway
Dallas, Texas 75201

Gentlemen:

Please send me an examination copy of Steven T. McCaughey's
FOREST PRODUCTS MARKETING for consideration for adoption.

Name (Please Print)..

School ....

City...................... State................. ZIP.......

Notes: Merit has just published a new book, *Forest Products Marketing*. Copy for
an advertisement to appear in the *Southwest Journal of Marketing* is given above,
and descriptive material concerning the book appears on pages 302–303. The
objective of the ad is to encourage instructors to send for the book, examine it, and
order it for use in their classes. In anticipation of receiving many cards from instructors
as a result of the ad, you are to prepare a follow-up sales letter that you can send
to all those requesting an examination copy.

NEW BOOK INFORMATION

TITLE: FOREST PRODUCTS MARKETING

AUTHOR: Steven T. McCaughey
              Professor of Marketing
              University of the Northwest
              Seattle, Washington

SIZE: 6 3/8 x 9 1/4, 384 pp.

PUBLICATION DATE: March, 19--   PRICE: $7.50

TEXT:

Written for students in forestry schools or in business schools who aspire
to marketing or general management positions in the forest industries, the
book may also be used in management training programs or for general
reading by executives in the forest industries. It has a managerial, or
decision-making, focus, particularly in the cases it contains. This focus
will help train the student for any type of administrative job, not only
marketing. Policy decisions in any functional area are likely to have
major marketing implications, so that even the students who remain in
timberlands management or in production will find that some knowledge of
marketing is essential.

This book provides an economic, historical, and institutional background
against which the reader can assess the trends taking place in the forest
products industries today. While the book assumes no prior knowledge in
marketing or in the forest products industries, both the text material
and the cases are presented in such a way as to provide challenging
material for readers who already have backgrounds in these fields. The
34 cases, for instance, are of a fairly wide range of difficulty and
have been successfully used in both graduate and undergraduate teaching
and in management training programs. Concepts presented in the product
planning, distribution, and selling areas should provide new insights
into the many changes taking place in these fields.

In Part I of the book, containing Chapters 1, 2, and 3, the reader learns
what marketing is about and what role it plays in the forest industries.
The technique of analysis and solution of cases is explained, and an
approach to the understanding of market demand and customer buying habits
is presented.

Part II deals with the four basic elements of the marketing mix--product
policy, pricing, channels of distribution, and promotional programs--plus
marketing organization and marketing research. The material in these
chapters, both text and cases, is presented in terms of the marketing of

lumber and wood products, with an emphasis on the marketing function as playing a central role in the total operations of the forest products enterprise.

Part III also deals with the elements of the marketing mix, plus marketing organization and marketing research. The setting here, however, is in the pulp and paper segment of the forest industries. The reason for this division is that the markets and customers served, and the marketing problems involved, are rather different in pulp and paper, as compared with lumber, plywood, and other panel and wood products.

Finally, Part IV, with its concluding chapter (Chapter 16), provides the capstone to the structural sequence of Parts II and III. Throughout the earlier chapters the author has emphasized the importance of setting goals and objectives; determining marketing strategy and tactics to achieve the objectives; planning the marketing program to carry out the strategy; developing an appropriate marketing organization to put plans into effect. In the concluding chapter, methods for the control and evaluation of marketing performance are described. These methods may be used by the marketing executive to gauge the effectiveness of his company in perform-ing the essential parts of the marketing function.

SPECIAL FEATURES:

34 major Harvard Business School-type cases based on actual company situa-tions and successfully proven in use in both graduate and undergraduate teaching and in management training programs.

An Instructor's Manual containing teaching notes and solutions to the cases.

Full text coverage of all major aspects of marketing as applied to the forest industries.

Emphasis on a managerial approach to marketing in forest products companies, supported by a description of the economic, historical, and institutional background of the forest industries.

Explanation of the use of the case method of teaching.

ALPHA UNIVERSITY

ENID, OKLAHOMA 73705

October 1, 19--

Merit Publishing Company
1640 Stemmons Freeway
Dallas, Texas 75201

OCT 4 REC'D

Dear Sir:

Would you please send me a copy of CHEMISTRY FOR EVERYONE, by Kevin Burgess, which I would like to consider for use in my general chemistry course for nonscience majors.

Your attention will be very much appreciated.

Sincerely,

Carla J. Schweitzer
Assistant Professor

CJS:cw

NEW BOOK INFORMATION

TITLE: CHEMISTRY FOR GENERAL APPLICATION

AUTHOR: Professor Frieda N. Persons
          State University
          Klamath, Oregon

SIZE: 7 1/4 x 10 1/4, 448 pp.

PUBLICATION DATE: March, 19--   PRICE: $9.95

TEXT:

The presentation of the field of chemistry to groups of college students who have virtually no background in mathematics and who are not interested in a career in science requires very special treatment. The author has taught large non-science major classes in chemistry and has recognized the shortcomings of existing textbooks designed for these students.

Initially basic concepts of structure, bonding, and writing of formulas and equations are introduced to the student. He is then guided through a number of current and crucial topics of the day in which chemistry plays a significant role. These topics include air pollution, water pollution, household chemicals, drugs, agriculture chemicals, radio-chemistry, nuclear energy, and polymers. While the student is examining these subjects, additional principles are drawn in and expanded.

Questions and projects are included with each chapter and a glossary of scientific terms is in the back. In the appendix there are listed for the instructor a number of excellent short films that can be worked into the lecture material. In addition, there are suggestions for audio-visual aids, laboratory work, and student atomic model kits. Although quantitative reasoning is frequently called for, the text does not require the use of formal mathematics. Removal of the mathematical barrier is of extreme importance to non-science students, who will gain from this book not only a foundation in the important chemical theories and principles but also an understanding of the relevance of chemistry to their day-to-day living.

CONTENTS:

General. Structure of the Atom. The Elements and Their Families. Chemical Bonding. Research in Schools. Research in Industry. Drugs and Clinical Chemistry. Agricultural Chemicals. Polymers I. Polymers II. Food Additives. Water Pollution. Air Pollution. Household Chemical Products. Radiochemistry and Nuclear Energy.

■■■■■■■■■■■■■■■■■■■■■■■■■■■■■■■■■■■■■■

Notes: Merit does not publish the Burgess book (it is published by First-Rank Press, a competitor). However, Merit has just issued a new book, *Chemistry for General Application,* by Professor Frieda N. Persons, which is designed for the student who is not a science major. Naturally, you think your book is far superior to that published by First-Rank Press. Descriptive material on the Persons book appears above.

■■■■■■■■■■■■■■■■■■■■■■■■■■■■■■■■■■■■■■

COLLEGE OF SOUTHERN ARKANSAS

TEXARKANA, ARKANSAS 75501

Arts and Science Department

October 2, 19--

OCT 4 RECD

Merit Publishing Company
1640 Stemmons Freeway
Dallas, Texas 75201

Gentlemen:

I have adopted and am now using your text, <u>Principles of Anthropology, Second Edition</u>, by Coulsen.

On August 30, I requested an answer key for this book, and I was sent a key for another book by mistake, which I returned with a second request. Any effort that you could make to see that I receive the correct answer key for the above-mentioned text in the shortest possible time would be greatly appreciated.

Thank you.

Sincerely yours,

James A. Patterson
Professor

■ ■

Notes: When a professor adopts a textbook, he is supplied an answer key without charge.

■ ■

MᶜKᴇɴᴢɪᴇ Mᴇᴍᴏʀɪᴀʟ Lɪʙʀᴀʀʏ

Levitan-Todd College

CARSONVILLE, ARIZONA 85703

October 1, 19--

OCT 4 REC'D

Dear Sirs:

Please mail and bill me for the following books:

    1 Louvrain: THE BEGINNING OF EDUCATION IN AMERICA

    1 Morrissey: THE INFLUENCE OF HORACE MANN ON PUBLIC EDUCATION

    1 Black: EDUCATION IN TRANSITION

I am aware that the first two items listed above are no longer listed in your catalog and may be out of print. If you cannot supply these items, will you please tell me where I may be able to secure these books.

Sincerely yours,

Abraham R. Kosy

Abraham R. Kosy

■ ■

Notes: The first two books listed are Merit publications, but they are out of print, as Mr. Kosy suggested. You have tried on other occasions to locate copies by writing to the New York office, but they can't help. Such books are sometimes available at bookstores. You also know of two firms that specialize in finding hard-to-obtain books: Aardvarks Booksearchers, Box 668, San Diego, California, and International Book-finders, Box 3003-S, Beverly Hills, California. The third book listed, Black's *Education in Transition,* has not yet been published; it is due off the press sometime next January.

■ ■

MONSERRAT UNIVERSITY

LaMar, New Mexico 87509

Graduate School

October 1, 19--

OCT 4 RECD

The President
Merit Publishing Company
Dallas, Texas 75201

Dear Sir:

I have just had the opportunity to read a pamphlet called "History as Literature," by D. F. Acheson, which you have been distributing to educators. It is a delightful essay, and I should appreciate it if you would send me a copy for my use. If it is not asking too much, could you spare me two dozen copies for distribution in class? In any case, I should like at least the one for myself. Are there others in this pamphlet series?

Thanking you for your cooperation and for your encouragement of history and historians, I am

Very truly yours,

Alvin D. Rausche
Graduate Adviser
Department of History

■ ■

Notes: Merit published and distributed free to customers five pamphlets, each by a different author, entitled *History as Literature*. You have 20 copies of the one Mr. Rausche wants and will give them to him. The only copy left of each of the others is in the company archives. Because there has been some demand for them, however, these were typed and mimeographed; single manuscripts, with permission to reproduce them, are given those requesting them. The person to contact is Miss Isabelle Lancer, Company Communications, in New York.

■ ■

Bagnold OIL AND REFINING COMPANY

440 SCOTT STREET   LITTLE ROCK, ARKANSAS 72201

Marketing Department

I didn't answer
this since you at want to
have the copyright — so
please handle.
JMG

OCT 4 RECD

October 1, 19--

Professor J. Morrison Gunther
Cherokee Nation Community College
Poteau, Oklahoma 74953

Dear Professor Gunther:

   We are preparing an operations manual for our service
station dealers in the Southwest, and we would like to reproduce Chapter 11 ("Keeping Customers Coming Back") from your
book, SERVICE STATION OPERATION AND MANAGEMENT. May we have
your permission to do so?

   We expect to print about 2,500 copies, which will be
supplied free to our dealers. The materials will not be
sold and will not, of course, be in competition with your
book (which we think is excellent, by the way).

   I would appreciate an early reply.

                              Sincerely yours,

                              William A. Perkinson

                              William A. Perkinson
                              Marketing Manager

WAP:mst

■ ■

Notes: All requests for permission to reproduce copyrighted Merit books must be
directed to Miss Kathryn DuPree, Manager of Permissions and Copyrights, in New
York. No one else in the company is authorized to grant such permission.

■ ■

Rayburn Junior College

PURCHASING DEPARTMENT

Ropesville, Texas 79358

October 2, 19--

OCT 5 REC'D

Merit Publishers
Stemmons Freeway
Dallas, Texas 75201

Gentlemen:

Many thanks for sending me a replacement copy of
Symonds: PRINCIPLES OF GENETICS for my defective copy. I
appreciate your fast service.

Would you please send me the instructor's manual for
this book? Thank you.

Sincerely,

John G. Harding

John G. Harding
Purchasing Assistant

Notes: Merit has a strict policy about sending instructor's manuals and answer keys to unauthorized people because they may eventually find their way into the hands of students. The procedure is for the appropriate department head in the college or university to authorize the issuance of the manual—which could be as simple as an OK on the above letter, signed by the department head. The key will be billed to Mr. Harding (the book has not been adopted by Rayburn Junior College) at the usual discount.

CLOVIS
TECHNICAL INSTITUTE

347 Commerce Street   Clovis, New Mexico 88101

October 2, 19--

OCT 5 REC'D

Manager, College Department
Merit Publishing Company
1640 Stemmons Freeway
Dallas, Texas 75201

Dear Sir:

    Would you please send me the instructor's manual and
key to a HISTORY OF ELECTRICITY, Third Edition. Also if
there are tests to accompany this book, I would like to see
them. I assume these materials are free.

    Thank you.

Sincerely,

Richard L. Loganberry

Richard L. Loganberry
Lecturer

■ ■

Notes: As you know, Merit's policy is to provide instructor's keys without charge
only when the book has been purchased for class use; otherwise, a charge is made
(in this case, $2.40, including the discount). Your records show that Clovis Technical
Institute has not adopted the book. However, there is a chance that it will be adopted
(Mr. Loganberry only recently requested an examination copy). Separate tests have
not been published for this book. However, the instructor's manual contains 12 tests
that may be duplicated for use by the teacher.

■ ■

WESTERN ARKANSAS STATE COLLEGE

PINE BLUFF, ARKANSAS 71601

October 2, 19--

OCT 5 REC'D

Merit Book Co., Inc.
1640 Stemmons Freeway
Dallas, Texas 75201

Gentlemen:

Thank you for the fifty tests for MOLECULAR STRUCTURE AND
ATOMIC CONCEPTS, by Rich and Wasstone.

The enclosed invoice indicates that I have been charged $41
for these tests. It was my understanding that these tests
were furnished free to instructors using your textbook.

I have placed an order through the college bookstore for
several copies of this particular textbook for use during
the coming quarter, but if you are going to charge me for
this supplementary material I will simply cancel the order
and return your tests.

I shall appreciate your checking this matter as I do not
wish to pay this $41 invoice.

Very truly yours,

Gerald F. Fisk

Notes: Although a few publishers furnish free tests when books are adopted, most charge for them. If free tests were provided, the cost of producing them would have to be included in the price of the textbook—and those schools that don't want the tests might object. Too, establishing a modest price for the tests enables the publisher to invest more editorial and production excellence in them.

You don't want the customer to cancel his textbook order with the bookstore; yet you would set a dangerous precedent by giving away the tests.

Free Examination Invitation Card

PEDERSEN: HANDBOOK OF POLLUTION CONTROL

Merit Publishing Company
1640 Stemmons Freeway
Dallas, Texas 75201

OCT 5 REC'D

I accept your invitation. Please send me this handbook for ten days' examination on approval. Within 10 days of receipt I will send you (*check one*) ☑ the full purchase price of $12.00 or ☐ $4.00 down and $4.00 monthly until the price of the book is paid. (We pay delivery costs if you remit with this card. Same return privileges.)

Print Name *Duane R. Stapleton, Ph.D.*
Street *College of Engineering, Room 440*
City *Maywood City* State *Arizona* ZIP *86124*
Company *Crofton University*
Position *Professor of Engineering*

■ ■

Notes: The above postcard was included in an advertising circular for a new book, *Handbook of Pollution Control,* by Pedersen. Today you received 33 cards such as the one above, 11 of which were each enclosed in an envelope with a check for $12 and 3 of which were each accompanied by a $4 check. Professor Stapleton was one who sent $12.

Unfortunately, an error was made in the printing of the card. The price of the handbook is $23.50; the amount to be paid down is $5.50 and the monthly payments are $6. The circular of which the card was a part listed the price correctly.

Merit can't afford to honor orders at the $12 price; it wouldn't be economically feasible.

■ ■

SANDSTONE STATE UNIVERSITY

SAYRE, OKLAHOMA 73662

DEPARTMENT OF CHEMISTRY AND
CHEMICAL ENGINEERING

October 2, 19--

OCT 5 REC'D

Merit Publishers
1640 Stemmons Freeway
Dallas, Texas 75201

Gentlemen:

A recent flood in Western Oklahoma just about wiped out
our chemistry laboratory here at the university. Among some
valuable possessions lost were about 25 Merit textbooks,
reference books, and handbooks in chemistry and chemical engineering. These were my personal property, and I valued
them highly. Incidentally, I feel that Merit books are
excellently made.

I wish to replace these volumes. Is there a special
discount you might give me in a situation of this kind? As
soon as I have your answer, I will try to put together a
list.

Sincerely yours,

F. P. Dekker
Associate Professor

FPP:tn

■ ■

Notes: You are pleased to give Professor Dekker a special discount of 25 percent
on the Merit books he wants replaced. Professor Dekker should place his order with
you directly so that you can make sure he gets the discount promised.

■ ■

PURVIS-ADDISON TEACHERS COLLEGE

Fort Lee, New Mexico 88037

DEPARTMENT OF EDUCATIONAL
PSYCHOLOGY AND SOCIOLOGY

October 2, 19--

OCT 5 REC'D

Chief Executive
Merit Publishing Company
1640 Stemmons Freeway
Dallas, Texas 75201

My dear Sir:

    Recently I bought a copy of Popham's WRITINGS ON MENTAL DEFICIENCY (for which I paid $18.50), and I was shocked to discover a few days later that the binding is falling apart.

    I think $18.50 is a high price, and I do not understand how a company of Merit's reputation could send out such shoddy merchandise. I expect a high quality book. I am very distressed and annoyed.

Very truly yours,

J. William Walton

Professor of Psychology

■ ■

Notes: Now and then, but very rarely, a defective book is shipped to a customer. Although each book is inspected by the manufacturer before it is shipped to Merit's warehouses, and again by Merit's order fulfillment clerk, sometimes a defective one slips through. You replace such books without charge, of course, taking the customer's word for it (the customer does not need to return the defective book in order to receive a replacement, but you'd like him to do so).

■ ■

St. Ann's SCHOOL OF NURSING
HOSPITAL OF TULSA

Morningside Heights
Tulsa, Oklahoma 74114

AREA CODE 918
808-8080

October 4, 19--

Merit Publishing Company
1640 Stemmons Freeway
Dallas, Texas 75201

OCT 6 REC'D

Gentlemen:

We recently purchased thirty (30) copies of <u>Elements of
Nutrition, Second Edition,</u> by Russell and Finkelstein, for
use in our classes. (Purchase Order A 6369)

Do you have instructional aids to accompany this book?
If so, I would appreciate knowing about them.

Very sincerely yours,

Sarah L. Bacardi
Sarah L. Bacardi, Chairman
Department of Nutrition

■■■■■■■■■■■■■■■■■■■■■■■■■■■■■■■■■■■

Notes: Miss Bacardi, you find, did purchase the book and is entitled to the instructor's source book without charge. Also available are objective tests (48 pages, $1.20 list price), a laboratory manual (224 pages, $4.60 list), and a set of transparencies (a kit of 12 four-color transparencies that sells for $48 net). You are glad to send the instructor's source book, a set of objective tests, and a laboratory manual without charge. You enclose a flyer on the transparencies.

■■■■■■■■■■■■■■■■■■■■■■■■■■■■■■■■■■■

RED RIVER AGRICULTURAL COLLEGE

FORT TOWSON, OKLAHOMA 74735

October 4, 19--

OCT 6 RECD

Merit Publishing Company
Dallas, Texas 75201

Attention Manager

Dear Sir:

On August 17, I sent you a check for $62.48 in payment
of my book order (invoice 468-2) of July 12. Today I
received another bill. Of course, I will not pay it; indeed,
I don't understand how you could make such an error because
I have my canceled check to prove that I paid you. This is
not the first time this has happened to me.

Yours truly,

Milton H. Grannitt

Milton H. Grannitt, Chairman
Agronomy Department

Notes: Mr. Grannitt is right; the second invoice was sent in error. After careful searching by the Customer Billing Department, it was discovered that Professor Grannitt's check was credited to M. O. Grannet, another customer. As chairman of the Agronomy Department, Mr. Grannitt is an important purchaser, and it is especially embarrassing that he should be the victim of such an error, not only once but on other occasions.

TEXAS GULF COLLEGE

Center for Continuing Education

BEAUMONT, TEXAS 77708

October 4, 19--

OCT 6 RECD

Merit Publishing Corporation
1640 Stemmons Freeway
Dallas, Texas 75201

Gentlemen:

Do you have a new text in world geography that might be
suitable for our continuing education classes (these people
use high school level books)? We are planning to introduce
this course in our Center for Continuing Education next
spring, and I am examining the various books available.

Sincerely,

Craig L. Mooter

Craig L. Mooter
Director

Notes: Merit has just published *Our World Environment—Patterns and Cultures,* by Morris L. Jason and Michele T. DuBois, which you believe would be ideal for Mr. Mooter's classes (several colleges have adopted it for their adult education evening classes). You will send a complimentary copy of the book. It lists for $9. Assume, in writing to Mr. Mooter, that you will enclose a colorful brochure describing the book and its accompanying workbook, tapes, transparencies, tests, and facsimile key for the instructor.

MOUNT TILFORD HIGH SCHOOL

Mount Tilford, New Mexico 88501

SUPERINTENDENT: Curtis J. Davis, Ph.D.
PRINCIPAL: Miriam Alvarez, Ed.D.

Area Code 505 • 414-1001

October 4, 19--

OCT 6 REC'D

Merit Publishing Company
1640 Stemmons Freeway
Dallas, Texas 75201

Gentlemen:

Please send me a free examination copy of SWITCHING CIRCUIT
AND FINITE AUTOMATA, by Charles Bohrmann. I would also like
a copy of the instructor's handbook and student's guidebook
for this book.

Sincerely yours,

(Miss) Donna Bustamente

Donna Bustamente
Mathematics Teacher

■ ■

Notes: The book referred to in Miss Bustamente's letter is designed for graduate
school courses in colleges and universities; it is not suitable for high schools. It is
possible that Miss Bustamente teaches in a local university and wants the book for
a graduate class, but you think it is unlikely. She may purchase the book, of course.
The list price is $17.50.

■ ■

Southern Arizona College of Fine Arts

Phoenix, Arizona 85012

October 2, 19--

OCT 6 RECD

General Manager
Merit Publishing Company
1640 Stemmons Freeway
Dallas, Texas 75201

Dear Sir:

The enclosed letter arrived from your attorney, and I find it so ridiculous that I thought I ought to share it with you.

I have been constantly harangued about a bill that I have already paid. It was paid in two installments, and I have the canceled checks to prove it. Due to inefficient bookkeeping, Merit Publishers (where did you get that name Merit?) has continued to pester me with bills. I have received no acknowledgments of my payments or my letters telling you that I had paid the bills—only more bills.

So, I say to your attorney, come and get me. I would welcome a suit which would cause you more unflattering publicity than we have already been able to spread. I am a professor here, and I have certainly let the faculty know of this incident and the very rude manner in which our letters have been ignored. Please instruct your college book salesman not to bother contacting me here, as I want no part of such an organization.

Yours truly,

Claud Quillan

Claud Quillan, M.F.A.

CQ:nn
Enclosure

■ ■

Notes: You made a very thorough investigation of this situation, and you find that Mr. Quillan is right. Through a series of errors in the Customer Accounts Department, Mr. Quillan did not receive credit for his payments, and his letters unaccountably got filed without being answered. Records show that Mr. Quillan is a good customer (he uses several Merit art books in his classes) and has always paid his bills on time.

Theodore R. Watkins
Counselor at Law

416 Brooker Building
One Fillmore Circle
New York, New York 10022

September 28, 19--

OCT 6 REC'D

Mr. Claud Quillan
304 Quigley Avenue
Phoenix, Arizona 85018

Dear Sir:

As attorney for Merit Publishing Company, I have been
requested to commence legal action to enforce payment on your
account.

Before doing so, however, I want to continue my policy
of attempting to settle collection matters in a friendly way.

Therefore, rather than proceed immediately with measures
which will ultimately add a considerable amount to what you
now owe, I suggest that you take advantage of this opportunity to settle your account IMMEDIATELY.

Sincerely yours,

Theodore R. Watkins

Theodore R. Watkins

IRG

The only excuse you have to give Mr. Quillan is that Merit's billing and collection
system has been undergoing conversion to a computerized system, and correspondents
and others have been tied up in learning new procedures brought about by the change
in the system. (Several other people got similar letters who shouldn't have.) You think
now that all the bugs are ironed out.

■ ■

327 Dogwood Lane
Kirkwood, Missouri 63122
October 2, 19--

OCT 6 REC'D

Merit Publishing Company
1640 Stemmons Freeway
Dallas, Texas 75201

Gentlemen:

    I would like to apply for a sales job with Merit Publishing Company, and I am particularly interested in selling college textbooks.

    I am a college graduate, with a major in political science. Since I finished school two years ago, I have been working in the research department of Krutchfield-Samuelson Oil Company. I find this work too confining, however, and I want a job that will give me a chance to travel and meet interesting people. I believe a sales job where I would travel to college campuses and meet with professors would be ideal.

    I can come to Dallas at your convenience for an interview. Please write me at the address above, or if you would prefer to telephone me, my number is 314-TA2-4149.

Very truly yours,

Ronald S. Burris

Ronald S. Burris

Notes: You have an opening in the Arizona-New Mexico territory and another in the Oklahoma-Arkansas territory for which you have been interviewing candidates.

ARGYLE COLLEGE BOOKSTORE

Pine Canyon, Texas 75968

OCT 6 REC'D   October 4, 19--

General Manager, College Department
Merit Publishing Company
1640 Stemmons Freeway
Dallas, Texas 75201

Dear Sir:

Well, you've done it again! I ordered items 3, 9, and 13 as follows:

Item	Quantity	Title
3	312	Beers: Nursing Procedures, 3rd Edition
9	50	Monk and Freed: Elements of Botany
13	210	Archer: Cost Accounting, 6th Edition

Instead of the above, I received the following:

	312	Colfax: Internal Medicine, 4th Edition
	53	Zabor: Plant Pathology
	210	Mays-Gerber: Legal Secretary's Handbook

I have sent back the books I did not order and request <u>urgently</u> that
you ship me the right ones. Classes for the second semester are already
under way, and we're in a real bind. You can imagine what kinds of names
I'm being called.

Very truly yours,

Cynthia Hindemith

Mrs. Cynthia Hindemith

■ ■

Notes: Investigation shows that Mrs. Hindemith's complaint is fully justified—the wrong books were shipped. (The same thing happened in September to an order from Argyle College Bookstore.) You're making arrangements to ship items 3 and 13 immediately by rail express. Unfortunately, Monk and Freed: *Elements of Botany* is out of stock, and you don't expect a new supply for about three weeks.

■ ■

ALPHA ZETA COLLEGE

Montego, New Mexico 87734

October 5, 19--

OCT 7 REC'D

Merit Publishing Company
1640 Stemmons Freeway
Dallas, Texas 75201

Dear Sir:

    Please rush me 30 copies of Kunsthalle: ANTHOLOGY OF
EASTERN LITERATURE and bill me at the regular discount.

                   Yours truly,

                   M. J. Thomas
                   Instructor

■ ■

Notes: The college owes Merit Publishing Company $647.80 for books purchased
at various times during the year, and although many letters have been written by Merit,
the bill has not been paid nor has any explanation been offered. You have been notified
by the New York office not to ship Alpha Zeta College any more books on credit; it
will be a cash-only transaction. The books requested above amount to $402.60.

■ ■

Middleton Furniture Company

814 Dallas Avenue   *Houston, Texas 77002*

October 5, 19--

OCT 7 RECD

Merit Publishing Company
1640 Stemmons Freeway
Dallas, Texas 75201

Gentlemen:

One of our customers, Professor Lucas R. Manger, is, I, understand, an author of yours. We have had a great deal of difficulty collecting an amount he owes us and have had to threaten suit.

Would you please tell me what Professor Manger's royalty income is from his book? This information will help me to prove his capacity for paying his bills.

Thank you.

G. S. Lemon

Notes: Information about authors' royalties is maintained in the New York office, and you cannot grant Mr. Lemon's request. At the same time, you know that such information is not released by the company.

LANCASTER CITY COLLEGE

Lancaster, Missouri 63548

October 5, 19--

OCT 7 RECD

Merit Publishing Company
1640 Stemmons Freeway
Dallas, Texas 75201

Gentlemen:

Please send me the following books and bill me at the regular discount.

40 Clampett: GEOLOGY FOR PETROLEUM ENGINEERS, 2d Edition
20 Gregory-Mischler: STRENGTH OF MATERIALS, 8th Edition
16 Levine: OIL WELL CEMENTING, 2d Edition
36 Likert-Bast-Moore: PETROLEUM PHYSICS

I should like to have these books by October 16 when my fall classes
begin, so please rush shipment.

Very truly yours,

A. W. Rusmisel, Chairman
Petroleum Engineering Department

Notes: Your office does not serve the Missouri area, and you must refer the letter
to Merit's St. Louis office at 517 North Fourth Street, 63144.

anniversary reminder

To: (Your Name)

Date: October 5, 19--

OCT 7 Rec'd

Next month's anniversaries in your department are as follows:

Name		Anniversary	
		Date	Year
Mrs. Deborah Bertrand (10 years)		October 25	19--

Personnel Relations Department

■ ■

Notes: The document above is sent by the Personnel Relations Department on first, fifth, tenth, fifteenth, twentieth, etc., anniversaries to the appropriate supervisors and is their signal to acknowledge the occasion appropriately.

As indicated, Mrs. Bertrand has been an employee of Merit for ten years; for the past four years she has been a sales correspondent in the College Department. She is very personable and effective in her job. She is a skillful letter writer, who has made many friends among Merit's customers because of her personal attention to their problems—wrong books shipped, delayed shipments because books were out of stock, incorrect billings, and so on. In fact, she is a great asset to your department and you value her highly.

■ ■

Interoffice Memorandum

TO   All District Sales Managers   **FROM**   Stanley G. Wright

SUBJECT Expenses   **DATE**   October 5, 19--

OCT 7 RECD

Again I want to remind you that sales expenses for the year are far ahead of budget and nearly twice what they were last year. Of particular concern to me are expenses of your salesmen in the following categories:

1. <u>Entertainment</u>. Although I am aware of the need for entertaining important customers, I am very doubtful that our men are being really selective about whom they entertain and realistic about the amounts being spent. For example, I have an expense account on my desk for a single dinner party of two customers that came to $97.40. Although this may be completely justifiable, I think it calls for an explanation.

2. <u>Conventions</u>. I think we must be more selective about the conventions at which we are represented and the number of people we send. For example, I note that we had four salesmen at a recent regional speech convention which, according to figures, drew only 34 professors. I would question whether even one salesman was needed at such a meeting, but certainly we didn't need four.

3. <u>Automobile Expenses</u>. Mileage expenses this year are shockingly out of line with previous years, which makes me wonder whether our salesmen are properly planning their trips or are, in fact, running helter-skelter without any kind of itinerary.

4. <u>Complimentary Copies</u>. I am well aware that we can sell books only when professors have a chance to examine them, but I am seeing far too many requests from salesmen to send complimentary (as opposed to examination) copies to professors. The salesmen must make sure that when copies are sent on a complimentary basis the recipient is a very hot prospect. On my desk at the moment is a request from a salesman to send a complimentary copy of Campbell's CANADIAN GEOGRAPHY to a professor of music!

Will each of you audit your salesmen's expense and sales reports carefully and let them know immediately that you are doing so. I know that I will see a far different picture in October than I have seen in August and September. By the way, it is only fair that I tell you that I am continuing to spot-check expense reports of all sales personnel and that I will call to your attention situations that require an explanation.

■ ■

Notes: Mr. Wright is vice president and general manager of the College Department of Merit Publishing Company in New York.

■ ■

Y' ALL COME!

SOUTHWEST MUSIC EDUCATORS NATIONAL CONFERENCE

Annual Meeting
December 27-30

Sam Houston Hotel

San Antonio, Texas

PROGRAM HIGHLIGHTS

       Keynote Address: "Changing Moods of Modern Music,"
                            Dr. Stuart Gaines, Midwood Music School

       Banquet: 7 p.m., December 29--All-musical program!

       Twelve Challenging Workshops (See attached list.)

ADDED ATTRACTIONS

       Special "live music" demonstrations

       Continuous film showings

       Exhibits of the newest in equipment and publications

REGISTRATION

       Fill in and return enclosed card.

       Special rates offered at Sam Houston Hotel.

       Register early for best accommodations.

■ ■

Notes: The Southwest Music Educators National Conference has announced it is having its annual meeting December 27–30, in San Antonio. Merit Publishing Company has planned a special exhibit (other publishers, musical instrument manufacturers, and various other educational suppliers will also exhibit).

At Merit's exhibit, all the latest textbook materials in music education will be on display. In addition, Merit has a large selection of records, cassette tapes, etc., which it sells to libraries, music educators, and others. A special feature of the exhibit is a soundproof booth in which teachers can play records and tapes. The College Department has also arranged to show its films continuously in a "Little Theater," which has been arranged for with the hotel.

You want to attract as many convention members as possible to the Merit exhibit booth and to the special movies scheduled. You are to prepare a promotion letter to those who are likely to attend the convention (you have a good, up-to-date mailing list of music educators in your district).

■ ■

LAMONT COMMUNITY COLLEGE

LAMONT, NEW MEXICO 88338

October 4, 19--

OCT 7 REC'D

Merit Publishing Company
1640 Stemmons Freeway
Dallas, Texas 75201

Gentlemen:

I want to tell you how much I am enjoying using the Friedson-McKenna book, DYNAMIC RETAIL MERCHANDISING TECHNIQUES, in my classes. This is precisely the book I have been searching for, and the result I am obtaining in my classes is evidence that the students like it, too. They especially like the cases that introduce each chapter and the Continuing Retailing Project that applies in a most practical way the principles they have learned.

The laboratory manual is exceedingly helpful, as is the very excellent teacher's guide. Are you planning transparencies? I am anxious to obtain some--indeed, I have developed some of my own, though I'm afraid the art and the reproduction is somewhat crude. I have also prepared some tapes for use in the section on retail selling, and my students like them very much. Essentially, they consist of dialogues between customer and salesman, showing the right and wrong ways to sell.

In any event, I thought you would want to know that I'm an ardent fan of the Friedson-McKenna approach, and I'd like to see anything else your company publishes in the retail merchandising field.

Sincerely yours,

Frederick Marck

Frederick Marck, Professor
Distributive Education

Notes: There was some discussion about transparencies at the last sales meeting in New York, but as far as you are able to determine, there are no plans to publish them. You do think the editor in New York, Marcia Stebbins, would be interested in seeing Professor Marck's transparencies and also hearing the tapes he spoke about.

Wichita Falls Institute of Technology

WICHITA FALLS, TEXAS 76301

October 6, 19--

OCT 8 RECD

Merit Publishing Company
1640 Stemmons Freeway
Dallas, Texas 75201

Gentlemen:

Enclosed is our purchase order (3Y7621) for 300 copies of INTEGRATED CIRCUITS--Theory and Applications, by Stroll and Travis. I hope you will be able to get these books to me early in December for use in a special industrial training program which our institute is conducting.

Sincerely yours,

O. L. Fairchild, Ed.D.

OLF:eh
Enclosure

■■■■■■■■■■■■■■■■■■■■■■■■■■■■■■■■■■■■

Notes: This is the first order Dr. Fairchild has placed with Merit in two years. There was some difficulty between Dr. Fairchild and a Merit salesman over two years ago (the salesman is no longer employed by Merit). At that time Dr. Fairchild said he was "through with Merit and will in the future order every one of my textbooks from other publishers."

■■■■■■■■■■■■■■■■■■■■■■■■■■■■■■■■■■■■

Interoffice Memorandum

TO   (Your name)   **FROM**   Travis Funseth

SUBJECT   Professor Lucius Goldman   **DATE**   October 6, 19--

OCT 8 REC'D

     Today Professor Lucius Goldman informed me that he will become Dean
of the School of Architecture at Crockett University in July of next
year. He has wanted this position for a long time (he thinks the department is much too conservative), and is very excited about it. Apparently
the appointment is no secret--the professors in the department know about
it.

■ ■

Notes: Professor Goldman is one of Merit's most distinguished authors, having written
two very successful textbooks and collaborated on a "picture book" on architecture
for trade sale. He is a somewhat flamboyant man, in his late 30s, and is a special
friend of Merit's VIPs. You have met him on several occasions, but you cannot consider
him a close, personal friend.

■ ■

Here's the form letter we send customers about books they return in unsalable condition.
D.W.

Dear Customer:

Our Receiving Department has notified us that your return of Merit books contains books that are not salable. (Date)

Specifically, the following books are (either/or): 1. Out of Print 2. Soiled or Shopworn 3. Beyond Cleaning 4. Price-Marked (which has proved too costly to remove) 5. Price-Marked (which cannot be removed) 6. Cover Damaged.

(List quantity, author, title, and condition--taken from receiving ticket; e.g., 20 Bailey: RENAISSANCE POETS - Out of Print)

You will agree, we are sure, that the present Merit Returns Policy is very liberal. Basically, our main concern is that books returned be in resalable condition. To this extent we feel justified in requesting that customers remove prices and, in general, be certain that books being returned are in salable condition.

Since no credit can be issued, may we please have your decision relative to the disposition of these books. Please reply to my attention by noting at the bottom of this letter your decision.

Sincerely,

Returns Section

Notes: It has come to your attention that your customers who return books for credit have been receiving a form letter that is not altogether satisfactory in wording and general tone, and you asked to see a copy. In the interest of good customer relations, you decide to offer suggestions to the Returns Section on how the letter might be improved. (You do not supervise this department; Darlene Wilson does.)

Interoffice Memorandum

TO (Your name)   **FROM** Stanley G. Wright

SUBJECT Exhibit   **DATE** October 6, 19--

OCT 8 RECD

    Concerning your need for a new exhibit, which we discussed on the telephone last week, I understand that Dramatic Visuals, in Tulsa, has come out with a new portable exhibit that is very good looking, reasonably priced, and easy to pack, transport, and store. It's called, I understand, "Port-a-Visual." Why not write these people for information? Their address is 3000 South Harvard, Tulsa 74114.

■ ■

Notes: With several end-of-year regional conventions in the offing, you have been looking for a compact, "foolproof" exhibit to use in displaying Merit books. You want one that is attractive but not too high-priced since you would like to order several so as to keep them moving around the convention circuit. Last week when you discussed this need with your boss, Stanley G. Wright, he promised to get details on one he had seen and liked. His memo is shown above.

■ ■

Interoffice Memorandum

TO (Your name) **FROM** Ed Lancaster

SUBJECT American Marketing Association **DATE** October 6, 19--
Meeting

OCT 8 REC'D

Last night I attended a dinner meeting of the American Marketing
Association, in Phoenix, as a guest of Professor John Fleming. The featured speaker was Clement K. Richter, vice president for marketing, of
Ramsing Corporation, in Kansas City (I understand Ramsing manufactures
automotive parts). Mr. Richter talked on professionalism. I know that
sounds like a pretty dull topic, but he made it really exciting. His
theme was that we are all managers no matter what our job title; we
manage ourselves and we manage the territories assigned to us. He
thinks selling is the highest "calling" a person could aspire to and
that a salesman today is actually the customer's buying consultant.
This may not sound like heady stuff, but I must confess that he gave
me a completely new perspective of my job. The guy speaks extremely
well, uses slides and tapes for dramatic effect, and relates perfectly with an audience.

Perhaps you may wish to consider Richter as a possible speaker
at our March sales conference. Professor Fleming tells me that Richter
does a lot of speaking throughout the country; apparently he enjoys
it, and his company thinks it's good PR.

■ ■

Notes: You are putting together now a program for the next sales conference in March,
and you have been considering getting an outside speaker. The theme you have settled
on for your conference is "Market Management," in which you plan to emphasize
the need for better sales planning, territory coverage, product knowledge, and customer relations. The conference dates are March 12–14. You expect to use your field
sales supervisors as discussion leaders. The outside speaker would kick off the conference at 10 a.m. on the first day (he can have all the time he wants, but you think
an hour would be about right). The conference site is the Lakeway Inn and Marina
in Austin, Texas.

■ ■

2330 Northwest 16 Street
Oklahoma City, Oklahoma 73106
October 5, 19--

OCT 8 REC'D

Merit Publishing Company
1640 Stemmons Freeway
Dallas, Texas 75201

Gentlemen:

The Maple Gardens Parents Association is holding a bazaar in February
for the purpose of raising money for the Maple Gardens Elementary School.
Several companies are contributing products that will be auctioned off to
the highest bidders. The proceeds will go toward new playground equipment,
a sound movie projector (the one the school now owns is beyond repair),
and a larger freezer for the school cafeteria.

It was suggested that an ideal item for our bazaar is your ENCYCLOPEDIA
OF MODERN SCIENCE, which several people have seen at the local library.
Would you be willing to donate this set of books for our bazaar? We would
certainly appreciate it, and you would be doing a marvelous thing for our
community.

Yours sincerely,

Abigail Harrison

Mrs. Abigail Harrison

■ ■

Notes: The *Encyclopedia of Modern Science,* to which Mrs. Harrison refers, is a
20-volume set that sells for $495 net, and Merit is not in a position to honor Mrs.
Harrison's request. Merit does, however, have a large inventory of a book called *Faces
and Places,* a picture book on world cultures, which has proved to be unsalable. It
is priced at $17.95, and you can supply a copy of this book for the bazaar.

■ ■

SOUTHERN CALIFORNIA PAPER CORPORATION

500 Mission Valley Center West   San Diego, California 92914

PERSONNEL RELATIONS

October 5, 19--

OCT 8 REC'D

Merit Publishing Company
1640 Stemmons Freeway
Dallas, Texas 75201

Attention College Department

Gentlemen:

Mr. E. Walter Boudreau has applied to us for a sales
position. In his résumé, Mr. Boudreau lists your firm as an
employer for the year 19--.

Can you make any comments concerning Mr. Boudreau's
qualifications, his character, and his performance? I assure
you that any information you give me will be kept in strictest confidence.

Very truly yours,

Janice Nance

Ms. Janice Nance
Personnel Specialist

ene

Notes: Mr. Boudreau was a salesman under your supervision for a year. Although
he showed considerable ability when he tried, you had difficulty getting him to be
productive. He did not seem to like selling; although he was very good at developing
friendships, he made few sales, and you concluded that he was not forceful enough
to succeed in selling. You liked him (everybody did) and you did not want to let him
go, but after several talks with him the two of you decided that selling college textbooks
was not his forte, and he left the company.

reference section

BUSINESS REFERENCE BOOKS

FORMS OF ADDRESS AND SALUTATION

ABBREVIATIONS FOR NAMES OF STATES,
TERRITORIES, AND POSSESSIONS
OF THE UNITED STATES

ABBREVIATIONS FOR NAMES OF
PROVINCES OF CANADA

PROOFREADER'S MARKS AND SYMBOLS

BUSINESS REFERENCE BOOKS

The American Heritage Dictionary of the English Language, American Heritage Publishing Co., Inc., and Houghton Mifflin Company, Boston, 1969.

Amy Vanderbilt's New Complete Book of Etiquette, Doubleday & Company, Inc., Garden City, N.Y., 1967.

Bartlett's Familiar Quotations, 14th ed., Little, Brown and Company, Boston, 1968.

Books in Print, R. R. Bowker Company, New York. (An author-title-series index to the *Publishers' Trade List Annual;* published annually.)

Bullinger's Postal and Shippers Guide for the United States and Canada, Bullinger's Guides, Inc., Westwood, N.J. (Published annually.)

Congressional Directory, U.S. Government Printing Office, Washington. (Published annually.)

Directory of International Mail, U.S. Government Printing Office, Washington.

Dun & Bradstreet Reference Book, Dun & Bradstreet, Inc., New York. (By subscription only; published bimonthly.)

Gavin, Ruth E., and William A. Sabin, *Reference Manual for Stenographers and Typists,* 4th ed., Gregg Division, McGraw-Hill Book Company, New York, 1970.

Hotel & Motel Red Book, American Hotel Association Directory Corporation, New York. (Published annually.)

Huffman, Harry, and Syrell Rogovin, *Programmed College English,* McGraw-Hill Book Company, New York, 1968.

Hutchinson, Lois Irene, *Standard Handbook for Secretaries,* 8th ed., Gregg Division, McGraw-Hill Book Company, New York, 1969.

Information Please Almanac, Atlas and Yearbook, Simon and Schuster, New York. (Published annually.)

Moody's manuals, Moody's Investors Service, Inc., New York. (There are five separate manuals: *Moody's Banks and Finance Manual, Moody's Industrial Manual, Moody's Municipal and Government Manual, Moody's Public Utilities Manual,* and *Moody's Transportation Manual;* published annually.)

N. W. Ayer & Son's Directory of Newspapers and Periodicals, N. W. Ayer & Son, Inc., Philadelphia. (Published annually.)

National ZIP Code Directory, U.S. Post Office Department Publication 65, Washington. (Revised periodically.)

The New York Times Index, The New York Times Company, New York. (Published semimonthly.)

Perrin, Porter G., *Writer's Guide and Index to English,* 4th ed., Scott, Foresman and Company, Glenview, Ill., 1965. (Consists of two parts: a writer's guide, which discusses general English topics, and an index to English, which gives details of grammar arranged alphabetically.)

Poor's Register of Corporations, Directors and Executives, Standard & Poor's Corporation, New York. (Published annually.)

Post, Elizabeth L., *Emily Post's Etiquette,* 12th rev. ed., Funk & Wagnalls Company, New York, 1969.

Postal Manual, U.S. Government Printing Office, Washington.

Rand McNally Commercial Atlas and Marketing Guide, Rand McNally & Company, Chicago. (Published annually.)

Readers' Guide to Periodical Literature, The H. W. Wilson Company, New York. (Published semimonthly, September–June; monthly, July–August.)

Roget's International Thesaurus, 3d ed., Thomas Y. Crowell Company, New York, 1962. (A word book for finding a word to fit an idea.)

Standard Corporation Records, Standard & Poor's Corporation, New York. (Published bimonthly.)

Webster's Biographical Dictionary, G. & C. Merriam Company, Springfield, Mass., 1966.

Webster's New World Dictionary of the American Language, College Edition, The World Publishing Company, Cleveland, 1968.

Webster's Seventh New Collegiate Dictionary, G. & C. Merriam Company, Springfield, Mass., 1969. (Desk-sized.)

Webster's Third New International Dictionary, G. & C. Merriam Company, Springfield, Mass., 1966. (Unabridged.)

Who's Who, St. Martin's Press, New York. (A biographical dictionary of notable persons, mostly British; published annually.)

Who's Who in America, Marquis-Who's Who Incorporated, Chicago. (A biographical dictionary of notable living Americans; published biennially. Similar biographical dictionaries covering persons in various fields are *Who's Who of American Women, Who's Who in Commerce and Industry,* etc.)

The World Almanac and Book of Facts, Doubleday & Company, Inc., Garden City, N.Y. (Published annually.)

FORMS OF ADDRESS AND SALUTATION

The following forms of address and salutation are among those accepted and commonly used. The salutations shown after each address are listed in decreasing order of formality.

NOTE: Only the masculine forms of address have been used in order to save space and avoid the repetition of *Ms., Miss,* and *Mrs.* Whenever an office is held by a woman, substitute the appropriate feminine form, as follows:

FOR:	USE:
Mr.	Ms., Miss, *or* Mrs.
Sir:	Madam:
Dear Sir:	Dear Madam:
My dear Mr. (*Surname*):	My dear Ms., Miss, *or* Mrs. (*Surname*):
My dear Mr. Secretary:	My dear Madam Secretary:
My dear Mr. Mayor:	My dear Madam Mayor:

GOVERNMENT OFFICIALS

President of the United States
The President of the United States
The White House
Washington, D.C. 20500

Mr. President:
My dear Mr. President:

Vice President of the United States
The Vice President
The United States Senate
Washington, D.C. 20501

Sir:
My dear Mr. Vice President:

Chief Justice of the United States
The Chief Justice of the United States
Washington, D.C. 20543

Sir:
My dear Mr. Chief Justice:

Cabinet Member
The Honorable (*Full Name*)
Secretary of (*Department*)
Washington, D.C. (*ZIP Code*)

Sir:
Dear Sir:
My dear Mr. Secretary:

United States Senator
The Honorable (*Full Name*)
The United States Senate
Washington, D.C. 20510

Sir:
Dear Sir:
Dear Senator (*Surname*):

United States Congressman
The Honorable (*Full Name*)
House of Representatives
Washington, D.C. 20515

Sir:
Dear Sir:
Dear Mr. (*Surname*):

Governor
The Honorable (*Full Name*)
Governor of (*State Name*)
(*City, State ZIP Code*)

Sir:
Dear Sir:
Dear Governor (*Surname*):

State Senator
The Honorable (*Full Name*)
The State Senate
(*City, State ZIP Code*)

Sir:
Dear Sir:
Dear Senator (*Surname*):

State Representative or Assemblyman
The Honorable (*Full Name*)
House of Representatives *or*
The State Assembly
(*City, State ZIP Code*)

Sir:
Dear Sir:
My dear Mr. (*Surname*):
Dear Mr. (*Surname*):

Mayor
The Honorable (*Full Name*)
Mayor of (*City*)
(*City, State ZIP Code*)

Sir:
Dear Sir:
My dear Mayor (*Surname*):

MILITARY AND NAVAL PERSONNEL

Army Officers
Lieutenant General (*Full Name*)
United States Army
(*Address*)

Sir:
Dear Sir:
My dear General (*Surname*):
NOT: My dear Lieutenant General
  (*Surname*):
Dear General (*Surname*):

Colonel (*Full Name*)
United States Army *or*
United States Marine Corps
(*Address*)

Dear Sir:
My dear Colonel (*Surname*):
Dear Colonel (*Surname*):

Naval Officers
Admiral (*Full Name*)
United States Navy
(*Address*)

Sir:
Dear Sir:
My dear Admiral (*Surname*):
Dear Admiral (*Surname*):

Commander (*Full Name*)
United States Navy
(*Address*)

Dear Sir:
My dear Commander (*Surname*):
Dear Commander (*Surname*):

ROMAN CATHOLIC DIGNITARIES

Cardinal
His Eminence, (*First Name*) Cardinal
  (*Surname*)
(*Address*)

Your Eminence:

Archbishop or Bishop
The Most Reverend (*Full Name*)
Archbishop *or* Bishop of (*Place*)
(*Address*)

Your Excellency:

Monsignor
The Right Reverend Monsignor
(*Full Name*)
(*Address*)

Right Reverend Monsignor:
Dear Monsignor (*Surname*):

Priest
Reverend (*Full Name*), (*Initials of Order*)
(*Address*)

Reverend Father:
Dear Father (*Surname*):

Mother Superior
The Reverend Mother Superior
Convent of (*Name*)
(*Address*)

Reverend Mother:
Dear Reverend Mother:
Dear Reverend Mother (*Name*):

Sister
Sister (*Name*), (*Initials of Order*)
(*Address*)

My dear Sister:
Dear Sister (*Name*):

PROTESTANT DIGNITARIES

Protestant Episcopal Bishop
The Right Reverend (*Full Name*)
Bishop of (*Place*)
(*Address*)

Right Reverend and Dear Sir:
My dear Bishop (*Surname*):
Dear Bishop (*Surname*):

Protestant Episcopal Dean
The Very Reverend (*Full Name*)
Dean of (*Place*)
(*Address*)

Very Reverend Sir:
My dear Mr. Dean:
My dear Dean (*Surname*):
Dear Dean (*Surname*):

Methodist Bishop
The Reverend (*Full Name*)
Bishop of (*Place*)
(*Address*)

Reverend Sir:
Dear Sir:
My dear Bishop (*Surname*):
Dear Bishop (*Surname*):

JEWISH DIGNITARIES

Rabbi With Doctor's Degree
Rabbi (*Full Name*), D.D.
(*Address*)

Reverend Sir:
Dear Sir:
My dear Rabbi (*Surname*):
Dear Rabbi (*Surname*):

Rabbi Without Doctor's Degree
Rabbi (*Full Name*)
(*Address*)

(*Same salutations as preceding.*)

EDUCATION OFFICIALS

President of College or University
(*Full Name*), (*Initials of Academic
    Degree*)
President, (*Name of College or
    University*)
(*Address*)

or:

Dr. (*Full Name*)
President, (*Name of College or
    University*)
(*Address*)

Dear Sir:
My dear President (*Surname*):
Dear Dr. (*Surname*):

Professor
Professor (*Full Name*)
Department of (*Name*)
(*Name of College or University*)
(*Address*)

or:

Dr. (*Full Name*)
Professor of (*Subject*)
(*Name of College or University*)
(*Address*)

Dear Sir:
My dear Professor *or* Dr. (*Surname*):
Dear Professor *or* Dr. (*Surname*):
Dear Mr. (*Surname*):

ABBREVIATIONS FOR NAMES OF STATES, TERRITORIES, AND POSSESSIONS OF THE UNITED STATES

	NEW	OLD		NEW	OLD
Alabama	AL	Ala.	Missouri	MO	Mo.
Alaska	AK	. . .	Montana	MT	Mont.
Arizona	AZ	Ariz.	Nebraska	NE	Nebr.
Arkansas	AR	Ark.	Nevada	NV	Nev.
California	CA	Calif.	New Hampshire	NH	N.H.
Canal Zone	CZ	C.Z.	New Jersey	NJ	N.J.
Colorado	CO	Colo.	New Mexico	NM	N. Mex.
Connecticut	CT	Conn.	New York	NY	N.Y.
Delaware	DE	Del.	North Carolina	NC	N.C.
District	DC	D.C.	North Dakota	ND	N. Dak.
of Columbia			Ohio	OH	. . .
Florida	FL	Fla.	Oklahoma	OK	Okla.
Georgia	GA	Ga.	Oregon	OR	Oreg.
Guam	GU	. . .	Pennsylvania	PA	Pa.
Hawaii	HI	. . .	Puerto Rico	PR	P.R.
Idaho	ID	. . .	Rhode Island	RI	R.I.
Illinois	IL	III.	South Carolina	SC	S.C.
Indiana	IN	Ind.	South Dakota	SD	S. Dak.
Iowa	IA	. . .	Tennessee	TN	Tenn.
Kansas	KS	Kans.	Texas	TX	Tex.
Kentucky	KY	Ky.	Utah	UT	. . .
Louisiana	LA	La.	Vermont	VT	Vt.
Maine	ME	. . .	Virgin Islands	VI	V.I.
Maryland	MD	Md.	Virginia	VA	Va.
Massachusetts	MA	Mass.	Washington	WA	Wash.
Michigan	MI	Mich.	West Virginia	WV	W. Va.
Minnesota	MN	Minn.	Wisconsin	WI	Wis.
Mississippi	MS	Miss.	Wyoming	WY	Wyo.

ABBREVIATIONS FOR NAMES OF PROVINCES OF CANADA

Alberta	Alta.	Nova Scotia	N.S.
British Columbia	B.C.	Ontario	Ont.
Manitoba	Man.	Prince Edward Island	P.E.I.
New Brunswick	N.B.	Quebec	Que. or P.Q.
Newfoundland	Nfld.	Saskatchewan	Sask.

PROOFREADER'S MARKS AND SYMBOLS

∧	Insert word	and∧it
—	Omit word	and so it
....	No, don't omit	and so it
\	Omit stroke	and sob it
/	Make letter small . . .	And so it
=	Make a capital	if he is
≡	Make all capitals	I hope so
⌐⌐	Move as indicated . . .	and so—⌐
=	Line up, even up . . .	TO: John
‖	Line up, even up	‖ If he is
ss [	Use single spacing . .	[and so it
∽	Turn around	read it so
ds [	Use double spacing . .	[and so it
=	Insert a hyphen	white-hot
5⌐	Indent — spaces . . .	5⌐If he is

#	Insert a space	and∧so it
⸜	Insert a space	and so it
⊂	Omit the space	10 a. m.
___	Underscore this	It may be
∽	Move as shown	it is (not)
_	Join to word	the port
word	Change word	and if he
o	Make into period . . .	to him.
⊂⊃	Don't abbreviate	(Dr.) Judd
○	Spell it out	① or ② if
¶	New paragraph	¶If he is
∨	Raise above line	Hale says
#→	More space here	It may be
—#→	Less space here	If she is
2#	2 line spaces here . . .	It may be

INDEX